Planning Reagan's War

Related Titles from Potomac Books

Dean Acheson and the Creation of an American World Order
  —Robert J. McMahon

*The Triumph of Internationalism: Franklin D. Roosevelt
and a World in Crisis, 1933–1941*
  —David F. Schmitz

John F. Kennedy: World Leader
  —Stephen G. Rabe

How the Cold War Ended: Debating and Doing History
  —John Prados

Obama's War: Avoiding a Quagmire in Afghanistan
  —James Gannon

*The Wars of Edvard Shevardnadze, Second Edition,
Revised and Updated*
  —Melvin Goodman and Carolyn M. Ekedahl

Planning
Reagan's War

*Conservative Strategists and
America's Cold War Victory*

FRANCIS H. MARLO

Potomac Books
Washington, D.C.

Copyright © 2012 by Francis H. Marlo

Published in the United States by Potomac Books, Inc. All rights
reserved. No part of this book may be reproduced in any manner
whatsoever without written permission from the publisher, except in
the case of brief quotations embodied in critical articles and reviews.

Library of Congress Cataloging-in-Publication Data
Marlo, Francis H.
    Planning Reagan's war : conservative strategists and America's
cold war victory / Francis H. Marlo.
        p. cm.
    Includes bibliographical references and index.
    ISBN 978-1-59797-667-1 (hardcover)
    ISBN 978-1-59797-742-5 (electronic)
    1. United States—Foreign relations—1981–1989. 2. United
States—Foreign relations—Soviet Union. 3. Soviet Union—
Foreign relations—United States. 4. Reagan, Ronald—Political and
social views. 5. Cold War—Diplomatic history. 6. Cold War—
Political aspects—United States. I. Title.
    E876.M356 2012
    973.927—dc23
                                                    2012004501

Printed in the United States of America on acid-free paper that
meets the American National Standards Institute Z39-48 Standard.

Potomac Books
22841 Quicksilver Drive
Dulles, Virginia 20166

First Edition

10 9 8 7 6 5 4 3 2 1

CONTENTS

Acknowledgments   vii

1   Defining Grand Strategy   1
2   The Reagan Administration's Grand Strategy   11
3   Beliefs   37
4   Goals   71
5   Tools   101
6   The Role of Reagan and His Advisors   129
7   Conclusions   161

Notes   181
Bibliography   213
Index   237
About the Author   243

ACKNOWLEDGMENTS

This work would not have been possible without the support of three exceptional scholars: Richard Shultz, Robert Pfaltzgraff, and Carnes Lord. These three men have had a profound impact on me since my days at the Fletcher School of Law and Diplomacy, and it has been an honor to call myself their student.

It also could never have been written without the generous assistance of a number of former Reagan administration officials. In particular, I would like to thank Edwin Meese III, Richard Allen, Richard Perle, Roger Robinson, and Frank Gaffney for their insights into Reagan and the workings of his administration, as well as their patience in answering my too-often-misguided questions. I would also like to acknowledge the passing of Fred Iklé, Caspar Weinberger, and Jeane Kirkpatrick, three other former Reagan administration officials who were kind enough to pass along to me their recollections and knowledge of this era.

I would also like to thank my colleagues at the Marine Corps Command and Staff College for their friendship and support. Having the opportunity to work with such an impressive collection of scholars is a genuine privilege. I would especially like to thank Doug Streusand for his own insights into the Reagan years and Bruce Bechtol for his invaluable help in guiding me through the publication process. And while I am enormously grateful to Marine Corps University for its support, I must emphasize that responsibility for the content of this book is mine alone. The views expressed here do not necessarily reflect the views of the Marine Corps Command and Staff College, the Marine Corps University, or the U.S. Government.

No one can complete a task such as this one without external support. I have been blessed with a fantastic network of friends and family whose unquestioned encouragement and support made the long hours devoted to this work bearable.

Most of all, I would like to thank my beautiful wife, Karen, without whose love and support no professional accomplishment would matter, and my two wonderful sons, Stephen and Alex.

Defining Grand Strategy

The late 1970s and early 1980s were times of tremendous change in U.S. national security policy. A nation humbled by its demeaning withdrawal from Vietnam in 1973, wracked with indecision and distrust following the revelations of Watergate, and increasingly concerned about Soviet advances in the Third World began to seek a new direction and more vigorous national strategy by the beginning of the 1980 presidential election. In November 1980, Ronald Reagan was overwhelmingly elected the fortieth president of the United States, in large part due to the perception that he had a better strategic vision for standing up to Soviet pressure.

The foreign policy of the Reagan administration has been the subject of countless books, articles, and analyses, which have congealed to form the conventional history of the administration that is so prevalent today. This conventional history tends to take one of two forms. For some, the very notion that the Reagan administration developed and implemented a genuine grand strategy is unthinkable,[1] thus rendering the search for its foundation pointless. This version of conventional history, probably the most common, is rooted in the idea that Reagan knew virtually nothing about such matters and was therefore easily swayed by individuals within his administration. In this view, Reagan himself amounted to little more than (as Clark Clifford once put it) an "amiable dunce" whose decisions were "based on instinct and deeply rooted prejudices, and [whose] advisors often tend[ed] to tailor their recommendations to fit his presumed views and biases."[2] Reagan, his critics claim, relied heavily on his subordinates to explain foreign policy to him and "did not really understand the foreign policy debates swirling around him."[3] As a result, Reagan is depicted as little more than a figurehead who chose from a carefully screened list of foreign policy options, but who made no meaningful intellectual contribution to his own foreign policy.[4] At best, Reagan is described as an "inside-out sandwich," with a set of strong beliefs and great political skill, but completely ignorant of foreign policy issues.[5] Those holding this view of the Reagan presidency argue that his ignorance of foreign affairs, when combined with his allegedly extreme beliefs, essentially drove U.S. foreign policy down a path far removed from the accepted, mainstream approach.

Others, holding an only slightly more charitable view of Reagan, attempt to find the sources of the administration's strategy in the bureaucratic politics and personality clashes within his administration. In this view, it is not Reagan's supposedly simplistic ideas or prejudices that caused his administration's radical departure from a mainstream foreign policy, but rather Reagan's alleged inability to control the internal struggles within his administration. The fact that there were deep divisions within the Reagan administration is well known, with conventional wisdom listing the factions as the "pragmatists" (George Shultz, James Baker, Michael Deaver) versus the "Reaganauts" (Caspar Weinberger, William Casey, Jeane Kirkpatrick, Edwin Meese).[6] According to this view of the Reagan administration, both "pragmatists" and "Reaganauts" were convinced that they represented the "real Reagan," and therefore viewed any policy decision that they did not support to be a result of bureaucratic politics or personal betrayal. Analysts holding this view argue that Reagan's unwillingness to take sides in the struggle led to an erratic, inconsistent, and unpredictable foreign policy.[7] According to these conventional accounts, it was not until Reagan decided (sometime during his second term) to side with the so-called pragmatists that anything resembling a "real" foreign policy emerged.

These two depictions of the Reagan administration have existed since its earliest days and have achieved an almost unquestioned validity among many scholars.[8] Yet the plausibility of both descriptions of the Reagan strategy have come under increasing scrutiny in recent years, as scholars have challenged Reagan's alleged ignorance of foreign affairs by releasing his own writings on the subject. A recent series of books have provided unprecedented insight into Reagan's personal views on a number of topics, including foreign policy.[9] These writings reveal a Reagan far different from the commonly held caricatures of him as either an intellectually empty ideologue or a closet "moderate" captured by his "hard-line" advisors. Instead, recent scholarship proves that Reagan had a very clear understanding of American foreign policy and had already outlined, in his own mind, long before entering office, the direction in which he would ultimately lead his country. Unsurprisingly, his foreign policy thinking mirrors closely the thought of a number of key conservative strategists who shared his ideological perspective. His writings also reveal that, contrary to the claims of some, his views on foreign policy did not change appreciably, nor did Reagan feel any need to side with either the "pragmatists" or the "Reaganauts." Rather, Reagan pursued the course that he believed to be right, based on his own beliefs and foreign policy goals. While recognizing the need for making pragmatic tradeoffs in foreign affairs, he never allowed such tradeoffs to moderate his determination to achieve his key goals. While philosophically committed to conservativism, he was completely willing to sacrifice ideological purity for real results. In truth, Reagan played the central role in his administration's strategy, a role that will be more thoroughly explored in chapter 6.

This book's goal is to explain the development and implementation of grand strategy during the early years of the Reagan administration by focusing on President Reagan and his key foreign policy advisors. In particular, it will first identify the key components of the Reagan administration's strategy, paying special attention to Reagan's efforts to roll back the Soviet empire and destroy the Soviet state. It will then demonstrate the intellectual linkage between Reagan's strategy and post–World War II conservative strategic thought and explain the roles Reagan and his closest advisors played in creating and implementing this fundamentally different strategic concept. Finally, it will identify some enduring lessons to be learned from the Reagan strategy and suggest a possible post-9/11 U.S. grand strategy.

In order to conduct such analysis, however, grand strategy itself must be defined clearly and accurately. The goal of this chapter, then, is derive the elemental principles of grand strategy.

DEFINING GRAND STRATEGY

For a concept as central to a nation's survival and well-being as grand strategy, the term's meaning remains murky and contentious. Since this term did not really emerge until the twentieth century, most of history's greatest strategic thinkers, such as Sun Tzu and Carl von Clausewitz, offer no definition of this concept (though their concepts can certainly be applied to the level of grand strategy). While more recent strategists have attempted to define grand strategy, their efforts have largely been unsatisfying. In many cases, while (briefly) acknowledging that grand strategy includes all elements of national power, their discussions of grand strategy quickly devolve into the analysis of the role of military power, largely ignoring the critical contributions of other elements of national power. In other cases, strategists wrongly imply that grand strategy can only be found in wartime and is little more than a nation's wartime policy.[10] Such a claim is fundamentally absurd, as nations unquestionably pursue grand strategies during peacetime as well. Certainly these strategies need not be the multifaceted, global strategies of the Cold War. They can instead resemble the grand strategy of the early American republic, which was extremely limited and local, or the grand strategies of much of the developing world today, which focus on little more than political stability and economic survival.

While academic disagreements over an "official" definition of grand strategy are likely to continue for as long as there are academics, there are certain characteristics of grand strategy that most contemporary strategic thinkers recognize. First, it is generally understood that grand strategy must be comprehensive, serving to guide the use of all of a nation's powers and capabilities. Second, it is widely accepted that grand strategy is primarily focused externally, on a state's survival as an independent actor and on its relations with other actors in the international system. Finally, most strategic thinkers recognize that grand strategy focuses on the "big picture" and is directed toward achieving major objectives. Ironing out a cultural exchange or deconflicting tourist visa policies are simply not the stuff of grand strategy. Any working definition of grand strategy must reflect these broadly accepted elements of grand strategy.

However, a reasonable definition of grand strategy must also recognize not only that a strategy is the result of human thought, but that the numerous inputs to the development of strategy must be prioritized, gathered, analyzed, and incorporated into a reasonably consistent whole by individuals with specific views of the world. Whatever this view is called—ideology, baseline assumptions, or biases—history has shown that it plays the central role in the process of strategic formulation. Thus, for the purposes of this study, grand strategy (or national strategy) will be defined as *the planned use of all available tools of statecraft to achieve first-order national goals based on a given understanding or belief regarding the nature of the international system.* This definition, therefore, argues that there are three central components to grand strategy: beliefs, goals, and tools. Each of these components will be analyzed in more detail later.

Before analyzing the various components, however, it is important to make equally clear what falls outside the scope of grand strategy and to note that grand strategy itself is subsumed by a broader, more encompassing concept: statecraft. While the term statecraft is rarely used in modern social science, its close relationship with grand strategy is worth exploring. If grand strategy is responsible for balancing the pursuit of various national goals, then statecraft is responsible for balancing the pursuit of a nation's grand strategy with other pressing concerns. Grand strategy is concerned almost exclusively with a nation's relationship with the outside world; statecraft is concerned with both "securing the state against foreign adversaries and ensuring at least a modicum of justice and social peace."[11]

Thus, while developing a grand strategy is one of the most important tasks a statesman faces, it is not the only one. Making the difficult tradeoffs between pursuing one's grand strategy and preserving domestic stability, or between improving one's international position and strengthening one's domestic political base, are tasks of statecraft. However, as some have noted, the internal logic of both strategy and statecraft are quite similar.[12] Both must contend with one or more potential adversaries, both must be practiced in a realm of imperfect information, and both seek to achieve specific goals. In fact, the overlap between these two concepts is considerable, since the leader is ultimately responsible for both strategic and statecraft decisions. Put in terms of the definition of grand strategy earlier outlined, defining beliefs and goals is a task of statecraft; planning for and using the various tools is strategy.[13]

Beliefs

At strategy's most basic level, its purpose is to create a connection between ends and means, to develop a causal link between goals and tools. In a simple world, this connection would be direct, obvious, and ultimately uninteresting as a field of study. Just as the shortest distance between two points is a straight line, so too the best method for achieving a goal would be the obvious and "rational" one. States seeking peace would disarm, invest power in international institutions, and cooperate with one another. Differences among states would be resolved through negotiations genuinely aimed at accommodation and mutual satisfaction.

But such a simple world does not now, nor will it ever, exist. Statesmen instead must navigate through a world of conflict and uncertainty, one in which states pursue numerous goals, including power, position, and wealth, while information on real or potential adversaries is always incomplete and of uncertain value. Because of these unalterable realities of the international system, national leaders' view of the world around them necessarily drives the vital art of strategy.

The impact of a national leader's beliefs on the domestic goals a country pursues is fairly obvious. Candidates for elected office frequently run on entirely different platforms and set forth radically different domestic policies. One would be hard-pressed to argue, for example, that American domestic life would have remained constant regardless of whether Walter Mondale or Ronald Reagan won the 1984 presidential election. Most serious political analysts understand and accept this reality. However, the ready acceptance of these differences rapidly disappears when the subject turns to foreign policy. Many international relations theorists have a great deal of difficulty in accepting such a reality, as it makes theory more challenging to develop and, ultimately, less useful as a predictive or proscriptive tool. While it is certainly true that many countries have a general "strategic culture," there are nonetheless important differences within a given culture regarding national priorities. Announcing, clarifying, and pursuing these priorities are core tasks of national leadership. Further complicating the job of the statesman is the need to balance the unavoidable tradeoffs between goals. Answering the question of how many "guns" versus how much "butter" is a central task of the president and his advisors, and directly reflects their beliefs about the hierarchy of national goals.

More importantly, a leader's core beliefs play a critical role in the development of his grand strategy. As highlighted by Alexander George, a statesman's belief system or "operational code" serves as the prism through which he views and interprets the world around him.[14] These beliefs serve to structure his thinking and permit him to deal with the unavoidable fact that information in the real world is often incomplete, inaccurate, or deliberately falsified. If, in fact, Clausewitz is right when he states that "most intelligence is false,"[15] then the statesman must rely on some baseline understanding of how the world, and his adversary, operate. It must be hastily pointed out, however, that such an understanding should not be equated with irrational, mindless prejudice, nor does it preclude rational analysis. "Such a belief system influences, but does not unilaterally determine, decision-making."[16]

Consider, for example, the often wildly differing opinions on such issues as the future of stock prices, inflation, interest rates, or national income. Different economic analysts, all with access to roughly identical information, frequently have different predictions about how the market or individual firms will behave in the future. These differences are the natural outgrowth of different beliefs about how the financial world works, which pieces of data are most important, and which economic tools are most useful. Similarly, different national leaders have different views regarding how the international system works and which tools are most useful for achieving national objectives. These differing views lead to fundamentally different strategic choices and, therefore, to different grand strategies.

Goals

Grand strategy is ultimately about achieving certain national objectives. Beyond a set of obvious, minimal goals, such as the preservation of the country and some basic level of material well-being, defining the goals of the state is also primarily a task for the national leader and his close advisors. While numerous factors play a role in the development of a state's goals, the national leadership is ultimately responsible for setting priorities and monitoring pursuit of these goals. Certainly such factors as national power, geography, national history, and real or potential external rivals have a significant impact on the objectives of the state. Additionally, internal factors such as culture, political ideology, and electoral considerations rank as important considerations for many national leaders. Still, it is the leader and his core advisors who, based on their beliefs and view of the world, define and prioritize national goals.

It is critical, from the standpoint of developing a successful grand strategy, that these national goals be mutually reinforcing and focused on remedying specific problems or exploiting certain opportunities. Their function, after all, is to direct the efforts of the government toward some reasonably well-defined "end state." While it is inevitable that the leader will, at some point, be forced to make trade-offs between competing goals, on the whole the effective pursuit of these goals requires coherence and unity of purpose. Without such coherence, the pursuit of national goals becomes fragmented, confused, and haphazard, leading to strategic incoherence and the stagnation of national will. Only the national leadership, entrusted with the ultimate responsibility for national strategic success, is capable of providing that coherence and unity of effort.

Tools

Simply having well-defined goals, however, is no guarantee of strategic success. These goals must still be linked to specific tools of state power. While placing the various "tools of statecraft"[17] into political, military, and economic categories may be an overused approach, it is nevertheless a reasonably useful way of thinking about the various means a state has to pursue its goals. Rather than an exhaustive listing of all possible tools of national power, this section seeks merely to highlight the wide variety of tools available to the national leader.

The political tools of statecraft are almost certainly the most numerous and wide-ranging of those available to a world leader. However, they are also inherently difficult to differentiate from one another, as so many of them are mutually reinforcing. With this caveat in mind, it is nevertheless possible to discuss several types of political tools available to the statesman. The first and most heavily used tool is that of traditional diplomatic interactions. Modern diplomacy, whether conducted via the State Department, Defense Department (DOD), another federal agency, or through the president himself, is a constant feature of the international scene and a critical component of national power.[18] These diplomatic tools include the negotiation of international agreements, the routine maintenance of friendly or cordial relations between states, the coordination or discussion of political cooperation in all its forms, and the use of various forms of political or diplomatic sanctions.

A second, and increasingly important, political tool is public diplomacy. With the explosion of international communication technology and the increasing reach of media coverage, the ability of Americans (both inside and outside the government) to bypass foreign governments and speak directly to the people of the world offers tremendous opportunities for the advancement of U.S. national interests. It should hardly be surprising that this tool is inextricably linked to the idea of "soft power,"[19] a term referring to the attractiveness of American ideals and ways of life. By enabling him to influence an audience beyond his borders, a president's speeches and rhetoric, which are often overlooked in discussions of national power, can become important tools for achieving state objectives.

Unlike the political tools, which can often seem abstract and without concrete form, the military tools of statecraft are certainly more easily quantified and more widely understood. Outside of the central role of the military to deter, threaten, or actually use force to achieve national objectives, however, other aspects of the military tool are worthy of attention. The provision or withdrawal of military aid, whether in the form of actual hardware or training, is a tool available to the statesman. Closely related is the use of intelligence, both as a means of obtaining necessary information and making that information selectively available to friends and allies. Additionally, the use of covert action must be considered an important tool of statecraft. Such actions can consist of virtually anything, ranging from clandestine support to like-minded states or groups, to clandestine broadcasts aimed at stirring up domestic unrest among an adversary's population, to concrete steps designed to undermine the political or military power of the adversary.

Finally, some of the least understood but most important sets of tools are economic ones. The very notion of economic statecraft seems somewhat unusual and at odds with the basic capitalist tenet of a market free from excessive governmental regulation. Yet there can be little doubt that states pursue economic policies designed to advance their own interests. The provision of economic aid, support for loans from international lending institutions, and drafting of trade agreements are all important economic tools for achieving national ends. Similarly, the withdrawal of such aid or the imposition of unilateral or multilateral economic sanctions can also be valuable tools in advancing the goals of the state.

As mentioned earlier, the discussion of the various tools available to a state in implementing its grand strategy is, by necessity, limited. The fact is that national leaders have numerous potential tools for achieving the desired strategic ends and no single tool will be useful in all cases in the pursuit of all goals. Just as Clausewitz stressed the need for genius on the part of the military commander, so too does grand strategy require a form of genius on the part of the statesman in the selection and use of specific tools toward specific ends.

CONCLUSION

Strategy in general, and grand strategy in particular, represents the most important and difficult task for the statesman of any era. History has demonstrated repeatedly that a leader's strategic failure can lead to catastrophe, while strategic brilliance pays rich rewards. It is also a uniquely human endeavor heavily influenced by the worldview and beliefs of the individuals wielding national power. Some of the most important and influential thinkers on grand strategy, such as Sun Tzu and Clausewitz, have stressed repeatedly the central role that individual genius plays in the success of a state's grand strategy. Indeed, one can only understand and explain the three central elements of any nation's grand strategy—beliefs, goals, and tools—by understanding the people who ultimately develop and implement it.

The goal of this chapter was to develop a reasonable definition of grand strategy with which to analyze the grand strategy of the Reagan administration. This definition bears repeating, as it forms the intellectual basis for the rest of this book: grand strategy is the planned use of all available tools of statecraft to achieve first-order national goals based on a given understanding or belief regarding the nature of the international system. Subsequent chapters will demonstrate that

- the Reagan administration developed and implemented a fundamentally different American grand strategy that set out to roll back the Soviet sphere of influence and undermine the bases of the Soviet state;
- the beliefs, goals, and tools used by the Reagan administration represent the culmination of almost forty years of conservative foreign policy thought; and
- the individual ultimately responsible for the development and implementation of this strategy was Reagan himself.

The Reagan Administration's Grand Strategy

With the nature of grand strategy thus analyzed and its core elements identified, it is now necessary to discuss the grand strategy of the Reagan administration, particularly in the formative period of the early 1980s. Under the Reagan administration, the United States followed a fundamentally different approach to national strategy that challenged old assumptions about how best to deal with the Soviet threat and which tools were most useful in resisting Soviet expansionism. The administration's beliefs, goals, and tools reflected a new assertiveness and determination that hastened the end of the Cold War.

Identifying any administration's grand strategy can prove a difficult task, and the Reagan administration is no exception. As noted in chapter 1, much of the conventional history of the administration, drawn as it is from journalists' accounts, is deeply flawed. Memoirs of senior administration officials, while more reliable, are also incomplete. In fact, most were written at a time when the key documents outlining Reagan's grand strategy were classified and thus could not be discussed publicly.[1] Because of this fact, even these generally useful memoirs provide only a limited insight into the administration's real strategy.

Instead, the best sources for uncovering the Reagan administration's grand strategy are National Security Council (NSC) documents. NSC documents represent the highest-level agreement possible within the U.S. government. Since they represent direct orders from the president himself, they are negotiated, debated, and finalized throughout the interagency community. A large number of key Reagan administration documents were declassified during the late 1990s, revealing a vastly different administration than the one commonly portrayed and leading to a significant rethinking of Reagan's foreign policy. These documents, while quite broad in scope, are surprisingly specific in the beliefs, goals, and tools that characterized the Reagan strategy. When combined with memoirs and interviews with senior administration officials, they provide the best possible source material for a more accurate analysis of the administration's grand strategy. This strategy, to be later outlined, consisted of a sustained military, economic, political, and ideological campaign targeting key Soviet weaknesses with the goal of winning, rather than managing, the Cold War.

BELIEFS

At first glance, one might be tempted to doubt that any effort to classify the central foreign policy beliefs of the Reagan administration is possible. There were, after all, serious differences of opinion among members of Reagan's inner circle on several important national security issues, often reflecting fundamentally different views about which courses of action were most likely to advance U.S. interests. Despite these differences of opinion on policy implementation, however, the administration's foreign policy team did share a set of well-established operating assumptions about the international system that, when studied as a whole, form a coherent worldview upon which to build a distinctly different American foreign policy. These assumptions included a rejection of both détente and containment as useful frameworks for U.S.-Soviet relations; a belief that Soviet aggression was rooted in the internal nature of the Soviet state; a conviction that power, not accommodation, was critical to dealing successfully with the Soviet Union; an understanding that the Soviets had important weaknesses that could be effectively targeted; and a belief in the moral and political superiority of democracy and capitalism.

Rejection of Containment and Détente

Virtually all accounts of American Cold War strategy revolve around two central concepts: containment and détente. Formulated under Harry Truman, the concept of containment would rapidly become the overarching intellectual approach successive administrations took in dealing with the Soviet Union. While different administrations implemented it in different ways, at its core containment was a defensive strategy aiming to prevent the expansion of Soviet control or influence, while waiting for internal factors to lead to a "gradual mellowing"[2] of Soviet behavior and its eventual transformation into a responsible, traditional "great power." Reflecting its roots in balance-of-power theory, the strategy of containment called for the United States to take actions based solely on the external policies of the

Soviet Union, while rejecting any effort to promote or accelerate change within the Soviet empire.

Nevertheless, containment was never as widely accepted as is commonly assumed. Indeed, the policy had been actively opposed and denounced by members of both the political Left and Right since its inception. Events of the 1960s and 1970s, including the Cuban Missile Crisis, the rise of Soviet military power, and the social turmoil growing out of the anti–Vietnam War movement, energized the political Left and "mainstreamed" their ideas of détente, which liberal circles had been advocating for years.[3] Liberals would find many of their ideas embraced by the most unlikely of allies, President Richard Nixon. By the early 1970s, this unusual alliance between liberals and the pro-détente wing of the Republican Party had replaced containment with détente as the intellectual framework for U.S.-Soviet relations. Under this strategic approach, the United States would actively seek to negotiate common ground with the Soviet Union by means of trade deals and arms control agreements, which would lessen the competition for influence in the Third World, reduce mutual suspicion, and give the Soviets a stake in the existing international system. This approach would remain largely intact until the inauguration of Ronald Reagan, when the United States embarked on a fundamentally different approach.

In his failed effort to win the Republican nomination for president in 1976, Reagan made Gerald Ford's support for détente a major campaign issue. Following Ford's defeat, Reagan remained actively involved in opposing and criticizing the Jimmy Carter administration's pursuit of détente. From its earliest days of office, the Reagan administration made clear that it no longer considered détente a reasonable goal of American foreign policy. Reagan himself denounced it in his first press conference as "a one-way street that the Soviet Union has used to pursue its own aims."[4] Instead of leading to international peace and stability, the Soviets had taken advantage of détente to expand their military arsenal, accelerate their efforts to destabilize Third World countries, and increase Soviet influence around the world. As Reagan later wrote, "the Russians had interpreted [détente] as a freedom to pursue whatever policies of subversion, aggression, and expansionism they wanted anywhere in the world."[5] This view of the Soviet interpretation of détente was heavily criticized at the time but was later confirmed by Anatoly Dobrynin, who acknowledged that détente drove the Soviets to become more deeply involved in the Third World.[6] As stated in a memo to National Security Advisor William P. Clark, the Reagan administration's approach seeks "to neutralize the efforts of the USSR to increase its influence" and "to foster restraint in Soviet military spending, adventurism, and to weaken the Soviet alliance system." The Soviet Union is "to bear the brunt of its economic shortcomings." The formula is not détente.[7]

While Reagan's personal rejection of détente was recognized at the time of his election, his administration also refused to consider the hallowed goal of containment a viable long-term approach for dealing with the Soviet Union. The administration considered traditional notions of containment too defensive and timid to deal with the Soviets' sustained, intense, global challenge, which had begun in the 1970s. Secretary of State George Shultz, in testimony before Congress, argued that the global reach of Soviet power had rendered containment unworkable and that the United States instead needed to begin actively pursuing its own interests.[8] Outside of a few notable exceptions,[9] there was widespread recognition at the time that the Reagan administration was uninterested in pursuing containment. Indeed, the administration's critics repeatedly attacked Reagan for abandoning containment in favor of a more confrontational approach that, in their view, substantially raised the likelihood of a military conflict with the Soviet Union.[10]

Roots of Soviet Aggression

A second core assumption of the Reagan administration's strategy was that the Soviets' aggressive behavior was a direct and natural outgrowth of its internal social and political processes. In particular, the administration focused on the link between Soviet aggression and communist ideology. Thus, Reagan argued that a state regularly violating the basic human rights of its own citizens, engaging in the brutal repression of any and all challenges to the Communist Party's monopoly on power, and being itself led by a small and unrepresentative elite with no accountability to the general population would inevitably use deceitful and violent measures against its foreign opponents as well.

The heavy emphasis the administration placed on communist ideology ran counter to the popular view of the Soviet Union put forth by many "Kremlinologists," the media, and much of the academic establishment, who argued that the role of communism in Soviet foreign and domestic policy was negligible and pro forma. According to George Kennan, one of the intellectual leaders of this view, belief in the ideals of Lenin had long since died off within the

USSR by the 1980s. While the Soviet Union remained a "communist" state, communism had become "a lifeless ideology" that was almost entirely ceremonial.[11] Although Soviet leaders continued to publicly espouse Marxist-Leninist ideology, in private they saw the pursuit of world revolution as unachievable and unrealistic in the short term.[12] Instead, Kennan and his supporters argued that a combination of great-power geopolitics and age-old Russian territorial ambitions had become the primary drivers of Soviet foreign policy. Rather than seeking international proletariat revolution and global domination, the leadership of the USSR focused primarily on preserving its superpower status and was increasingly willing to ignore ideological goals in its pursuit of Soviet national interests.[13] Nor did these analysts view Soviet domestic policy as particularly ideological in nature. They argued that "in domestic affairs, few governments are as conservative as the Soviet regime"[14] and that the Russian mentality and (alleged) preference for economic and political security over civil liberties made much of the repression a natural outgrowth of Russian political culture.[15]

The Reagan administration and its intellectual allies vehemently rejected this view and repeatedly stressed the powerful influence communist ideology had on Soviet behavior. In an NSC-drafted report entitled "Response to NSSD 11-82: U.S. Relations with the USSR," the administration set forth its collective view on the primary determinants of Soviet behavior.[16] While not ignoring the impact of Russian imperial traditions or Soviet geopolitical realities, the report highlighted the central role of communist ideology in Soviet aggression. It stressed that communist ideology "provides the intellectual prism through which Soviet leaders perceive the outside world," thus ensuring that the Soviet leadership "views non-socialist states both as potential targets for revolution and as potential threats."[17] For example, the report stated that Moscow's increased focus on "active measures," such as "political training, covert support to insurgencies, grooming of agents of influence and propaganda activities," demonstrated the Soviets' dedication to winning the "ideological struggle."[18] Additionally, communism continued to provide the primary source of the regime's legitimacy and the only justification for the repression and brutality of Soviet domestic policy. In its review of Soviet domestic policy, the report repeatedly highlighted the powerful influence communism exerted over Soviet policymakers and the unwillingness or inability of Soviet authorities to consider noncommunist solutions to their mounting internal problems.[19] This report provided the intellectual basis for National Security Decision Directive (NSDD) 75, which defined the official administration strategy toward the Soviet Union.

While the Reagan administration clearly viewed communist ideology as a central driver of Soviet foreign policy, contrary to the claims of many of its critics[20] it did not believe that the Soviets intended to conquer the world militarily, nor did it believe the Soviets had a single "master plan" for world domination. Instead, it recognized that the Soviets were ideologically committed, opportunistically expansionist, and would seek "continuing opportunities to exploit and foster international tensions and instabilities to their own advantage."[21] The administration made this assessment of the role of communist ideology in Soviet foreign and domestic policy explicit in NSDD-75, which stated that "Soviet aggressiveness has deep roots in the internal system."[22] From this assumption, the administration logically deduced that changes in the internal nature of the Soviet regime could lead to more acceptable behavior in the outside world.

Power the Key to Dealing with Soviets

A third, and closely related, assumption underlying the Reagan grand strategy was the belief that the United States could only deal successfully with an expansionist, revolutionary state such as the Soviet Union through superior power. While this conviction was certainly derived, in part, from the failure of appeasement prior to World War II, it was also founded on the recognition that a state such as the Soviet Union, whose internal politics were based on the brutal and arbitrary exercise of power, would only submit to superior power when confronted on the international scene.

The president and his advisors rejected the approach taken by the Carter administration, which Reagan characterized as "having to beg [the Soviets] to negotiate seriously with an appeal to their better nature."[23] In their view, efforts to accommodate "legitimate" Soviet concerns were counterproductive. Rather than enhancing relations with the Soviets and assuaging their (alleged) fears of Western hostility, such efforts merely encouraged further Soviet intransigence and reinforced Soviet beliefs in the inevitable triumph of communism worldwide. The Reagan team understood that, in the Soviets' ideological view of the world, international affairs was a struggle for power and all efforts at accommodation were a sign of weakness. The administration recognized that U.S. efforts to encourage Soviet involvement in solving regional issues during the period of détente had resulted in renewed Soviet expansionism and increased regional tension. Instead of peace through mutual accommodation, the motto of the Reagan administration became "peace through strength."[24] With a clear understanding of the importance the Soviets placed on power relationships, the administration believed that only overwhelming power and the willingness to use it would deter the Soviets from continued expansionism. Although this belief did not rule out the possibility of negotiations with the Soviets, it did make clear that such efforts could only supplement, not replace, genuine national strength.

While this approach may seem obvious today, opponents of the administration bitterly criticized this belief on a number of grounds. Many Soviet specialists, such as Strobe Talbott, argued that this approach was dangerous, destabilizing, and excessively confrontational, claiming that it "had forced the Soviets into a corner from which they might yet lash out."[25] They argued that pressure of any kind on the Soviets was counterproductive, as it would only provoke them into greater hostility and less flexibility. Others argued that the United States had no choice but to seek some form of mutual accommodation with Moscow, if for no other reason than that "neither superpower can realistically expect to achieve a position of dominance except at astronomical costs."[26] Since both sides had limited resources, the only wise choice was to reach a mutual understanding on the "rules of the road" so as to constrain superpower competition within specific areas. In short, they believed that the only solution to the resource limitation problem was some form of détente. While acknowledging that the Soviets were becoming increasingly active in the Third World—particularly in Angola, Nicaragua, and Afghanistan—the administration's critics insisted that these actions were essentially defensive in nature and rooted in Soviet fear and insecurity, not their desire for power.[27]

Significant Soviet Weaknesses

Although none of the core beliefs of the Reagan administration were without controversy, perhaps the most contentious (and important) was the administration's intense focus on the Soviet Union's political, economic, and demographic weaknesses. While Reagan administration officials were extremely concerned about the rapid growth of Soviet military strength and political influence that took place during the 1970s, they also firmly believed that the Soviets had important vulnerabilities that could be effectively targeted by U.S. policy. This belief served as a primary driver of U.S. policy toward the Soviet Union.

The Reagan administration understood that the Soviets' success in expanding their global influence had come at a staggering cost. By the early 1980s, it had become increasingly clear to administration officials and their supporters that the

Soviets faced massive economic and political problems that their feverish military buildup had exacerbated. The Soviet economy was facing severe, systemic challenges that raised serious questions in the minds of Reagan and his staff about its long-term viability. As Reagan stated in his autobiography, "I had always believed that, as an economic system, Communism was doomed."[28] In the early days of the administration, at the request of Director of Central Intelligence William Casey, the Central Intelligence Agency (CIA) began a detailed analysis of Soviet economic weaknesses. When presented with these findings, President Reagan became increasingly convinced of the ultimate frailty of the Soviet economy.[29]

As outlined in "Response to NSSD 11-82: U.S. Relations with the USSR," the Soviet economy was stagnating, with economic growth and labor productivity steeply declining while raw material costs were skyrocketing.[30] At the same time, the Soviets' hard currency earnings were dropping and the costs of maintaining their empire were steadily increasing: "Assistance to East European and Third World clients rose dramatically from $1.7 billion in 1971 to $23 billion in 1980—some 1.5 percent of GNP."[31] Finally, the technological backwardness of the Soviet economy, especially in the area of natural resource extraction, and the ideological blinders that prevented the regime from instituting any meaningful reforms made it heavily reliant on Western support.[32] This reliance on Western technological and financial assistance would play an important role in defining the administration's economic policy toward the Soviet Union.

As difficult as these economic troubles were for the Soviet Union, the political problems that the Soviet leadership faced were, if anything, even more challenging. At the international level, "the return of the Chinese Communist Party to active involvement in the international [communist] movement" posed a serious challenge to the Soviets' status as de facto leader of Marxist groups worldwide.[33] This need to compete with the Chinese for influence would further tax Soviet economic resources, as Soviet leaders felt compelled to offer ever more generous aid to pro-Soviet regimes. Nationalist sentiment had begun to reemerge in Eastern Europe, partially as a result of the Polish Solidarity movement. The spread of Eastern European nationalism posed a dire threat to Soviet control of the region and complicated its efforts to expand its influence in Western Europe.

Meanwhile, declining standards of living and rampant political corruption at home contributed to a widespread "loss of commitment to the [Soviet] system and to the political order" among the Soviet public.[34] Ethnic nationalism was also on the rise in Central Asia, the Ukraine, and the Baltic States, with increasingly urgent demands for greater ethnic autonomy and improved standards of living. These demands coincided with a serious demographic change within the Soviet Union, in which the non-Russian population was steadily growing while the ethnic Russian population declined. The growing importance of the nationalities problem and the gradual rise of separatist movements in the Soviet Union caught the eye of DCI Casey, who ordered the CIA in September 1981 to more closely follow these issues.[35] The Soviet leadership found nationalist demands impossible to accommodate, due both to their own ideological rigidity and the looming ideological challenge posed by China. Finally, the long-running problem of political succession continued to plague the rapidly aging Soviet leadership, making it increasingly difficult to inject new ideas into the Soviets' intellectually stagnant policies and creating the potential for internal power struggles and a divided leadership.[36]

While administration officials were not alone in recognizing the serious challenges facing the Soviet regime, they were the only ones who believed that the United States could use these weaknesses to its advantage or that these weaknesses could have any significant impact on Soviet behavior. The administration's critics argued that, while the Soviets faced serious economic and political problems, Reagan's approach was "based on an overly optimistic assessment of Soviet vulnerabilities."[37] The main criticisms of the administration generally followed two principle lines of argument. One set of critics insisted that the administration was overstating the severity of the challenges facing the Soviet Union. The other, while acknowledging the serious problems within the Soviet state, insisted that any U.S. effort to capitalize on these weaknesses would be counterproductive and end in failure. Instead, they argued that the United States should support Soviet efforts to solve these problems by reducing American pressure on the Soviet regime and expanding economic ties to the struggling Soviet economy.

While acknowledging the existence of economic and political challenges, for example, some critics argued that the Soviet Union was still strong enough to maintain its international position vis-à-vis the West without significant reform.[38] Rejecting the administration's belief that the fundamental basis of the Soviet economy was irredeemably flawed, they argued that those who "predict the imminent collapse of the economy . . . underestimate not only the basic stability of the system, but also the vast difference that would be made if things as they now are were simply made to work properly," through relatively minor improvements in bureaucratic efficiency.[39] The administration's critics took a similar view of the political challenges facing the Soviet regime, insisting that relatively minor changes would resolve the growing political challenges. While recognizing the potential problem of demographic trends that would undermine the dominant role of ethnic Russians in the Soviet Union, they insisted that it was largely manageable, primarily because these ethnic groups had materially benefited from membership in the USSR and because the central authorities could still resort to population relocation and the selective liquidation of anti-Soviet ethnic leaders.[40] The problems of corruption and popular discontent could be readily solved by the rising generation of Soviet leaders who understood the need for greater discipline and more centralized control than had existed in the late Leonid Brezhnev period. This optimistic view of Soviet strength was best summarized by the claim put forth in 1982 by two well-regarded Sovietologists who insisted that the Soviet Union "is not now nor will it be during the next decade in the throes of a true systemic crisis, for it boasts enormous unused reserves of political and social stability that suffice to endure the deepest difficulties."[41]

Another set of critics argued that even if the Soviets were facing major political and economic problems, the United States was incapable of using these problems successfully to pressure the Soviet Union or extract any meaningful advantage. In fact, they argued that any effort to do so would greatly worsen the U.S.-Soviet relationship and make real progress on the outstanding issues between the two countries more difficult. For example, one Soviet expert argued that the Soviet leadership understood that ethnic nationalism posed a very real danger of destroying the USSR but insisted that any efforts to place pressure on the regime's weaknesses were useless.[42] Others insisted that the United States lacked both the understanding and the capability to promote any meaningful change within the Soviet Union, making any such effort a waste of time and money. In the view of these critics, any resources used to attack Soviet weaknesses in an effort to obtain a strategic advantage would be wasted and better spent on improving U.S.-Soviet relations and reducing mutual tension.

Superiority of Democracy and Capitalism

The final core assumption of the Reagan grand strategy was the belief that the moral superiority of democracy represented a powerful asset in the West's battle with totalitarianism. While the administration understood very well the power wielded by the Soviet Union and its allies, it never questioned the ability of democratic societies to compete with the Soviets at the moral, political, economic, or military levels. Just as the administration emphasized the importance of communism to the behavior of the Soviet state, it also highlighted the importance of the Western ideals of natural rights and individual freedom to the United States. Rejecting the self-doubt that had infected the American approach to foreign policy since the Vietnam War, Reagan and his advisors had tremendous optimism that victory over the Soviets in the battle for the "hearts and minds" of the world was inevitable. "Reagan believed staunchly in the power of freedom"[43] and had no doubt about the attractiveness of Western ideals. The administration believed that, ultimately, it was at the level of ideas and values that the West's struggle with communism would be won.

To critics and supporters alike, Reagan's belief in the strength of free-market capitalism and democratic institutions was well known and understood. A firm believer in American exceptionalism, Reagan tirelessly emphasized the latent power of Western ideals and the vast gulf between the West's admittedly imperfect pursuit of its ideals and the Soviets' morality of convenience. For him, the Cold War was "a battle of values—between one system that gave preeminence to the state and another that gave preeminence to the individual and freedom."[44] He drew a sharp contrast between the West's belief in an objective moral code with the Soviet view that "any crime including lying is moral if it advances the cause of socialism."[45] In the administration's view, the "morality gap" was an important element of U.S. power and a fact worth highlighting internationally. NSDD-75 makes clear that U.S. policy would be based on "the superiority of US and Western values of individual dignity and freedom, a free press, free trade unions, free enterprise, and political democracy over the repressive features of Soviet Communism."[46]

GOALS

While there remains some debate over how to best characterize the worldview of the Reagan administration in general, and the beliefs of Reagan and his core advisors in particular, there is considerable evidence to indicate that the overarching, first-order goals of the administration remained remarkably consistent over time. These fundamental goals represented the preferred end state for America's strategic position and provided the "aim points" for the administration's foreign policy initiatives. The five core U.S. goals, as described in NSDD-32 and NSDD-75, consisted of the preservation and strengthening of deterrence, the expansion of U.S. global influence, the continuation of dialogue with the Soviet Union, the reversal of Soviet expansionism, and the undermining of the Soviet Union and its empire.[47]

Preserve Deterrence

During the Cold War, the most basic, fundamental goal of every administration was to protect the nation and its armed forces from a direct Soviet military attack, whether nuclear or conventional. Closely related to this necessity was the need to deter any attack on America's allies or regional partners and to successfully defeat any Soviet attack. These goals were enshrined in the administration's first official document to set forth a comprehensive statement of U.S. national strategy, NSDD-32, which President Reagan signed on May 20, 1982. In the document, he stated that the United States would seek to "deter military attack by the USSR and its allies against the US, its allies, and other important countries across the spectrum of conflict; and to defeat such attack should deterrence fail."[48]

However, while the administration was dedicated to preserving conventional and nuclear deterrence, it was not interested in preserving Mutual Assured Destruction (MAD), which had been the cornerstone of U.S. nuclear doctrine for over twenty years. Under the logic of MAD, the fact that each superpower had a large enough nuclear arsenal to wipe out a high percentage of the other's population deterred each side from starting a war. Administration officials questioned the logic behind the doctrine, arguing that MAD was rooted in highly questionable assumptions about what the Soviet leadership valued and how it might react to a crisis. Emphasizing the limited knowledge the United States had about the inner workings of the Soviet state, these officials questioned MAD's premise that "on the big issues of nuclear strategy, [the Soviets] would act as we would; they would take no risks we would not."[49]

On a personal level, Reagan was deeply offended by the moral implications of MAD and set out, early in his administration, to lay the groundwork for a different approach to deterrence. At his direction, in September 1981 he began meeting with a small group of his advisors, including Edwin Meese, National Security Advisor Richard Allen, Science Advisor George Keyworth, and presidential advisor Martin Anderson, as well as Lt. Gen. Daniel Graham, William Van Cleave, and Edward Teller, to discuss and develop what would eventually become the Strategic Defense Initiative (SDI).[50] Representing the most significant change in U.S. nuclear doctrine since the early days of the Cold War, SDI would play an important role in the administration's confrontation with the Soviet Union.

Expand U.S. Influence

The Reagan administration's second major goal was to "strengthen the influence of the U.S. throughout the world."[51] During the 1970s, Soviet global influence, particularly in the Third World, steadily increased, while the American experience in Vietnam convinced many in the West that the United States was no longer able to exert global leadership. In their view, it was a declining power whose ability to influence international events was in an unalterable decline. Many (including some conservatives) argued that the United States needed to accept that a new, multipolar world was emerging and reduce its international commitments.[52] They insisted that the administration's belief that Western cohesion relied on American strength was irrational. Instead, they insisted that U.S. retrenchment would spur Western Europe and Japan to improve their own defenses and ultimately improve the U.S. relationship with its allies.[53] Finally, some insisted that the United States had neither the moral right nor economic resources needed to expand American influence.[54] The Reagan administration rejected these claims and set out aggressively to pursue American political and economic interests.

In rejecting the claims of its critics, the Reagan administration also refused to choose between strengthening relations with its Western allies and enhancing its ties to critical Third World countries. Recognizing that the Soviets viewed the shaky political cohesion of the North Atlantic Treaty Organization (NATO) as a major strategic opportunity, the administration understood that "[s]trengthened Western unity and continued U.S. resolve" were critical U.S. foreign policy goals.[55] At the same time, however, Reagan and his team were committed to expanding U.S. influence in the Third World, which had declined so drastically in the previous decade. Particularly important were "efforts to rebuild the credibility of the US commitment to resist Soviet encroachment on US interests and those of Allies and friends, and to support effectively those Third World states that are willing to resist Soviet pressures."[56]

Such a focus on the willingness to resist Soviet advances or pressure was the critical component of this foreign policy goal. As demonstrated in both the 1981 gas pipeline controversy and the 1983 effort to deploy intermediate-range nuclear forces (INF), the Reagan administration refused to seek Western unity for its own sake. Instead, it sought to create a unified group of nations dedicated to standing up to Soviet intimidation worldwide.

Maintain Dialogue with USSR

Third, contrary to the claims of Reagan's critics,[57] the administration saw the pursuit of dialogue with the Soviet Union as an important goal of American policy. In fact, Reagan himself, early in his administration, began efforts to engage in dialogue with Soviet Premier Brezhnev through a series of personal letters.[58] Unlike arms control enthusiasts, however, the administration never equated dialogue with arms control, nor did it make the reaching of an arms control agreement, regardless of its provisions, the central U.S. goal. Instead, the administration pursued a significantly more nuanced, subtle, and strategic approach, leaving the door open to discussions on a wide range of topics while making clear that the United States would not moderate the pursuit of its long-term national interests in exchange for negotiated settlements.

In the administration's view, dialogue with the Soviet Union comprised three key elements: arms control, human rights, and Soviet international behavior.[59] In terms of arms control, the administration rejected the liberal view of arms control negotiations "as codifications of equality and as mutual commitments to preserve and honor that equality,"[60] instead insisting on agreements that "protect and enhance U.S. interests and which are consistent with the principle of strict reciprocity and mutual interest."[61] It argued that arms control agreements could not be an end in themselves, but rather a single component of a much broader effort to enhance U.S. security. The administration also insisted, contrary to Soviet wishes, that the human rights situation within the Soviet Union and Soviet conduct in the Third World were equally important topics of discussion and central elements of U.S.-Soviet dialogue. In the administration's view, dialogue on these issues was a useful tool to maintain pressure on the Soviets to behave responsibly in the Third World and highlight the high costs of Soviet misbehavior.[62]

The first three goals outlined can hardly be considered unusual. After all, every administration during the Cold War recognized the need for preserving deterrence, expanding U.S. influence, and interacting with the Soviet Union. While each pursued different approaches for achieving them, every president understood the importance of these goals. What truly set the Reagan administration apart were its fourth and fifth goals, which represented a shift away from the passive, defensive strategic approach of the past. By taking up these objectives, the administration seized the strategic offensive and pursued a "theory of victory" that guided U.S. policy toward the Soviet Union. Understanding that victory was the only outcome that could permanently eliminate the threat the Soviets posed to the West, the administration emphasized the need for "building and sustaining a major ideological/political offensive which, together with other efforts, will be designed to bring about evolutionary change of the Soviet system."[63]

Reverse Soviet Expansionism

The fourth goal of the Reagan administration was to "contain and over time reverse Soviet expansionism,"[64] not only in conventional political-military terms, but also in terms of the persistent ideological struggle. In response to steadily increasing Soviet activity in the Third World, the Reagan administration set out to challenge the fundamental bases of communist thinking and exploit the weaknesses in the Soviet's global position in order to diminish the attractiveness of the Soviet model. In time, this desire to eliminate Soviet influence and expansionism in the Third World became known as the Reagan Doctrine. However, it must be pointed out that the goal of reversing the Soviet "sphere of influence" was not limited to the developing world. The administration also set out to undermine Soviet control over Eastern Europe and eliminate the artificial division of Europe dating back to the Yalta agreements.

One of Reagan's primary efforts was attacking the so-called Brezhnev Doctrine, which stated that the spread of communist governments, in both Europe and the Third World, was irreversible. Successfully disproving the Brezhnev Doctrine, in the administration's view, would reap tremendous benefits. First, by reversing Soviet expansionism, the administration saw the opportunity to undermine the geopolitical gains the Soviets received from its client states. For example, a Soviet defeat in Afghanistan would greatly limit their ability to threaten the oil-rich Persian Gulf region, while a setback in Central America would weaken the Soviets' ability to pressure the United States in a region of special interest and sensitivity. Second, the administration believed that reversing Soviet global expansionism "might well increase the likelihood that other Third World countries would resist Soviet pressures."[65] Finally, and most importantly, the rollback of Soviet control posed a fundamental challenge to the basic ideological validity of communism by demonstrating that there was nothing inevitable or historically predetermined about communist expansion. Given the importance the Soviets placed on the ideological element of power, the administration understood that the successful overthrow of a Soviet-backed regime would have a major impact on Soviet strength and confidence.

While the Reagan Doctrine focused on Soviet expansionism in the Third World, the administration also saw Eastern Europe as an important East-West battleground. Rejecting the arguments of those who insisted that the United States had a greater interest in international stability than in a free and democratic Eastern Europe, the Reagan administration also sought to undermine Soviet control over Eastern Europe and eliminate the ability of the Soviets to effectively threaten Western Europe. As stated in NSDD-75, the administration's central goal in Eastern Europe was "to loosen Moscow's hold on the region while promoting the cause of human rights in individual Eastern European countries."[66] In pursuing this goal, the administration recognized both the need to reward Eastern European states that sought to reduce their dependence on the Soviets and to punish those that reversed or halted liberalization efforts.

Undermine the Soviet Union

Finally, and most controversially, the Reagan administration, from its earliest days, deliberately set out to undermine the cohesion of the Soviet Union and ultimately destroy the Soviet state.[67] Mindful of the Soviet Union's political, economic, and social weaknesses discussed earlier, the Reagan administration sought to decentralize the Soviet economy, weaken the power of the ruling elite (*nomenklatura*), and gradually democratize the Soviet state by forcing it to deal with its own economic weaknesses, exacerbating its own internal problem of ethnic minorities and promoting the movement within the Soviet Union toward political and economic reform.[68] This effort to undermine and destroy the Soviet Union represented the most significant change in U.S. Cold War strategic thought since the rollback theorists of the early post–World War II period. But whereas John Foster Dulles and the Dwight Eisenhower administration talked about rollback, the Reagan administration actually pursued it.[69] By taking the strategic offensive, the administration sought to break out of the "essentially reactive and defensive strategy of containment"[70] and pursue an active strategy of victory.

In pursuing this ambitious goal, the administration understood the very real dangers its strategy entailed.[71] Administration officials accepted that some segments of the U.S. and Western population would reject this goal as incompatible with détente-style efforts to reach a comprehensive East-West settlement. It also understood that, at least in the short term, this effort would raise tensions with the Soviet Union and worsen Soviet political repression and militarism. Finally, it acknowledged that U.S. policies designed to force Soviet internal change could succeed in creating a more successful, advanced, and powerful adversary. Indeed, the administration's critics raised these very concerns repeatedly during the early 1980s, attacking the administration for taking (what they viewed as) a reckless gamble with virtually no chance of success. A noted advisor to the Carter administration on Soviet policy denounced "hard-liners" within the administration for orchestrating "an ideologically driven campaign to force either capitulation on our terms or collapse of the Soviet regime by exploiting its serious economic problems and its related troubles in Eastern Europe."[72] Some critics, while acknowledging the major challenges facing the Soviets, insisted that American assistance and inducements would be more effective in promoting gradual change within the Soviet Union than would the administration's confrontational approach.[73] Others insisted that the United States should pay no attention to the Soviets' internal situation and instead should focus solely on the USSR's international behavior.[74] Finally, the intense, negative reaction in some quarters to Reagan's prediction that the West would "leave Marxism-Leninism on the ash heap of history"[75] demonstrated the widespread belief of many knowledgeable administration critics that the Soviet system was extremely stable and largely immune to external pressure.

Despite this criticism and the risks inherent in their new strategic approach, administration officials remained committed to this strategy throughout Reagan's presidency. Convinced that the internal nature of the Soviet state was the principal driver of Soviet foreign policy, Reagan and his team made Soviet internal change a centerpiece of U.S.-Soviet relations and crafted U.S. foreign policy to maximize pressure on Soviet weaknesses. Neither the rise of Mikhail Gorbachev nor the improvement in U.S.-Soviet relations in the late 1980s changed the administration's fundamental strategic approach or reasoning. While it understood that success was never guaranteed, the administration vehemently disagreed with those who saw the Cold War as a permanent feature of international affairs and set out to prove the inherent weakness of the Soviet empire.

TOOLS

As controversial as some of Reagan's goals were, the tools his administration used to pursue these goals were even more contentious. Opponents of the administration regularly denounced the approach taken by the administration as unrealistic, reckless, dangerous, and destabilizing. When viewed as a whole, however, these tools reinforced one another and directly contributed to the successful pursuit of the administration's strategic goals already outlined. The four principle tools that the Reagan administration used to weaken and defeat the Soviet Union were a large-scale defense buildup seeking to restore American military superiority; a sustained program of economic warfare aimed at undermining the ability of the Soviets to compete with the United States; an unrelenting ideological and political assault highlighting the moral differences between the United States and the Soviet regime; and an aggressive campaign of clandestine operations designed to roll back Soviet power and undermine the Soviet state.

Military Buildup

Perhaps the most obvious and well-known tool the Reagan administration used to implement its grand strategy was a large-scale, wide-ranging military buildup consisting of several important components, each having an important strategic impact on the U.S.-Soviet competition. First, the significant improvements the administration made to both nuclear and conventional forces was meant to strengthen deterrence and dissuade Soviet adventurism by sending a message to the Soviets that "we were going to spend whatever it took to stay ahead of them in the arms race."[76] The administration understood that, since Soviet leaders considered military power the "principal basis of their influence and status in international relations,"[77] a successful U.S. challenge to their military superiority could have major strategic effects. The administration's success in fielding Pershing II and cruise missiles greatly enhanced Western European defenses and undermined Soviet efforts to intimidate NATO allies. At the same time, its efforts to improve America's power-projection capabilities also forced the Soviets to reconsider its expansion into the Third World.

The second critical component of the military buildup was SDI. Representing one of the most important "paradigm shifts" in the history of nuclear theory, SDI played a major role in Reagan's confrontation with the Soviet Union. By opening the door to a sustained U.S. effort that could quickly surpass the Soviet anti–ballistic missile (ABM) efforts (which had continued in direct violation of the ABM Treaty), the administration raised the possibility of an entirely new arms race, which the Soviets could not afford, especially since such a race would emphasize high-technology systems that the Soviets had great difficulty designing and building on their own. With the potential to render worthless the massive Soviet efforts to modernize their ballistic missile force, SDI also threatened to eliminate the Soviets' first-strike capability and greatly complicate any effort to use its nuclear superiority for political advantage.

The final component of the buildup, a new assertiveness in the use of military force, also played an important role in the administration's Soviet strategy. From the beginning of the Reagan administration, the United States demonstrated that it was both willing and able to deploy military force. During the early 1980s, U.S. forces engaged Libyan fighters over the Gulf of Sidra (1981), deployed to Lebanon on two separate occasions (1982 and 1983), and invaded Grenada (1983). While each of these operations were planned and executed in response to specific threats to U.S. national interests, as a whole they represented a new willingness to confront regional insecurity with military means and a weakening of the "Vietnam syndrome" that had inhibited the United States from conducting military operations throughout much of the 1970s. These operations—particularly the Grenada invasion—also sent a clear message to the Soviets that the United States would not shrink from protecting and advancing its interests in the Third World. Additionally, this new assertiveness was aimed at reasserting U.S. leadership and expanding U.S. influence, not only in the Western alliance, but throughout the world.

Economic Warfare

The fact that the United States deliberately sought to exploit Soviet economic weakness is rarely discussed these days in discussions about the end of the Cold War. When it is mentioned, it is often dismissed as either ineffective or counterproductive.[78] Yet, throughout the early 1980s, there was widespread recognition that the Reagan administration was conducting a broad campaign of economic warfare against the Soviet Union, the goal of which was to contain Soviet power, limit the Soviets' hard currency earnings, and promote change within the Soviet Union itself. The plan that guided this effort was NSDD-66, which Reagan signed on November 16, 1982. Drafted by Roger Robinson, Director of International Economic Affairs for the National Security Council, this plan outlined a sustained Western effort to force the Soviet Union to deal with its own economic shortcomings and to weaken the Soviet economy.[79]

In exchange for lifting the highly contentious and divisive U.S. sanctions against Western companies working on the natural gas pipeline running from the Soviet Union to Western Europe, Reagan obtained from the NATO allies a firm commitment to a set of principles that would guide the West's economic dealings with the Soviet empire. In NSDD-66 (and restated in NSDD-75), he outlined the four central principles agreed to by the United States and its allies. First, in order to limit the West's vulnerability to a Soviet cutoff during a crisis, the allies agreed not to commit to any increase in the purchase of Soviet natural gas beyond the first strand of the pipeline and to accelerate development of secure Western supplies of oil and gas, such as in the Norwegian Sea.[80] This agreement virtually guaranteed that the planned second strand of the pipeline, which was expected to provide the Soviets billions of dollars in hard currency earnings, would never be built.

The allies also agreed to two other major steps that greatly limited the flow of high-technology goods to the Soviet Union. First, the West agreed to expand the list of critical technologies and equipment subject to Coordinating Committee for Multilateral Export Controls (COCOM) restrictions.[81] Doing so would enable the United States to block any transfer of sensitive technology to the Soviet Union. Second, the allies agreed to reach an early agreement on similar controls on the export of gas and oil drilling and production equipment.[82] This effort was particularly important to the Reagan administration, which understood that limiting the ability of the Soviets to develop their extensive gas and oil reserves in Siberia would greatly reduce hard currency earnings. Given the fact that these exports accounted for between 60 percent and 80 percent of the Soviets' hard currency, any serious reduction in their production capabilities would represent a significant blow to their financial health.[83]

The final component of the agreement between the United States and its allies was an understanding that Western nations would greatly curtail the provision of official credits to the Soviets for purchasing Western goods.[84] Until this agreement, Western European states had regularly offered the Soviets and their Eastern European allies extremely generous terms of credit, with very low interest rates and lengthy repayment schedules. Despite these attractive terms, Soviet and Eastern European loan repayment was unreliable and marked by frequent threats of default. In view of this problem, the administration feared that extending further credits to the East raised the very real danger of "reverse leverage," in which the lender, fearing that the loan may never be repaid, is forced to offer steadily more generous terms to the borrower. By eliminating these generous terms, the Soviets lost access to the critically needed capital sustaining their struggling civilian economy, funding their military buildup, and financing their adventurism in the Third World.

Finally, one must also see the heavy emphasis that the administration placed on the development of high-technology weapon systems as another component of this campaign of economic warfare. There is no better example of such an effort than SDI. While, as discussed, SDI was primarily aimed at redefining deterrence and ending MAD, Reagan and his aides were also well aware that the Soviets would be under immense economic pressure to compete with such a system.[85] Mindful of the Soviets' mounting economic problems, the administration understood that the scope, size, and high-technology focus of the buildup would exacerbate the Soviets' economic difficulties. It is hardly a coincidence that one of the most frequent Soviet criticisms of the defense buildup was that it was an attempt "to sabotage [Soviet] economic programs by forcing the shift of money to the military sector."[86]

Political Warfare

A third major tool that the Reagan administration employed was a heated ideological and political campaign attacking the legitimacy of the Soviet system, exposing the fallacies of Soviet propaganda, and demonstrating the value and power of American ideals. The administration deliberately planned this attack on the basic legitimacy of Marxism and mandated that the U.S. policies toward the Soviet Union maintain "a strong ideological component" aimed at communism's ideological flaws.[87] A critical component of this effort was the use of public diplomacy and international broadcasting as tools. In a series of decisions made during his first term, Reagan outlined his vision for revitalizing America's efforts to sell its ideals abroad while attacking communist ideology. Early in his first year, Reagan directed major improvements to America's public diplomacy efforts, which had been virtually ignored under the Nixon, Ford, and Carter administrations.[88]

First, recognizing that much of the equipment used by Voice of America (VOA) and Radio Free Europe/Radio Liberty (RFE/RL) was hopelessly outdated and easily jammed by the Soviets, he ordered a broad technological modernization effort to increase the broadcasting power of the radio stations and to counter (at least partially) the Soviets' jamming. Over the next several years, the administration would spend nearly $1 billion to upgrade its broadcasting facilities.[89] Second, concerned about the Soviets' increasing use of Cuban troops to support its expansionist efforts in the Third World, the administration also proposed the creation of Radio Martí, which was designed to "generate difficulties for the Castro regime at home and limit its ability to support Soviet global interests," particularly in Central America.[90] However, despite these important early efforts, a broader plan for the strategic use of public diplomacy had not yet been developed.

The first step toward correcting this shortfall occurred in July 1982 when President Reagan signed NSDD-45, which identified public diplomacy as an important tool of national policy and directed VOA to "incorporate vigorous advocacy of current policy positions of the US government."[91] This directive represented a significant change from the approach taken by previous administrations, which generally tried to eliminate any overt statements from VOA supporting the United States or attacking Soviet policies. As a result, this new, more aggressive use of information was not popular with some analysts, who argued that using VOA and RFE/RL to attack the Soviet Union was unlikely to change the views of the Soviet or Eastern European people, more likely to harden anti-U.S. sentiment, and could incite an uprising in Eastern Europe resulting in greater Soviet repression.[92] Rejecting such gloomy predictions, the administration accurately foresaw that its media campaign would strengthen internal opposition movements, weaken central control, and enhance the political standing of the West.

As a further sign of the importance President Reagan placed on public diplomacy, in January 1983 he signed NSDD-77, which created a special planning group within the NSC to coordinate, oversee, and integrate America's public diplomacy efforts into its broader national security policy.[93] These efforts to improve the ability of the United States to conduct political and ideological warfare against the Soviet Union were further enhanced by NSDD-130, which made clear that public diplomacy was a "key strategic instrument for shaping fundamental political and ideological trends around the globe" and thus vital to marginalizing and discrediting communist ideology.[94] Stressing that honest and accurate information would be the most effective means of influencing key foreign audiences, NSDD-130 directed the U.S. government to target both elites and the general population of key countries and to pay special attention to overcoming barriers to the flow of information into closed societies such as the Soviet Union and Eastern Europe.[95] Two remarkably successful programs would best reflect this new effort to engage in political warfare: Project Truth and Project Democracy.

Project Truth was the outgrowth of attempts by the U.S. Information Agency (USIA), led by Reagan's longtime friend Charles Wick, to defend against the increasingly aggressive Soviet disinformation campaign, "restore an anti-Soviet focus and mission to US international information programs," and attack the underlying behavior and morality of the Soviet state.[96] Perhaps the most potent weapon in this effort was Reagan himself. A powerful, influential speaker with a deep sense of purpose, Reagan succeeded through his speeches not only in capturing the attention of the press, but in publicizing the ideological failures of Marxism and the brutal, dehumanizing impact of communist ideology. He began his ideological battle with the Soviets at his very first press conference, attacking Lenin's statement that communists had the moral right to lie, cheat, steal, and commit virtually any crime provided it advanced the cause of communism.[97] His willingness to use his rhetorical skills to engage in ideological warfare helped effectively turn back the Soviet "peace offensive" of the early 1980s, which aimed at derailing U.S. and NATO military modernization. By pointing out the brutal, repressive policies of the Soviet regime, he reminded the West that the Soviets' one-sided peace proposals were unworthy of consideration. By highlighting the Soviets' repeated violations of international law and basic human rights, he reclaimed the "moral high ground" for the West and reminded Western publics of the fundamental differences between East and West. As Carnes Lord has noted, "to the extent that American public diplomacy as a whole came to be infused with this spirit, it represented a strategic threat of an altogether different order than the one to which the Soviets had become accustomed over the years."[98]

But the administration also understood the need to highlight not only what it opposed, but what it supported. From this understanding came Project Democracy, which was launched by Reagan himself in his famous speech to the British Parliament in June 1982, when he called on the West "to foster the infrastructure of democracy—the system of free press, unions, political parties, universities—which allow a people to choose their own way, to develop their own culture, to reconcile their own differences through peaceful means."[99] The goal of this effort was to provide support to private organizations working to strengthen democratic institutions and thereby demonstrate to both the Soviet bloc and the Third World the superiority of democratic ideals and practices. This effort quickly obtained broad, bipartisan support and led to the creation, in 1983, of the National Endowment for Democracy (NED). NED would provide overt support to nations around the world, while also serving as a conduit for covert aid to the Polish Solidarity movement as well as to Czechoslovakian dissidents.[100] While rarely discussed in most conventional histories of the Cold War, Project Democracy represented a significant change in American policy. By openly, publicly, and officially committing itself to spreading democracy, the Reagan administration expressed "a faith in the principles of liberal democracy and a confidence in the democratic future" that had a profound influence on the Soviet elites as well as the general population behind the Iron Curtain.[101]

Covert Action

The final major tool the administration used to implement its grand strategy was the vigorous use of clandestine operations to reinforce the other tools earlier outlined. Certainly the best-known set of covert operations involved U.S. material support to anti-Soviet forces, both in Europe and in the Third World. Under what eventually became known as the "Reagan Doctrine," the United States announced that it would seek to reverse Soviet expansionism by giving political, military, and economic support to anticommunist movements around the world. While this policy was not publicly announced until the 1986 State of the Union address, it was very clearly a component of Reagan's grand strategy from the outset of his presidency. Both NSDD-32 and NSDD-75 highlight the administration's goal of reversing Soviet expansionism and supporting friendly forces in the Third World.[102] Guided by this policy, the United States provided assistance to, among others, native Afghan resistance groups, the National Union for the Total Independence of Angola (UNITA), and the Nicaraguan contras. This support greatly increased the costs of Soviet aggression, demoralized the Soviet leadership, and forced the Soviets and their allies onto the defensive.[103]

While U.S. support for these movements was widely known and hotly debated during the 1980s, at least one other clandestine effort took place in the heart of Europe and remained secret until the end of the Cold War. Beginning in February 1982, the United States provided millions of dollars in aid to the Solidarity movement in an effort to help it survive martial law and ultimately overthrow Poland's communist government.[104] Most of the aid came in the form of communication equipment, fax machines, printing supplies, and photocopiers, all of which were important in keeping the movement active and its remaining leaders out of the hands of Polish authorities. While it would be a gross exaggeration to claim that U.S. aid alone saved Solidarity (the Vatican, for example, gave the movement significantly more support than did the United States), it was nonetheless an important component of the administration's grand strategy.

The administration engaged in several other covert operations to reinforce and support the overt military, economic, and political tools previously discussed. For example, the administration's public diplomacy and international broadcast efforts were supplemented by a covert CIA program that smuggled anti-Soviet propaganda into predominantly Muslim Soviet Central Asia.[105] The Soviet invasion of Afghanistan had generated significant unrest in Soviet Central Asia. These operations built on this unrest and on the Soviets' economic and political problems in the region and were designed further to complicate the Soviets' problem of internal control.

Finally, the Reagan administration ran a little-known but extremely important covert operation designed to undermine the Soviet economy. In the summer of 1981, French president François Mitterrand informed Reagan that French intelligence had successfully recruited a KGB colonel named Vladimir Vetrov who was assigned to Line X, the KGB's directorate dedicated to the theft of Western technology.[106] With the detailed information on Soviet technology theft provided by Vetrov (code name "Farewell"), the CIA and Federal Bureau of Investigation began feeding disinformation to the Soviets, greatly complicating their efforts to integrate high technology into their economy. Numerous faulty blueprints and schematics were sold to the Soviets, as were deliberately sabotaged computer chips and other flawed technologies, which caused system failures, plant shutdowns, and other economic disruptions. In addition, thanks to the information Vetrov provided, over two hundred Line X officers and sources were expelled or compromised, decimating the Soviets' technological intelligence operations and further weakening their ability to obtain critically needed Western material. By slowing their ability to obtain useful Western technology and raising doubts about the value of the material they were able to steal, this program, coming at a time of significant Soviet economic problems, had a devastating impact on the Soviet economy.

CONCLUSION

The three components of grand strategy—beliefs, goals, and tools—are particularly evident in the Reagan administration's national strategy. Unlike his predecessors, Reagan rejected containment, which had been the dominant belief system of America's Soviet policy during most of the Cold War, and instead espoused a belief that winning the Cold War was possible. The administration promoted radically new goals for the United States, including the destabilization and ultimate defeat of the Soviet Union, and made use of tools, such as economic and political warfare, which had been widely considered ineffective or counterproductive. While a change in any one of the core components of U.S. grand strategy would have been noteworthy, the fundamental changes the Reagan administration made to all three elements of grand strategy demonstrate the revolutionary nature of the Reagan strategy.

However, defining the Reagan administration's grand strategy is just the first step in understanding its intellectual roots. Given the highly personal nature of grand strategy and the pervasive influence individuals exert over the definition and implementation of strategy, it is necessary to identify the strategists whose thinking and writing were particularly important to the development of the Reagan foreign policy. The next chapter will trace the history of conservative thought following World War II and demonstrate the intellectual pedigree of Reagan's strategy.

Beliefs

As discussed in the previous chapter, the Reagan administration embraced from its earliest days a grand strategy fundamentally different from the approaches of its predecessors, both Democratic and Republican. At its core, this strategy focused on ending the stalemate of the Cold War by pursuing a goal of Western victory. Still, the core ideas and fundamental tenets of the Reagan strategy did not spontaneously generate in 1981, but rather they represent the embodiment of a long-standing conservative approach to foreign policy that had been developing since the beginning of the Cold War.

One of the most enduring myths of U.S. Cold War strategy is the belief that, in contrast to the heated, divisive debates that characterized domestic policy, there existed a broad consensus among the American people on foreign policy issues. Indeed, as the Cold War continues to recede into the past, there is a growing tendency among historians to gloss over, understate, or completely ignore the very real disagreements that routinely arose over critical foreign policy issues. Yet any fair-minded review of Cold War history will reveal numerous cases in which fundamental issues of grand strategy were hotly contested. In the early postwar period, the Truman administration was repeatedly criticized both by those who felt it was being too confrontational with the Soviets and by those who felt it was not being confrontational enough. During the 1950s, debates raged over the conduct of the Korean War, the Suez Crisis, the U.S. role in Eastern Europe, decolonization, and the defense budget. This pattern continued throughout the 1960s and 1970s, with highly divisive debates on Vietnam, arms control, and détente being the most widely recognized. In short, American Cold War history is replete with cases of presidents making difficult choices over critical strategic issues despite vehement opposition from some segments of society. In each case, the president's ultimate decision largely reflected his priorities, beliefs, and fundamental view of the world.

As a result, it should come as no great surprise that, in tracing Reagan's "strategic lineage," conservative foreign policy thinkers had an important formative influence on the eventual Reagan strategy. After all, Reagan was the first (and only) truly conservative president of the Cold War and had been a leading spokesman for the conservative movement for decades before his presidency. Contrary to the claims of many critics, Reagan had a long-standing interest in foreign affairs and a strong sense of what the United States needed to accomplish in the world.[1] The strategy his administration developed and successfully implemented was a direct descendent of the rollback theorists of the early Cold War, the Goldwater conservatives of the 1960s, and the neoconservatives of the 1970s, and represents a distinctive, conservative approach to foreign policy. This chapter will trace the development and evolution of each of the five core beliefs of the Reagan strategy and highlight its critical intellectual ancestors.

REJECTION OF CONTAINMENT AND DÉTENTE

As discussed in the previous chapter, the Reagan administration came to office with a fundamentally different approach to relations with the Soviet Union. Rather than rely on the timid, defensive approach of a containment policy or accept the strategic dangers of continuing the failed policies of détente, Reagan chose to take the initiative, seize the strategic offensive and seek a Western victory in the Cold War. This decision to pursue a policy of confrontation represented the culmination of almost forty years of conservative foreign policy thought.

Early Cold War Period

The end of World War II gave rise to an extensive and heated dialogue on the proper role of the United States in the world and, more specifically, the proper approach for it to take in dealing with its fellow superpower, the Soviet Union. Many Americans had hoped that the wartime allies, perhaps by working through the United Nations, could avoid the great-power clashes that had contributed to World Wars I and II. Nevertheless, as the euphoria of the defeat of Germany and Japan died off and the Soviets began tightening their grip on Eastern Europe and supporting communist insurgencies worldwide, it became increasingly clear that the political struggle between the United States and the USSR would not be resolved quickly or easily. While a small segment of the West continued to hold out hope for renewed cooperation between the two sides, the great debate on U.S. foreign policy shifted from whether the superpowers could work together, to how best to protect the United States and its allies from the Soviet threat. The dominant position was best expressed in the famous "X Article" written by George Kennan and published in *Foreign Affairs* in 1947.[2] According to Kennan, the most reliable method for preventing further Soviet expansionism was to confront the Soviets with "unalterable counterforce at every point where they show signs of encroaching upon the interests of a peaceful and stable world" until such time as the Soviets' own internal development led to the "breakup or gradual mellowing of Soviet power."[3]

While it would soon become the "default" U.S. grand strategy during the Cold War, containment was never widely accepted by conservatives, many of whom had deep reservations about its strategic wisdom and supported a fundamentally different approach to protecting the United States from the Soviet threat. At the same time, however, one must exercise considerable caution when tracing the history of conservative foreign policy thought, especially in the early days of the Cold War. Fighting and winning World War II caused radical changes in America's position in the world and its psychological outlook. Understanding and reacting to these changes posed a special challenge for conservatives, many of whom had been isolationists before the war. Although the vast majority of conservatives ultimately embraced a greatly enhanced U.S. role in the world, there were numerous foreign policy debates within the movement. While these debates sharpened and refined conservative foreign policy thinking, they also make it particularly difficult to identify specific individuals who can be seen as representing the "typical" conservative. Nevertheless, one individual in particular stands out as the focal point of conservative foreign policy thought during this period: James Burnham. A former Trotskyite turned dedicated conservative, Burnham provided the intellectual foundation for a distinctive, conservative approach to foreign policy and served as the "chief global strategist" of *National Review*, the most important conservative journal of the day.[4]

Despite their occasional internal differences, however, most conservatives focused on two major criticisms of containment. First, conservatives argued that containment was a fundamentally flawed approach because it was an entirely defensive strategy. Pointing out that a NATO-wide policy of containment could only work if the Soviets were willing to pursue a similar policy, conservatives stressed that there was no sign that the Soviets were even marginally interested in reaching such an accommodation.[5] While agreeing that Soviet expansionism needed to be halted, conservatives felt that containment failed to provide any meaningful end state that could guide American policy, other than the unfounded hope that one day the Soviet Union may "mellow." As Burnham noted, "a defensive policy . . . can never win."[6] Burnham went on to argue that "our present planning and policy cannot stop the communists more than temporarily, nor can any other plan or policy which is essentially defensive."[7] Others pointed out that constantly responding to Soviet efforts to subvert friendly governments worldwide committed "the free world to dealing with symptoms while ignoring causes" of international tension.[8] At best, such a defensive policy could slow the West's defeat and make victory more difficult for the Soviets, but it could not, in itself, change the ultimate outcome. Mindful of the West's experiences with Nazi Germany, conservatives stressed that a stable international order was impossible "between democracies and totalitarianism, or between free economies and economic dictatorship."[9] For this reason, conservatives urged the United States to seize the strategic initiative and force Moscow onto the defensive, arguing that "victory and even, in the long run, survival come only by carrying through an attack, only by passing to the offensive."[10] This belief in the need for a more assertive, offensively minded West would become a core element of conservative foreign policy thought during the Cold War.

The second key criticism that early conservatives leveled against the containment strategy was that it played to Soviet strengths while exposing Western vulnerabilities. Conservatives pointed out that the Soviets were making heavy use of indigenous communist parties and movements to undermine friendly governments. Given the ease with which these movements could infiltrate the open societies of the West and play on the anti-Western sentiment of the recently decolonized Third World nations, conservatives argued that defending against Soviet expansion would prove increasingly difficult for the West.[11] Particularly in the aftermath of the McCarthy hearings (which also caused deep divisions within the conservative movement), they argued that Western leaders were becoming steadily less willing to make the sustained, global effort required to challenge communist expansionism. Burnham was particularly concerned about this erosion of national will and insisted that the West needed an immediate reawakening or it would face possible destruction.[12] As evidence of the failure of containment, another important conservative author of this period, Eugene Lyons, pointed out that within a few years of containment becoming official U.S. policy, a popular government in Czechoslovakia was overthrown, China and Tibet were taken over by communists, and an anti-Western brand of neutralism had spread to portions of the Third World.[13] These events demonstrated to conservatives that containment could not lead to a lasting peace; in fact, conservatives strongly believed that superpower tension and the numerous conflicts of the period were "the inevitable products" of the containment policy.[14]

In short, conservatives in the early Cold War period argued that containment was both a deeply flawed strategic concept and a politically unsustainable policy offering no realistic hope of long-term security for the United States or its allies.

Middle Cold War Period

By the end of the postwar era, conservatives had reluctantly accepted that neither Democratic nor Republican administrations were willing to reconsider containment or give serious consideration to conservative foreign policy ideas. While the Eisenhower administration began by talking about "rollback" and "liberation," the president had secretly decided early in his first term not to seek any meaningful deviation from the containment strategy that Kennan had proposed.[15] Eisenhower's refusal to respond in any meaningful way to the Soviet repression of the 1956 Hungarian revolution made abundantly clear that he was uninterested in pursuing a genuinely conservative foreign policy.

Despite these setbacks, the conservative approach to grand strategy continued to develop, with a rising new crop of conservative strategists building on the ideas of their predecessors. This new set of conservative voices would finally find a true supporter in Barry Goldwater, who was dedicated to implementing the ideas they had been developing for almost two decades. Despite his landslide defeat in the 1964 presidential election, his candidacy proved a defining moment in American conservatism and fueled the further development of conservative foreign policy thought. While Goldwater was certainly the most well-known figure in American conservatism, several other notable figures emerged during this period to refine conservative foreign policy thought. Throughout the 1960s, these men reinforced and refined the conservative opposition to containment, while further challenging the arguments of an increasingly large segment of society seeking "peaceful coexistence" or détente with the Soviets.

One of the most important and influential conservative scholars during this period was Robert Strausz-Hupé, an Austrian-born professor and political philosopher.

Building on the criticisms that earlier conservatives had leveled against contain-ment, Strausz-Hupé argued that the United States had unwisely yielded the strate-gic initiative and accepted the Soviet distinction between the "peace zone," which consisted of Soviet-controlled areas, and the "war zone," which consisted of the rest of the world.[16] By accepting this distinction, the West had opened the door to large-scale Soviet subversion, while refusing to seize opportunities to disrupt Soviet control of Eastern Europe. This decision to acquiesce in a sustained Soviet effort to expand its influence came at a particularly dangerous time for the West. The widespread political upheaval resulting from decolonization had already gener-ated a significant amount of anti-Western sentiment in the Third World. By tac-itly accepting the Soviet argument that these areas were suitable grounds for superpower competition while accepting the inviolability of Soviet influence in Eastern Europe, the United States had essentially granted the Soviets the chance to make significant gains while limiting itself to, at best, preserving the status quo. To conservatives, such a policy represented an absence of rigorous strategic thought and demonstrated the intellectual failure of containment as a plausible theory for winning the Cold War.

Nor was this criticism of containment the only one conservatives would make during this period. Much like his predecessors, Strausz-Hupé expressed his con-cern that containment, by permitting the Soviets "to devote [themselves] full time to the job of aggression," would ultimately weaken the West's morale and under-mine its long-term willingness to resist communist expansion.[17] This criticism was echoed by several other conservative foreign policy analysts during this period, who argued that the status quo that containment sought to preserve was strategi-cally foolish and impossible to sustain in the long term. They argued that the USSR was not, and would never be, a status quo power and thus would never stop seeking to expand communism worldwide.[18] Thus, conservatives believed the theory that communism would "mellow" over time was neither plausible nor supported by any existing evidence.

Conservatives, sharing Burnham's concern about the ability of the West to sus-tain its willingness to confront Soviet aggression, were more convinced than ever that only a clearly stated goal of victory would sustain Western resolve to fight the "protracted conflict" of the Cold War. It was, therefore, critical for the United States to seize the initiative and go on the strategic offensive. As Goldwater pointed out, under the strategy of containment the United States witnessed a rapid expan-sion of Soviet influence throughout the Third World and an equally rapid decline in Western influence.[19] Only by making it clear to the world that the United States intended to not merely halt this trend, but reverse it, could the West achieve real security. In the view of these conservatives, the Cold War could not last forever and would end either in a Western victory over communism or the collapse and destruction of Western civilization.

Nor did this new breed of conservatives place much faith in the other major strategic approach that emerged during the 1960s: "peaceful coexistence" or détente. Indeed, most of the conservative criticism of U.S. foreign policy during this period focused on the dangers such a policy posed to the West. Using arguments strikingly similar to their criticisms of containment, conservatives stressed that the Cold War could not end without the capitulation of one side or the other. Thus, efforts to reduce tension were pointless, as they could never eliminate the fundamental incompatibility of the two competing systems. In Strausz-Hupé's view, the United States and the USSR had been engaged in a long-term "protracted conflict" since the end of World War II that could not be resolved by either negotiations or the relaxation of tensions. Because "permanent coexistence between systems so fundamentally opposed as closed societies and open societies is impossible," this conflict could never be resolved until either Western-style democracy or Soviet communism emerged as the dominant model of human society.[20] In the view of most conservatives, any effort to relax tensions with the Soviet Union was more likely to encourage increased Soviet expansionism and greater international instability than it was to reassure the Soviets of the peaceful intentions of the West. Harshly criticizing those who sought to change the fundamental nature of the superpower competition by demonstrating the West's goodwill and peaceful intentions, Burnham (who would remain a major figure in conservative foreign policy thought until the late 1970s) argued that the John F. Kennedy and Lyndon B. Johnson administrations' efforts to pursue a policy of détente and coexistence "disguised underlying attitudes of appeasement and capitulation" and could only result in a stronger, more dangerous communist movement and a weakened, demoralized West.[21] Not only would such a policy have a corrosive effect on Western will, but conservatives feared such a policy could actually increase the danger of war, as it could encourage the Soviets to take greater risks (particularly in the Third World) while misjudging the likelihood of a strong Western response.

Conservatives also pointed out that the very term "peaceful coexistence" had a vastly different meaning to Soviet leaders than it did to those in the West. To its advocates in the West, it represented a world in which the two blocs agreed to accept the status quo and halt all efforts to shift the balance of power or spread their respective political and economic systems. Conservatives criticized this policy's supporters in the United States for believing that détente could change Soviet perceptions and goals and thereby create an "emerging Communist Party of the Soviet Union that is worthy of the West's trust and friendship."[22] Such a belief, they argued, represented a fundamental misunderstanding of the Soviet concept of peaceful coexistence. Conservatives stressed that, to the Soviets, peaceful coexistence was not a description of their preferred end state, but rather a strategy to continue their political struggle against the United States, with the ultimate aim of global domination.[23] The core beliefs and central goals of Soviet grand strategy remained the same under détente—only the tools they would use had changed. Rather than resorting to direct military force, which risked a major response by the superior military power of the West, the Soviets saw political warfare and clandestine support to anti-Western movements as valuable and legitimate tools for use under a policy of détente. Conservatives further warned that the Soviets would use détente, and particularly the "gestures of mutual consultation and apparent goodwill," to undermine the legitimacy of anticommunism as a reputable policy within Western society and thereby weaken Western resolve.[24] Citing numerous public statements by Soviet officials, conservatives also argued that the Soviets sought to use the strategy of peaceful coexistence in the Third World as a way of "mobilizing the masses and launching vigorous action against the enemies of peace," namely, pro-Western rulers in the Third World.[25] By encouraging the spread of "neutralism" in the wake of decolonization, the Soviets saw an opportunity to convince the United States to withdraw its support for its anticommunist allies in the Third World. Once the ties to the United States were disrupted, the Soviets could then more easily make use of coups and subversion to topple "neutral" regimes and place reliable, pro-Soviet leaders in power.

This recognition that peaceful coexistence represented not a final settlement to the Cold War, but rather a new and more dangerous phase of Soviet aggression, would become a central tenet of conservative thinking and would be reinforced by later conservative and neoconservative strategists.

Late Cold War Period

As the 1960s came to a close, the United States was deeply divided over the conduct of American foreign policy. Protests against the Vietnam War were swelling, and large segments of the foreign policy establishment and the general public condemned the very notion of a forceful, vigorous, anticommunist U.S. foreign policy. Instead, much of the foreign policy elite insisted that the time was right for the United States to seek a more cooperative approach: détente. This leftward shift in American foreign policy thinking, especially within the Democratic Party, helped give rise to a new breed of conservatives, the "neoconservatives."

While their influence was never as great as some of their supporters (and critics) would later claim, these neoconservatives were destined to play an important role in further refining conservative foreign policy thought. Still, the neoconservatives' core arguments were surprisingly similar to, and in some cases derived from, those that traditional conservatives had been making for two decades. In particular, much of the intellectual rigor and flavor that would characterize neoconservative foreign policy thought can be traced back to traditional conservatives such as James Burnham.[26]

While conservatives (and now neoconservatives) continued to question the fundamental assumptions underlying containment,[27] the bulk of their critique of U.S. foreign policy focused on détente. In fact, by the mid-1970s, the debate over détente had become the single most important foreign policy issue dividing liberals and conservatives. Arising out of this debate and driven by a concern that détente had led to a weakening of American resolve and that the balance of power had begun to shift decisively in the Soviets' favor, a number of notable conservatives and neoconservatives joined to form an organization that would exert a profound influence on the strategic debate: the Committee on the Present Danger (CPD). Founded in 1950 by (among others) Paul Nitze, Charls Walker, and Eugene Rostow, the CPD was a bipartisan group that sought to alert the general public to the growing Soviet threat and to rally national decision makers to take the measures necessary to counter this threat.[28] While often depicted as a primarily neoconservative organization, CPD membership was extremely broad and included both traditional conservatives (such as Colin Gray and Robert Strausz-Hupé) and neoconservatives (such as Jeane Kirkpatrick and Richard Perle). Reagan himself joined in January 1979, and a number of CPD members were appointed to positions in the Reagan administration.[29] The CPD and other conservatives viewed the rise of détente as proof of their contention that Western publics would never support a static, defensive strategy such as containment over an extended period of time. For conservatives, détente had not only failed to promote any meaningful change in either Soviet goals or Soviet institutions, but had also given the Soviets a significant strategic advantage.

Many of its supporters in the West saw détente as a way to end the global strug-gle for power and influence that had, in their view, undermined relations between the superpowers. Believing that military superiority no longer had any meaning, they insisted that the United States take the lead in building a new relationship with the Soviets, founded on a set of clear principles.[30] These principles, which would eventually be enshrined in the U.S.-USSR "Statement of Basic Principles" signed in May 1972, included an agreement that both sides would avoid situations that could lead to military confrontation, cease efforts at unilateral advantage, work to avoid situations that contribute to international tension, and claim no spe-cial rights anywhere in the world.[31] At its most basic level, then, détente both required the superpowers to institute fundamental changes in their behavior and presumed that better economic and political relations between the two would reduce the Soviets' incentives to continue their arms buildup or exacerbate inter-national tension.

In the view of most conservatives, such an approach was built on "a monu-mental piece of fatuous misjudgment," namely, that the Soviets would ever will-ingly foreswear efforts to gain a unilateral advantage.[32] As conservatives pointed out, the Soviets steadfastly refused to make any significant change in their inter-national behavior and began violating the "Basic Principles" almost immediately, backing their Arab clients in the October 1973 Yom Kippur War and flagrantly violating the 1973 agreement on Indochina. Nor, indeed, did the Soviets show any signs of reducing their massive military buildup, instead continuing and acceler-ating its modernization efforts. Throughout the 1970s, conservatives stressed that Soviet foreign policy remained aggressive and expansionist, while détente's com-mercial and political agreements had done nothing to alter the Soviets' openly professed goal of destroying the Western democratic system.[33]

This behavior reinforced the long-standing conservative contention that the Soviet and Western concepts of peaceful coexistence were fundamentally different and incompatible. Conservatives continued to argue, as they had throughout the Cold War, that the Soviets saw détente not as a means of ensuring world peace, but as a grand strategy aimed at undermining the political and economic cohesion of the West while building up Soviet military power.[34] Ultimately, conservatives felt that Soviet behavior clearly indicated that overarching Soviet policy had not changed but had merely become "more sophisticated in style" and thus harder to stop.[35]

In addition to highlighting repeated Soviet violations of both the terms and spirit of détente, conservatives also argued that the U.S. pursuit of this policy had conceded to the Soviets two important strategic advantages. First, conservatives noted that the relaxation of international tension had enhanced the ability of the Soviets to influence Western policies. In particular, détente had granted them easier access to Western technology and financial credits, which were critically needed to sustain the Soviet economy while providing relatively little gain for the West.[36] Furthermore, by convincing much of the foreign policy establishment that the only alternative to détente was a third world war, the Soviets were able to pressure Western policymakers into make greater concessions, particularly in the area of arms control, thus further shifting the balance of power in the Soviets' favor. Second, conservatives argued that détente had allowed the Soviets to manipulate Western publics and politicians. By publicly attacking any Western policy that the Soviets did not approve of as inconsistent with détente and a threat to world peace, the Soviets were able to use the peaceful intentions of the general public to undermine the West's will to resist Soviet expansionism. At the same time, détente strongly implied a certain moral equivalence of the two superpowers that "divorced the idea of freedom from the US stance in international affairs" and thereby sapped a source of the West's ideological and political strength.[37] In short, conservatives believed that détente was not a solution to the East-West struggle, but rather a Soviet-supported tactic for achieving global superiority and a strategic disaster for the West.

As already outlined, conservatives throughout the Cold War consistently argued that containment and détente were unwise and unsound strategic approaches. They argued that these policies would encourage Soviet expansionism, weaken Western resolve, and render an acceptable outcome to the Cold War impossible. Instead, they called for the United States and its allies to seize the strategic initiative and develop a truly global strategy aimed at a Western victory.

MAJOR ROLE OF COMMUNIST IDEOLOGY IN SOVIET FOREIGN POLICY

While recognizing that Russian culture and long-standing Russian national interests did have some influence over Soviet actions, most conservatives argued that communist ideology was the primary driver of Soviet behavior. In particular, they argued that communism set forth the guiding vision of Soviet foreign policy, validating the Soviets' declared goals and justifying Soviet behavior. Because of the central role Marxist ideology had for the Soviet Union, conservatives argued that understanding, confronting, and defeating Soviet ideology was a critical element of any successful U.S. grand strategy.

Early Cold War Period

In the early days of the Cold War, there was a fairly widespread agreement among foreign policy analysts that Soviet foreign policy was heavily influenced by communist ideology. Even Kennan, who would in subsequent years deny that communist ideology played any significant role in Soviet behavior, highlighted that communism "has profound implications for Russia's conduct as a member of the international community."[38] But this consensus would not last very long. The rise of Sen. Joseph McCarthy and his accusations of widespread communist infiltration of the U.S. government made anticommunism a less reputable political position, while Nikita Khrushchev's "secret speech" denouncing Joseph Stalin raised the hopes of Western liberals that the Soviets had given up elements of their ideology and had become a more traditional great power. By the mid-1950s, the belief that communism remained central to explaining Soviet foreign policy was found almost exclusively among conservatives. Conservatives in the early days of the Cold War consistently argued that both the Soviets' goals and their behavior demonstrated the importance they placed on communist ideology.

Of the major conservative writers of this period, none played a greater role in highlighting the ideological dimension of the communist threat than Hannah Arendt. In her seminal work *The Origins of Totalitarianism*, Arendt analyzed the nature of totalitarian rule and identified the mindset that animated totalitarian movements. She noted that, when compared to other parties or political organizations, totalitarian movements were characterized by "their demand for total, unrestricted, unconditional, and unalterable loyalty of the individual member," a fact that made ideological moderation or internal reform unlikely.[39] Arendt stressed that, for totalitarian movements (such as Soviet communism), "the scientificality of totalitarian propaganda" was essential to maintaining control of the population, as it provided the only justification for the regime's political repression and use of terror.[40] Thus, for members of the Soviet leadership, communist ideology was neither a convenient cover masking Russian national objectives nor a passing intellectual fad, but rather the defining element of the Soviet system. Future conservatives (as well as her own contemporaries) would echo and build upon this assessment of ideology's critical importance to the Soviet Union.

While Arendt provided the philosophical basis for conservatives' focus on communist ideology, others were demonstrating the close linkage between communism and Soviet foreign policy goals. In that effort, none were as insistent as James Burnham and Whittaker Chambers. As former communists, they understood better than most the priority the Soviets placed on ideological indoctrination and the influence communist doctrine had on the worldview of the Soviet leadership. In Chambers's view, the Soviets saw communism as much more than merely a form of government rooted in Marxist thought. It was, instead, a "rival faith" that guided the Soviets' challenge to the West.[41] Similarly, Burnham argued that since the days of Marx, communism had always been an ideology with the absolute end of a global communist empire. The Soviet Union's core goal, which it repeatedly and publicly expressed, was to fulfill that ideological imperative.[42] While not denying the influence of traditional Russian interests on Soviet behavior, Burnham and his fellow conservatives insisted that the primary motive for Soviet expansionism was to encourage the spread of communist governments worldwide.[43] Nor was the pursuit of this goal mitigated by conventional morality. As one conservative noted, Lenin and his successors "repeatedly defined morality as whatever will advance the success of the communist cause."[44] Reagan himself would make an almost identical statement early in his presidency.

In addition to highlighting the influence communist ideology had on the professed goals of the Soviet Union, conservatives also noted that Soviet international behavior provided compelling evidence of the powerful influence of communist ideology. For conservatives, the Soviets' use of military force to suppress "bourgeois uprisings" in Eastern Europe was only the most obvious example of the Soviet dedication to maintaining and expanding communist influence. A number of other Soviet actions clearly demonstrated the centrality of communist ideology. Throughout the Cold War, conservatives were careful to emphasize both the wide range of tools and the inherent tactical flexibility that communist ideology afforded Soviet rulers. Some conservatives, for example, stressed that Stalin's postwar refusal to cooperate with the West, particularly in light of the Soviets' critical need for aid in rebuilding their country, could only be understood in light of communism's visceral opposition to the capitalist economic order and its deep-seated paranoia that widespread contact with the West (and particularly Western ideas) could destabilize the Soviet regime.[45] Similarly, conservatives argued that the Soviets' extensive use of infiltration, espionage, and propaganda to influence Western society represented a clear link to Lenin's use of similar techniques to facilitate his own seizure of power.[46]

Finally, conservatives noted that the Soviets' efforts to expand were truly global and thus reflected the universal ambitions of communist ideology. They stressed that the rapid increase in Soviet military and political support to communist movements in such areas as Malaya, Costa Rica, and the Philippines—areas far outside Russia's traditional sphere of influence—was a clear indication that ideology, not historical ambitions or geopolitics, was the primary driver of Soviet foreign policy.[47]

Middle Cold War Period

Unlike their more liberal counterparts, conservatives throughout the middle phase of the Cold War continued to emphasize the significant influence that communist ideology had on the goals and behavior of the Soviet Union. In fact, one of the most important disputes between liberals and conservatives during this period was over the role of Marxist ideology in determining Soviet actions.[48] Many liberals downplayed the differences between the leadership of the two superpowers, insisting that most of the Soviets' actions were defensive in nature and rooted in the fear of Western invasion. Liberals argued that the conservative view of the Soviet leadership as committed communists was wrong, instead insisting that Soviet leaders were more interested in improving the lives of their people than in pursuing larger, ideological goals.[49] Conservatives, on the other hand, continued to insist that the role of communist ideology in Soviet behavior had not diminished and increasingly saw the Cold War as a struggle between two inherently incompatible ideologies.

Throughout the 1960s, conservatives continued to argue that the Soviet Union remained committed to aggressive, ideologically based expansionism, with the ultimate goal of global supremacy. Building on the arguments of their predecessors, conservative strategists emphasized that the Soviet leadership's view of international politics was heavily colored by Marxist ideology and thus fundamentally opposed to a stable, long-term peace with the West. They pointed out, for example, that despite Khrushchev's "secret speech" and the denunciation of Stalin's crimes, the Soviets had shown no signs of reducing their support for global revolution or of abandoning their efforts to overthrow the existing global order.[50] If anything, they argued, the events of the 1960s had reinforced the ideological convictions of the Soviet leadership. Given the steady expansion of communist influence worldwide and the internal turmoil resulting from Western decolonization, conservatives rightly asked, "What reason does a man looking with Khrushchev's eyes have for abandoning the view that 'capitalist-imperialism' is decadent" and doomed to collapse?[51] Conservatives saw no evidence that the mellowing of ideological fervor, which liberals claimed was the inevitable outcome of Soviet economic growth, had begun. Instead, communist ideology remained the unifying factor and the primary motivation guiding the Soviet elite.[52]

In light of the continued importance of communist ideology and the sustained Soviet efforts to expand the reach of their ideology, conservatives during this period increasingly focused on the centrality of the ideological battle to the ultimate outcome of the Cold War. Winning this ideological battle required understanding the fundamental basis of Marxist thought. Communist theory, they pointed out, did not arise out of an altruistic desire for social justice, but rather from Karl Marx's claims to have discovered the fundamental laws of human history.[53] Conservatives argued that it was the belief in these "laws of history," not economic collectivism, that represented the key to understanding and defeating communist ideology.[54] The communist belief in historical determinism provided the justification and motivation for Soviet conduct, including the use of violence, subversion, and aggression as tools for achieving the historically inevitable communist world. Conservatives believed that rather than focusing solely on the expansionism and aggression resulting from communist ideology, the most practical and effective solution to resolving the Cold War was to undermine and destroy the root cause: communist doctrine. In particular, conservative strategists argued that it was critical to disprove the Soviets' claim that a communist world was a historical inevitability. For conservatives, the West's larger goal of a free and peaceful world could only come about after the decisive defeat and elimination of the world communist movement and the thorough discrediting of communist ideology.[55] Thus, American grand strategy needed to focus more heavily on the ideological battle between East and West.

Late Cold War Period

The dispute over the influence of communist ideology on Soviet behavior remained a major topic of debate during the 1970s. In fact, as has been discussed, one of the core assumptions of the détente policy was the belief that the Soviets no longer really believed in communism and had become a traditional great power. Détente supporters argued that traditional methods of statecraft, such as negotiations and mutual accommodation, were the best way to maintain international peace.

During this period, much of the foreign policy establishment focused primarily on the alleged continuity between the policies of prerevolutionary czarist Russia and those of the Soviet Union. Some, such as Kennan, argued that Marxism's influence on Soviet policies had evaporated within a few years of the Bolsheviks coming to power.[56] Others, while acknowledging that Soviet behavior during the early Cold War did have an important ideological component, insisted that the Soviets recognized the folly of such an ideological view of the world and had abandoned their efforts to change the international system.[57] In either case, however, the view of most liberals was that efforts to challenge the validity of communism or to conduct "ideological warfare" against communist doctrine was a waste of time that could only increase international tension without advancing American interests.

Given the close connection between détente and this view of Soviet ideology, it was logical that conservatives of the 1970s would continue to focus on the impact of communism on the goals and actions of the Soviet Union, arguing that the Soviets continued to strive for global communist domination. Both established conservative figures, such as Barry Goldwater, James Burnham, and M. Stanton Evans, and the emerging neoconservatives argued that the Soviets had not given up their goal of world domination, nor had they ceased their efforts to overthrow pro-Western governments and support pro-Soviet regimes in the Third World. This consistency in Soviet foreign policy was hardly a surprise, as conservatives pointed out that the ruling elite of the Soviet system viewed conflict and violence as the "natural regulators of all human affairs" and believed that conflict could only end when communism had spread worldwide.[58] After all, conservatives noted, the Soviet and Cuban intervention in Angola had no geopolitical or traditional Russian overtures. Such involvement *only* made sense if one recognized the Soviets' ideological commitment to "national liberation movements."[59] In her detailed criticism of the Carter administration's foreign policy, Jeane Kirkpatrick highlighted that the ideological goal of communist expansion drove Soviet support for similar movements in Latin America.[60] For the Soviets, this expansion of communism into the United States' own sphere of influence would not only demonstrate the historical inevitability of communist expansion, but would also serve to demonstrate the expansion of Soviet power and further accelerate the decline of American power and prestige. Another important neoconservative figure, Richard Pipes, argued that Marxism-Leninism remained "a militant doctrine" that would not accept an international system it could not control and drove the Soviet Union to seek global domination.[61] In the minds of conservatives, failure to understand the influence this ideology had on Soviet goals and actions could only lead to flawed Western policies and, ultimately, the West's defeat.

Conservatives also saw the lack of any significant structural or behavioral change within the Soviet state as further proof of the central role of communist ideology. Despite decades of industrialization and modernization, the Soviet state had remained largely unchanged, reliant on brutal repression and coercion to maintain domestic order. Conservatives argued that the Soviet leadership's refusal to make any significant domestic change demonstrated the sustained influence of communist ideology. Some pointed out that even Khrushchev's denunciation of Stalin's crimes, which some liberals hailed as evidence of the erosion of communist dogma, did not lead to meaningful change in the structure of the Stalinist state.[62] Despite years of the Soviet state being led by such "moderates" as Khrushchev and Brezhnev, none of its basic institutions had changed. The general population still had no say in the basic policies of the Soviet government, nor was there any relaxation of the economic or political power of the state.[63] Others pointed out that the Soviet leadership's refusal to make even modest changes to the Marxist agricultural policy, despite worldwide recognition of its absolute failure, demonstrated a deep, abiding commitment to communist doctrine.[64] In fact, most conservatives argued that the Soviet leadership could not afford to question or revise the role of communist ideology, as it represented the only remaining claim to the government's legitimacy. Since the Soviet Union remained a totalitarian state rooted in a utopian vision and dedicated to the destruction and wholesale remaking of society, any significant departure from the central teachings of Marx would destroy the only basis for the Communist Party's continued monopoly of power.[65] Stressing the fact that communist doctrine permitted temporary retreats in the face of overwhelming power, conservatives insisted that the core elements of communist ideology remained central to the worldview of the Soviet leadership throughout the Cold War.

CENTRALITY OF SUPERIOR POWER IN DEALING WITH THE SOVIET THREAT

Another common theme in conservative foreign policy thought was the central role that power played in assessing the U.S.-Soviet relationship. But conservatives did not merely focus on the reality of power. After all, many well-regarded analysts, such as Kennan, accepted the importance of power in international relations. Where the two groups diverged is over the impact and importance of the United States maintaining a significant power advantage over the Soviet Union. Beginning in the mid-1960s, Western liberals became increasingly convinced that power differentials, especially in the military arena, had ceased to play much of a role in influencing Soviet behavior. Rather, they argued that mutual goodwill, reassurances of America's peaceful intentions, and honest efforts at negotiation were the key to reducing U.S.-Soviet tension and encouraging Soviet moderation. Conservatives never accepted this claim and insisted that the Soviet leadership would only respond to superior Western power. The debate between these two fundamentally different views of international power would continue throughout the Cold War.

Early Cold War Period

In the early days of the post–World War II era, most foreign policy analysts, both liberal and conservative, recognized the dangers of appeasement and importance of dealing with the Soviet Union from a position of strength. Having witnessed the failure of British and French efforts to appease a rising Nazi Germany, there was little question in the minds of most Americans that it was both foolish and dangerous to yield to the demands of an aggressive, expansionist state. As the Soviets tightened their grip on Eastern Europe and sought to extend their influence in the rest of the world, the immediate reaction of both liberals and conservatives was to criticize Soviet actions and to call upon the West to resist further Soviet expansion. Many liberals argued that, by doing so, the West could strengthen the "peace group" within the Soviet leadership and bring about a more reasonable, moderate Soviet foreign policy.[66] Most also agreed with their conservative counterparts, who argued that the absolutist nature of Soviet demands (which themselves were rooted in communist ideology) made any effort at appeasement a grave mistake. Because the Soviets' goal was global domination, there was no concession, short of total surrender, that could satisfy their demands. In their highly ideological view of the world, the Soviets would view any friendliness or accommodation as either blatant capitalist hypocrisy or as a sign of Western weakness or stupidity.[67] Rather than easing Soviet fears and reducing their expansionist desires, concessions would, in the view of most Western strategists, merely lead to additional and more outrageous Soviet demands. As Arendt noted, the greatest mistake the West could make was failing to recognize that "important concessions and greatly heightened international prestige did not help to reintegrate the totalitarian countries into the comity of nations" but rather "clearly precipitated their recourse to the instruments of violence and resulted in all instances in increased hostility against the powers who had shown themselves willing to compromise."[68] In the view of both liberals and conservatives during this period, only Western resolve, backed by superior power, could dissuade Soviet aggression and lead to improved Soviet behavior.

Middle Cold War Period

This consensus on the centrality of power would not survive the turmoil of the 1960s. While American liberals moved steadily toward advocating peaceful coexistence and détente with the Soviet Union, conservatives continued to insist that superior power was crucial to preventing Soviet aggression and promoting Soviet reform. Liberals argued that superior American power was dangerous, as it exacerbated Soviet fears of invasion and made Soviet leaders less likely to moderate their international or domestic behavior.[69] Many liberals argued that the Soviet Union was a deeply insecure nation, absolutely convinced that the West harbored plans to attack and destroy it. At the same time (and somewhat contradictorily), they argued that power, particularly military power, was becoming increasingly irrelevant in the international arena. The destructive power of nuclear weapons, they claimed, had progressed to the point that these weapons were unusable, rendering nuclear superiority meaningless. As a result, many influential liberal voices called for the United States to not only renounce efforts to retain its military superiority, but to accept parity or even slight inferiority as a way of calming Soviet fears.[70]

Unsurprisingly, conservatives viewed this approach as highly dangerous and rooted in a serious misunderstanding of the Soviet Union. Echoing Arendt's argument from the previous decade, they insisted that unilateral Western concessions would not ease tensions, but rather spur additional, more extreme Soviet demands.[71] Drawing on the basic precepts of communism, conservatives further noted that Marxism-Leninism was an inherently "combative ideology" that viewed history as a series of conflicts whose outcome was dictated by the power differential.[72] In addition, since the Soviet leadership, in both its internal and external dealings, relied on the coercive threat and use of superior power to achieve its objectives, only a significant Western power advantage could dissuade the Soviets from further expansionism.[73] For conservatives, events such as the Berlin Blockade and the Cuban Missile Crisis demonstrated that the Soviets would only back down in the face of superior power. Given that Soviet international designs remained aggressive, conservatives argued that the only reasonable approach for maintaining international peace was unquestioned Western superiority. While acknowledging that this approach would increase international tension, conservatives believed that this tension would "produce the maximum disintegrative and weakening effect on the Communist bloc," while a relaxation in tension would help the Soviets to concentrate on their "social and economic failures" and thereby become an even more dangerous competitor.[74]

Late Cold War Period

This debate over the importance of power and military superiority continued to rage throughout the 1970s. By the end of the decade, the gulf between liberals and conservatives had widened, leading each camp to espouse fundamentally different views of the importance of national power. Liberals believed that any efforts to pressure the Soviet Union by building up Western military power was doomed to failure, arguing that such efforts would only heighten Soviet feelings of insecurity and fuel the arms race, thereby worsening East-West relations and diminishing American security. Conservatives, on the other hand, insisted that Western military superiority was critical and would provide important strategic and psychological advantages.

The liberal distaste for superpower competition, particularly in the military realm, steadily increased throughout the 1970s. Many liberals argued that the failure of U.S. military power to win the Vietnam War had demonstrated that military superiority and coercive power had become increasingly irrelevant in international affairs. After all, they argued, the United States had a sizable margin of military superiority, particularly in nuclear weapons, for most of the post–World War II era, yet had been unable to translate this superiority into meaningful political influence.[75] This belief in the futility of coercive diplomacy was enshrined in détente's "Statement of Basic Principles," in which each side renounced any effort to obtain unilateral advantage and pledged to work together to solve international problems. For most liberals, such a statement made eminent sense. Because there were no longer any issues between the United States and USSR that could possibly be solved by military conflict and because there was no political value in military superiority, the arms race had become "essentially devoid of political justification."[76] Liberals argued that rather than advancing American interests, military pressure would only diminish chances for a negotiated settlement between the two superpowers.

This view, unsurprisingly, was not shared by conservatives, who continued to emphasize two central points in arguing for ensuring and expanding Western military superiority. First, conservatives felt that the international psychological impact of Soviet military superiority could be dangerously destabilizing. They insisted that the Soviets, guided by their highly ideological view of the world, would see Western weakness as proof of the long-expected collapse of the capitalist world and would thus become more aggressive and less interested in reaching mutually beneficial agreements. As evidence, they pointed out that the Soviets responded to the unilateral restraint the United States showed in the mid-1970s not with a matching restraint, but with a renewed effort to achieve military superiority.[77] For conservatives, this Soviet action was hardly surprising, given the importance the Soviets placed on military power and particularly the nuclear balance. For the Soviets, the nuclear balance was "the fulcrum upon which all other levers of influence—military, economic, or political—rest."[78] Thus, in the view of most conservatives, it made little sense to expect the Soviets to willingly slight one of the defining elements of Soviet international importance.

Second, conservatives argued that, while Western liberals may have believed that military power was no longer an important factor in international politics, such a belief was not shared by others around the world. Nations throughout the Third World were closely watching the superpower competition to see which side would become the dominant power. As a result, the (self-imposed) decline of U.S. power could only raise concerns among pro-Western Third World governments about the wisdom of relying on American friendship.

In addition to expressing concerns regarding the impact Soviet superiority would have on international politics, conservatives also worried that, by forgoing military (and particularly nuclear) superiority, the West would undermine its entire approach to Cold War military strategy. Lacking the ability to stop a Soviet conventional assault on Western Europe, U.S. nuclear doctrine relied heavily on the threat of massive retaliation in response to any Warsaw Pact invasion. However, many conservatives questioned whether any such threat would be deemed credible when the Soviets also possessed nuclear superiority.[79] U.S. inferiority, then, would neither reassure the Soviets of the West's peaceful intentions, nor would it reduce the likelihood of East-West conflict. Instead, conservatives argued that it would encourage Soviet adventurism, undermine deterrence, and raise questions among America's NATO allies regarding the credibility of U.S. security guarantees.

At the same time, conservatives also emphasized that efforts to reach equitable arms control agreements were heavily dependent on the West having a clear margin of military superiority. Only with such a margin could the United States "expect successfully to negotiate hardheaded and verifiable agreements to control and reduce armaments."[80]

Finally, conservatives remained deeply concerned about the impact that Soviet superiority could have on the willingness of the Western public to stand up to Soviet pressure. Noting that "the political will to resist an expanding power is a precondition of stopping its expansion," conservatives feared that Soviet superiority (especially when compounded by the unwarranted hopes for détente) could weaken this will and thereby undermine the ability of the West to protect its vital interests.[81] In short, conservatives believed that power, and particularly military superiority, were central to ensuring Western security.

RECOGNITION OF SOVIET WEAKNESSES

While deeply worried over the threat posed by communist political and military expansion, conservatives throughout the Cold War argued that the Soviet Union had important weaknesses that, if properly exploited, could force the Soviets to alter their behavior. Whereas early conservatives tended to focus on the Soviets' economic vulnerabilities, conservative thought would gradually, over time, outline both political and economic weaknesses that could be exacerbated and manipulated by the strategic use of American power.

Early Cold War Period

As discussed, conservatives of the early Cold War period believed that the United States needed to take the strategic initiative and launch a more aggressive, assertive campaign against the Soviet Union. This belief was founded, in part, on an analysis of Soviet weaknesses that would prove to be remarkably prescient. In fact, the conservatives of this era accurately identified many of the economic and political weaknesses that would only become apparent to much of the foreign policy elite in the late 1980s. During this time, no one was more insistent on the inherent fragility of the Soviet domestic and international position than James Burnham. His review of Soviet vulnerabilities was remarkably foresighted, particularly in identifying some of the fundamental economic flaws in the Soviet empire.

Recognition of some of the Soviet Union's economic weakness following World War II scarcely required a great deal of insight. After all, Western analysts were well aware that the German invasion had inflicted massive damage on the Soviet economic infrastructure. Much of the mainstream discussion of Soviet weakness, then, had focused on the obvious problems of rebuilding infrastructure and overcoming the serious population losses from the war. While Burnham acknowledged these problems, he greatly expanded the scope of this analysis to identify more systemic flaws that could be exacerbated by Western policy and were not widely recognized in the West. Chief among them were the steadily increasing production costs, extreme inefficiency, and poor quality of manufactured goods throughout the Soviet empire.[82] While recognizing that the Soviet landmass had an abundance of

natural resources, he accurately predicted that the Soviets would have increasing difficulty extracting these resources, given their technological backwardness.[83] The
recognition of these flaws would, in the years to come, drive conservatives to argue
for economic and trade policies designed to worsen these fundamental economic
weaknesses.

While accurately predicting the economic difficulties that would plague the
Soviet Union in the 1980s, Burnham and his fellow conservatives also recognized
the serious political flaws in the Soviet system that could be worsened by the skill-
ful use of American power. Burnham pointed out the younger members of the
party were exhibiting signs of "a grave theoretical and . . . moral crisis" caused by
the inability of the Soviet leadership to justify its dominant role in the socialist
world or to develop a reasonable solution to the problem of political succession.[84]

Other scholars noted that, in addition to these challenges, the leaders of totalitarian states face a paradox that becomes increasingly difficult to manage. A totalitarian state's "disregard for facts, its strict adherence to the rules of a fictitious
world, becomes steadily more difficult to maintain, yet remains as essential as it
was before."[85] Leaders are forced to promise the impossible in order to seize power
and then must develop an all-encompassing governmental structure to pursue the
impossible in order to remain in power. Conservatives stressed that this structure,
while ensuring leadership control, stifled individual initiative and rendered Soviet
society so inflexible that Burnham accurately predicted that "it seems to me likely,
from its very nature, that the communist system can collapse fast once it starts col-
lapsing."[86]

Finally, he and many other conservatives pointed out the serious political challenges the Soviets faced in retaining control over their empire, particularly over the
captive nations of Eastern Europe and their own nationalities within the Soviet
Union.[87] Despite Soviet propaganda to the contrary, the peoples of Eastern
Europe, the Baltic states, and Central Asia welcomed neither Russian domination
nor the repressive and alien political system imposed on them. As with the economic vulnerabilities, future conservatives would advocate aggressive U.S. actions
to target these political weaknesses.

Middle Cold War Period

While much of the conservative analysis of Soviet weaknesses during the early
years of the Cold War focused on the serious economic challenges facing the
regime, by the 1960s conservatives had gradually begun to focus on the political

vulnerabilities inherent in communist systems. Whereas the earlier focus on economic difficulties reflected a recognition of the economic damage World War II had inflicted upon the Soviet Union, the focus on political factors can be seen as a response to three key factors: the political upheaval within the Soviet Union during the mid-1950s, the relative stabilization of the military balance in Europe, and the Soviets' increasing use of communist ideology as a tool of foreign policy. Since the United States was increasingly forced to deal with a political—vice military—threat, conservative foreign policy strategists responded by analyzing the USSR's political vulnerabilities.[88]

Among the first to highlight the serious political vulnerabilities of the Soviet regime was Robert Strausz-Hupé, whose analysis of the USSR's political failures were echoed by a number of conservative writers. Strausz-Hupé believed that the Soviet Union's greatest threat was also its greatest weakness, namely, its unending, ideologically driven desire for power.[89] He argued that this lust for control led the Soviets to implement foolish economic policies and made it impossible for the regime to develop any real support among the general public. Conservatives recognized that this popular opposition to communist rule was widespread not only among the captive nations of Eastern Europe, but also within the Soviet Union itself. Despite the Soviets' prediction that nationalism would wither away with the building of the socialist state, it remained a serious challenge to the political stability of the Soviet empire. If the Soviets, in response to nationalist pressures, moved toward greater federation, they risked splintering the empire. At the same time, if they moved toward greater centralization, they risked accelerating the growth of nationalist sentiment.[90] As demonstrated by the 1956 uprising in Hungary, rising nationalist sentiment caused the local communist regimes to be extremely unpopular in Eastern Europe, making them the Soviets' "Achilles' heel" and leading conservatives to urge sustained pressure on these regimes to increase the likelihood of upheaval and revolution.[91] In the view of many conservatives, the situation in Eastern Europe would not be easily remedied any time soon, making future revolts against Soviet domination inevitable.

As a result of the gradual buildup of Western military power in Europe, Soviet tactics shifted from the use of military pressure on Western Europe toward the use of communism's intellectual allure to gain influence within the recently decolonized Third World. In response, Strausz-Hupé and his fellow conservatives paid increasing attention to communism's inherent ideological vulnerabilities and urged the West to exploit these weaknesses. In particular, the conservatives highlighted that communist doctrine, which provided the basis of the Soviet state, was extraordinarily frail. First, conservatives pointed out that it was becoming increasingly clear that communism's "laws of history" did not exist and thus the worldwide spread of communism was not inevitable.[92] For example, whereas Marxist ideology claimed that living conditions for the working class in the West would worsen over time, the fact was that they had steadily improved. Second, conservatives pointed out that, despite the growing movement toward national independence, the Soviets' "insistence on retaining in political bondage alien national bodies inevitably leads to strains and frictions within the communist world."[93] Finally, conservatives recognized the political weaknesses caused by "the wide discrepancy between communist ideology and practice."[94] While the Soviet leadership promised the elimination of classes, wealth for all, and the elimination of the state, in practice it had established an entirely new class, appropriated almost the entire national product for use by the new elite, and created the most repressive totalitarian state in human history.[95] Strausz-Hupé and his colleagues argued that a victory in the Cold War required the West to target these political and intellectual failures.

While their focus may have been primarily on the Soviets' political weaknesses, conservatives during this period did expand upon their earlier assessments of the Soviets' economic vulnerabilities as well. At a time when most Western liberals denied that the Soviets faced any significant economic challenges, conservatives continued to highlight key economic trends within the Soviet empire that the West could use to its advantage. While recognizing that the Soviets had (for the most part) managed to recover from the destruction resulting from World War II, conservatives noted that a number of new, longer-term problems were emerging within the Soviet and Eastern European economies. The USSR's collectivized agricultural program was a disaster, forcing the country to become reliant on the outside world to feed its own people, and the transportation and energy sectors were mismanaged and grossly inefficient.[96] It continued to face severe manpower problems, in particular a shortage of skilled labor, as well as significant shortfalls in capital.

Beyond these specific weaknesses, conservatives also recognized the key problem underpinning all of the Soviets' economic weaknesses: an inability to rationally allocate its resources between "short-run strengthening of power, long-run strengthening of power, and raising standards of living."[97] The most effective, efficient method for managing the struggle between these three competing goals was greater decentralization of the economy. Yet the Soviet leadership had for years known that they could not meaningfully decentralize their economy without threatening the control and ideology of the Communist Party. Thus, conservatives of this period grasped the Soviets' key economic challenge some twenty years before the vast majority of the foreign policy establishment: the Soviets could either attempt to compete with the Western economies by embarking on a program of massive economic reform and risk the political collapse of their system, or they could retain central control of their political and economic system but fall further behind the West.

Late Cold War Period

During the 1970s, recognition of the Soviets' critical weaknesses became more widespread, even among some (but by no means all) American liberals. In fact, one of the intellectual justifications for détente was the belief that both the United States and the USSR were facing increasing political and economic difficulties that required greater cooperation to solve. Where liberal and conservative views diverged during this period, then, was not over the existence of these weaknesses, but rather their severity and the extent to which the West could exacerbate them to its own benefit. For most liberals, the Soviets' feeble economic growth and internal political problems were severe enough to provide an incentive to seek détente, but not so severe as to offer hope for a Western victory or a significant decline in Soviet power. This incentive on the Soviet side, combined with America's perceived decline, convinced most liberals that some sort of grand compromise with the Soviets was possible. By the end of the decade, conservatives had identified all the major economic and political vulnerabilities that would, in later years, lead to the collapse of the Soviet state. In fact, by the early 1980s, a few conservatives had already begun urging Western leaders to begin thinking about how to deal with the actual collapse of the Soviet regime.[98] This listing of vulnerabilities would become a virtual "target set" for the Reagan administration in its efforts to undermine and destroy the Soviet empire.

Whereas conservative writers of the previous decade had largely (though, as noted earlier, by no means exclusively) focused on the political difficulties facing the Soviet Union, the conservatives of the late Cold War period renewed their analysis of communism's economic vulnerabilities. Conservatives argued that the Soviets' declining economic growth was neither a transitory phenomenon nor merely the result of poor national leadership or individual corruption, though such problems did exacerbate matters. Instead, they stressed that the worsening economy was an inherent feature of the communist economic system. In particular, the economic weakness was the result of administrative overcentralization, the lack of genuine economic incentives, and the heavily militarized nature of the Soviet economy.[99] Symbolic of communism's failure, they argued, was the miserable state of Soviet agriculture, which was heavily dependent on the very small percentage of privately owned farmland in the Soviet Union, as well as Western grain sales.

Conservatives saw, in these weaknesses, opportunities that the West could exploit for strategic advantage. Increasingly, it became clear to conservatives that the Soviet Union was becoming heavily dependent on the West to sustain its economy, particularly in the areas of technology, energy exploration, and financial credits.[100] Even the Soviet military, which had long enjoyed privileged access to scarce technological and economic resources, had become increasingly reliant on Western technology, obtained from both legal purchase and outright theft.[101] It should hardly be a surprise, then, that years later the Reagan administration would target these specific areas in its effort to put pressure on the Soviet regime.

Conservatives of the 1970s also continued their efforts to assess the Soviets' key political vulnerabilities and had, by the time of Reagan's election, identified a set of weaknesses they believed could be effectively targeted by Western policies. At its core, conservatives argued, the Soviet Union was facing a serious crisis of legitimacy that was undermining its ability to control both its international empire and its domestic population. Despite its success in expanding its influence in Africa and the Middle East, the Soviet Union was facing serious questions about its political and intellectual credibility. Conservatives believed that the Soviets' inability to maintain control over their empire without resorting to force and repression revealed a critical vulnerability.[102] They argued that the continued opposition within Eastern Europe to Soviet rule, particularly in Poland during the 1970s, demonstrated the inherent illegitimacy of communist rule there, a view strengthened by international condemnation of the Soviet invasion of Afghanistan.

In addition to these threats to the Soviet Union's international authority, conservatives also identified the growing challenges the Soviets faced in merely controlling its own population. They argued that, despite over fifty years of communist rule, the regime had lost the respect and support of virtually the entire Soviet population and remained intact solely due to the coercive power of the ruling class.[103] As a result of this inherent illegitimacy (as well as its pressing economic problems), the regime had become increasingly fragile and prone to collapse.[104] Mirroring the argument Strausz-Hupé had made years earlier, conservatives of the 1970s pointed out the impact of "the gap between promise and fulfillment" on the Soviet population, stressing that "the more patent the failures of Soviet Communism are, the harder it is to justify the dogmas that constitute . . . the *only* source of legit-imacy of the Soviet autocracy."[105]

At the same time, conservatives highlighted the rise of ethnic nationalism within the Soviet Union, particularly in Central Asia and the Baltic states, and the dan-gers this rival ideology posed to Soviet internal stability. Making this rise of nation-alism even more dangerous were the demographic changes that had begun to occur during the 1970s, with the relative size of the better-educated, more highly skilled ethnic Russian work force declining, while the number of less-educated workers from Central Asia and the Transcaucasus was steeply increasing.[106]

During the Reagan years, conservatives would exploit these economic and political weaknesses in an effort to undermine the Soviet regime.

SUPERIORITY OF DEMOCRACY AND CAPITALISM

Even to many of his most bitter critics, Reagan's belief in the moral superiority of the West's political and economic system was unquestionable. "Ultimately, Reagan was a professed believer in freedom—economic, political and intellectual."[107] His optimism about the future of democracy and his belief in the ascendancy of Western ideals were core elements of his worldview and central to his adminis-tration's national strategy.

Yet, unlike the other four core beliefs discussed earlier, this idea is less easily found and was more heavily debated throughout the history of conservative for-eign policy thought. In almost every standard account of both the Reagan foreign policy and conservative intellectual history, the administration's belief in the inher-ent superiority of democracy is attributed to the rise and influence of neoconser-vatism. However, without denigrating the important contributions made by the neoconservatives, such a claim fails to recognize the long history of conservative thought in this area. In fact, with a few notable exceptions during the early stages of the Cold War, conservatives repeatedly made the superiority of democratic cap-italism a central element of their strategic thought.

Early Cold War Period

Reviewing the writings of both liberal and conservative foreign policy thought in the early days of the Cold War reveals surprisingly little discussion of the relative merits of Western society or the role of democratic ideology in American strategy, especially when compared with the intense debates on this subject that would occur in later years. In Burnham's writings, however, one finds a deeply conflicted view of Western democracy. On one hand, he repeatedly called for the establishment and spread of democratic institutions around the world. A common theme of much of his writing was the need to create a "non-communist world federation" that would be led by the United States and guarantee every member nation the right to organize its own political institutions and express its own cultural and religious values.[108] He also regularly emphasized the utilitarian value of Western ideology as a weapon against the Soviets and was one of the most committed supporters of assisting the nations of Eastern Europe in replacing their communist regimes with free institutions.

On the other hand, however, Burnham was extremely concerned about the many weaknesses he saw in Western societies. He regularly highlighted the dangers of democratic idealism and questioned the ability of much of the world to govern itself democratically without substantial Western assistance. Most of all, he worried about the dangerous tendency within democracies to underestimate the will and goals of totalitarian regimes (as they had prior to World War II) and to believe that reasonable, mutually satisfactory agreements could be reached with these regimes.[109] In summary, it would be fair to say that Burnham, while believing in the moral superiority of democracy, was not convinced that Western democratic institutions were capable of dealing with the political challenge posed by Soviet communism.

While Burnham's views were representative of many conservatives, it is important to note that not all conservatives shared Burnham's skepticism on this issue, nor was concern about the ability of democracies to meet the Soviet challenge limited to the conservative end of the political spectrum. Other well-known conservatives, such as Frank Meyer, criticized the moral relativism of some liberal writers (such as Walter Lippmann) and emphasized that the West needed to recognize and use the power of its own traditions.[110] Indeed, many conservatives saw the spread of communism as a fundamental challenge to the underlying assumptions of Western civilization, specifically the West's commitment to individual rights. Only by tapping into the strengths of the West, including individual freedom, economic opportunity, national unity, and the traditions of Western civilization, could the United States and its allies hope to counter the threat posed by communist ideology.[111] In addition, Burnham's concern about the ability of democratic societies to remain united was shared by many across the political spectrum. Even Arthur Schlesinger, a well-regarded anticommunist liberal, urged the

West to "make democracy a fighting faith" in large part because he recognized the difficulty democracies have in maintaining the political unity needed to implement a successful foreign policy.[112]

Nevertheless, unlike the other four beliefs, the direct linkages between early conservative thought in this area and the Reagan administration's strategic beliefs are tenuous. Not until the late 1950s and early 1960s would most conservative strategic thought begin to reflect the core beliefs that would eventually become part of Reagan's grand strategy.

Middle Cold War Period

The transition in conservative thought from concern to strongly held belief in democracy's power began in the late 1950s and culminated in the rise of Barry Goldwater, who made faith in Western ideas a core element of conservative philosophy. High-profile conservatives such as William F. Buckley and Robert Strausz-Hupé repeatedly urged the West to find, in its own great traditions, the will and strength to win the ideological war with communism. In his criticism of American liberals, Buckley argued that liberalism was unable and unwilling to provide a faith strong enough to motivate the West. While he agreed with Schlesinger and other liberals that democracies had not successfully rallied their people to resist the appeals of communism, he insisted that a revival of the people's faith in democracy was only possible by emphasizing the core political values of the West.[113] While some of Strausz-Hupé's earlier writings express concern about the impact of material wealth on the willingness of the United States to live up to its moral philosophy, by the early 1960s he made clear that a key strategic goal of the West was "to assure mankind a future of freedom" premised on the notion that "government is legitimate and genuine only so far as its ruling end is the protection of human freedom."[114]

This emphasis on the preservation and expansion of human freedom became a central tenet of the new conservative political revival sparked by Barry Goldwater. Goldwater argued that the United States needed to make clear to the world that it was "willing to fight and to die in defense of freedom" and was committed to take the actions required "to stop the ideas of communism with the better ideas of free men."[115] For him, victory over the Soviet Union in the Cold War was merely a stepping stone to the ultimate goal for the West, which was the creation of a world that placed a premium on democratic governance and human freedom.

This view of democracy was not universally shared and was criticized by both liberal and conservative critics. For some liberals, the notion that democracy was somehow morally superior to communism was rooted not in fact, but in the West's own psychological distortions.[116] In fact, a few argued that the democratic West had no hope of competing with command economies, which could better focus national resources on specific goals. Others, while acknowledging the superior morality of democratic principles, felt that there was no realistic hope of establishing democracies in the developing world.[117] This concern about the viability of democracy abroad was echoed by some conservatives, who felt that transforming the international system into a democracy was neither possible nor necessary to achieve the key goal of defeating communism.[118] Rather, these conservatives believed that the West needed to focus solely on defeating the external manifestations of communism, such as its efforts to subvert or intimidate other governments. There was, in their view, no meaningful strategic advantage to be gained by encouraging the spread of democracy.

Despite this limited opposition from a relatively small number of conservatives, by the end of the 1960s, belief in the power of democracy had gradually become an important element of conservative foreign policy thought.

Late Cold War Period

Throughout the 1970s, neoconservatives played an increasingly important (though by no means exclusive) role in the development of conservative thinking on the role of democratic principles in U.S. foreign policy. The primary neoconservative innovation to conservative strategic thought was its emphasis in the belief that the spread of democracy would enhance American security. Whereas earlier conservatives had generally focused on the impact of democratic capitalism on the material power relationship between the United States and the USSR, the neoconservatives also highlighted the broader ideological benefits that the spread of democratic systems would provide the West. Specifically, they argued that the spread of democratic governments worldwide would disprove the Marxist prediction of a communist world, limit the ability of the Soviets to expand their international influence, and create the political conditions necessary for an expansion of American political and economic influence. By endorsing the spread of democratic capitalism, they rejected the criticisms of American liberals who insisted, particularly in the aftermath of Vietnam, that the flaws in the U.S. system had rendered it unfit for global leadership and that the decadence of Western society made it unworthy of saving.[119]

Of all the Reagan administration's core beliefs, its belief in the superiority of democracy is the one most closely associated with neoconservatism. For neoconservatives, the ideological dimension of the Cold War was central to any Western strategy of victory. In the view of such notable neoconservatives as Norman Podhoretz and Sidney Hook, the gradual expansion of democratic institutions, including into the nations of the Soviet bloc, offered the only legitimate hope for a lasting peace. In addition, they argued that the only sustainable American foreign policy was one rooted in strengthening and spreading its core political and economic values.[120] Neoconservatives further believed that the most important U.S. weakness could be found not in the Western political and economic system, but rather in the morale of the elite, many of whom had lost faith in the ability of the West to solve its own problems.[121] While clearly influenced by Wilsonian thought, the neoconservatives differed from Wilsonians in part by focusing on the use of U.S. national power—vice international institutions—to advance America's democratic ideals. Yet both Wilsonians and neoconservatives shared a view that democratic institutions were inherently superior to other systems and that advancing democracy abroad was a moral obligation, albeit one to be advanced with great caution.[122]

While it is important to recognize the role neoconservatives played during this period, it should be stressed that other conservative authors made similar arguments about the moral and political superiority of Western democratic capitalism. Jean-François Revel, in his seminal work *The Totalitarian Temptation*, argued that in both economic performance and respect for basic human rights, communism was "vastly inferior" to capitalism and insisted that the spread of democracy would greatly improve living conditions worldwide.[123] Similarly, other conservatives pointed out the importance of the United States simply telling the truth about the Western system, emphasizing that, despite its flaws, democratic capitalism represented the best system available for both economic progress and individual freedom.[124] This conservative view of the power and superior morality of Western political and economic institutions would serve as the intellectual basis for the Reagan administration's aggressive efforts to undermine the communist system via public diplomacy and covert action.

CONCLUSION

As earlier demonstrated, the core beliefs of the Reagan administration represent the culmination of almost thirty-five years of conservative strategic thought that challenged mainstream foreign policy assumptions. In some cases, such as highlighting the need for a more offensively minded U.S. policy and explaining the role of communist ideology and power on Soviet behavior, conservative thought remained remarkably consistent throughout the Cold War. In other cases, such as analyzing Soviet weaknesses and assessing democracy's strength, conservative thought gradually evolved from the early days of James Burnham, through the Goldwater Revolution, to the rise of the neoconservatives. And while the beliefs outlined were by no means agreed upon by every conservative strategist, as a whole they represent a fundamentally different worldview that served as the intellectual and philosophical basis of the Reagan administration. As a result of these beliefs, the administration developed a set of more ambitious goals for the United States and designed a plan to wield more assertively all available tools of national power.

4

Goals

The previous chapter highlighted the commonality between the Reagan administration's strategic beliefs and those of mainstream conservative strategic thought. It showed how Reagan's key assumptions regarding the nature of the Cold War and the international system were representative of the larger conservative foreign policy community. This chapter will conduct a similar analysis to demonstrate that, just as in the case of the administration's core beliefs, its central goals reflected the steady evolution of conservative foreign policy thought.

PRESERVE DETERRENCE

The goal of deterring military conflict, particularly nuclear war, can hardly be described as unusual or unique to the Reagan administration. In fact, every administration since Hiroshima wrestled with the challenges of deterring World War III while pursuing other American goals and interests. Yet, as described in chapter 2, the approach Reagan took to preserving deterrence represented a fundamental shift from the widely accepted approach of Mutual Assured Destruction (MAD), toward an approach that sought to deter Soviet aggression through the development and fielding of superior Western power. This approach, which was captured by the oft-repeated phrase "peace through strength," emphasized strategic defense, robust counterforce capabilities, and improved conventional capabilities. Such a belief in peace through strength tracks closely with the thinking of several notable conservative strategists who saw efforts to prevent full-scale military conflict with the Soviets as a necessary, but by no means sufficient, condition for achieving larger strategic goals.

Early Cold War Period

The early years of the Cold War were, in many ways, the "golden age" of nuclear strategy. The advent of the Nuclear Age sparked a period of intense thought about the new strategic challenges resulting from the atomic (and later thermonuclear) bomb. While the actual terms may not have been used, the genesis of most of the key concepts of nuclear theory, such as "extended deterrence," "countervalue targeting," and "credible threat," can be found in the writings of the period.

Of the many strategic theorists to consider the problem of nuclear deterrence during this period, none was more influential than Bernard Brodie. His thinking would, by the end of the 1950s, exemplify the collective opinion of the foreign policy establishment and serve as the bedrock for most left-of-center nuclear strategists. Believing that nuclear weapons had fundamentally changed military conflict, Brodie argued that nuclear superiority offered no meaningful political or strategic advantages and thus could not contribute to U.S. national security.[1] In his view, the fundamental mission of the military had changed: whereas the military's role used to be to fight and win wars, "from now on its chief purpose must be to avert them. It can have almost no other useful purpose."[2] This statement reveals the fundamental basis of much mainstream and liberal nuclear strategy: nuclear weapons are so overwhelmingly destructive that their mere existence is more than enough to render military aggression pointless. As a result, the United States did not need to be overly concerned with numeric or technological superiority, nor with robust defenses or comprehensive plans for fighting a nuclear war. Provided its threat to destroy much of the Soviet homeland was credible, these strategists believed that the Soviets would be effectively deterred.

An underlying assumption of Brodie's writings (and those of virtually all of his contemporaries) was, of course, the acceptance of containment as the guiding strategic concept. If the United States was only seeking to dissuade or halt Soviet expansionism, then the reactive, defensive-minded approach endorsed by most mainstream nuclear strategists made perfect sense. A Soviet invasion of, for example, Western Europe would result in a full-scale conventional war that would likely escalate into a nuclear exchange. Since neither side could hope to emerge from such an exchange a "winner," the Soviets would be effectively deterred. Absent a commitment to roll back Soviet power, there was no reason for the West to seek or maintain nuclear superiority. Brodie's thinking on deterrence would remain influential throughout the Cold War, with later nuclear strategists building upon his belief that a secure and devastating second-strike capability was the centerpiece to a reliable deterrent posture.

While Brodie exemplified the thinking of most mainstream nuclear strategists, one can see in Burnham's writings the beginnings of a distinctively conservative approach to deterrence theory. For Burnham, the notion of relying solely on deterrence was dangerous and strategically unsound. Even before the Soviets' first nuclear test, he questioned whether a strategy that relied so heavily upon deterrence could actually keep the peace, arguing that the presence of nuclear weapons on both sides of the Iron Curtain would make a surprise attack increasingly likely and make the international system highly unstable.[3] While his concern that a nuclear-armed Soviet state would make war inevitable proved inaccurate, his concern regarding the dangers of a devastating surprise attack would become a central feature of later conservative thinking. In many ways, his critique of mainstream deterrence strategy mirrored conservatives' general criticism of containment: an approach based solely on defensive, reactive measures can never lead to victory. Rather, he believed that the United States needed to pursue a global, wide-ranging strategy containing both offensive and defensive elements, and saw the deterrent force of American nuclear weapons (and military power as a whole) as an important defensive component, but one that needed to support the pursuit of broader strategic goals.[4] By deterring Soviet military action against key Western interests, American military superiority would enable the United States to make offensive use of other, non-military means. This view that an effective deterrence required American superiority would be echoed and expanded upon by later conservatives.

Middle Cold War Period

As noted, the 1960s saw a rapid growth in the systematic study of nuclear deterrence and the development of more robust theories of deterrence. Drawing on the thinking of Brodie and others, most mainstream nuclear theorists argued that vast increase in the power and number of nuclear weapons held by the superpowers had made unthinkable any serious military conflict between the United States and the USSR and had forced both sides to recognize that maintaining the ability to cause massive devastation in response to a surprise attack was the only reasonable nuclear strategy. Secretary of Defense Robert McNamara strongly endorsed MAD, and at one point even suggested that the United States required only a second-strike capable of destroying 20–25 percent of the Soviet population and 50 percent of its industrial output to guarantee a stable nuclear deterrence.[5] For McNamara and other proponents of the MAD approach, the key to deterring a Soviet nuclear attack was to have a reliable and secure second-strike capability, aimed primarily at Soviet population centers. Provided this second-strike capability was developed and maintained, they argued that any other capability improvements were strategically meaningless, a waste of national resources, and potentially destabilizing.

As the codification of MAD progressed throughout the 1960s, conservatives became increasingly concerned about MAD's implications for overall American strategy. One of the most important, influential voices in the development of a conservative approach to deterrence was Strausz-Hupé. Deeply concerned about the West's rapidly shrinking military, and especially nuclear, superiority, he argued that "American policy relies upon a margin of military superiority vis-à-vis the communist bloc which is dangerously narrow by the measure of American global commitments."[6] In the view of most conservatives, nuclear superiority was critical both to maintaining the credibility of the U.S. commitment to Western Europe and to enabling the United States to resist Soviet aggression in more limited wars. Strausz-Hupé argued that the U.S. move toward MAD would further encourage Soviet piecemeal aggression, since the Soviets knew that the United States would never risk a nuclear war (and thus its own destruction) over a limited Soviet incursion in the Third World.

As a result, he stressed that any theory of deterrence must rest on an understanding of how such a war would be fought. "It is only by devising *operationally* effective forces that we will have at hand at the crucial moment adequate deterrent forces."[7] The mere existence of nuclear weapons was not enough to ensure deterrence. Rather, in order to maintain a credible deterrent, the West needed to think through and plan for the actual use of these weapons. Echoing Burnham's earlier writings, other conservatives also emphasized that deterrence was only one element of national power and needed to be integrated into a much broader strategic effort.[8] Central to such an effort was American nuclear superiority, which conservatives argued would enable the United States to more readily confront Soviet aggression by presenting them "with the same choice which they now purport to offer us: peaceful co-existence or the possibility of a war in which they would be destroyed."[9] This superiority would not only serve as an effective deterrent against a full-scale Soviet nuclear attack, but would also permit the United States greater freedom to pursue the more aggressive, offensive efforts required to win the Cold War.

Late Cold War Period

Perhaps the most important factor in the development of deterrence theory during this period was the loss of American nuclear superiority. By the early 1970s, the Soviet Union had reached (at least) rough equality to the United States in overall nuclear capability, if not outright superiority. This fact generated two fundamentally different responses, largely along liberal-conservative lines.[10] For adherents to the assured destruction approach, the growth of the Soviet arsenal was largely irrelevant. Provided that a sizable portion of the U.S. arsenal could reasonably be expected to survive a surprise attack (which the development of ballistic-missile submarines made increasingly likely), they believed that deterrence was unaffected. "Deterrence comes from having enough weapons to destroy the other's cities; this capability is an absolute, not a relative, one."[11]

Thus, proponents of MAD argued that the only way for this mutual deterrence to fail would be if either side developed the ability to prevent the destruction of their population centers and economic assets, primarily through the development and fielding of large-scale civil or missile defenses. Otherwise, they argued that the nuclear balance was ultimately meaningless. Since no advantage could be gained by achieving nuclear superiority, it did not matter how large or technologically advanced the Soviet arsenal became, so long as the United States retained the ability to devastate the Soviet homeland.

For the (mostly) conservative strategists who opposed MAD, the loss of American nuclear superiority represented a dangerous change to international stability and posed a major threat to Western security. It also served to intensify conservative criticisms of MAD, in particular highlighting two key weaknesses in America's nuclear strategy. First, they stressed that the Soviets' strategic writings and military policies indicated that they did not accept the notion of MAD and that they viewed nuclear superiority as valuable.[12] As evidence of the Soviets' rejection of MAD, conservatives cited the massive Soviet buildup that began in the 1960s, arguing that it far exceeded the amount necessary for the Soviets to implement MAD. This buildup, and the Soviets' own strategic writings, indicated that "Soviet strategists regard[ed] the possession of more and better strategic weapons as a definite military and political asset, and potentially the ultimate instrument of coercion."[13]

The problem this difference in views caused for superpower deterrence was obvious: were the Soviets to view America's deterrence strategy as either implausible or impossible to implement in light of Soviet nuclear superiority, they would be more likely to take greater risks to achieve Soviet global objectives. Since the key to deterrence was the ability to deny one's adversary any plausible hope of victory, conservatives argued that the development of a nuclear war-fighting capability was critical to deterring the Soviets effectively. Such a capability would "den[y] the Soviet Union any plausible hope of success at any level of strategic conflict; [offer] a likely prospect of Soviet defeat; and [offer] a reasonable chance of limiting damage to the United Sates."[14] Failure to develop such a capability, they argued, would weaken deterrence and make a nuclear war more likely.

Conservatives argued that the second key weakness in MAD was its failure to acknowledge that there were a large number of possible scenarios in which nuclear weapons might be used, only one of which was the large-scale, intercontinental destruction of population centers that preoccupied MAD supporters. In these situations, the ability to control the process of escalation was critical to deterring a conflict or preventing a conventional conflict from becoming a nuclear one. In considering these scenarios, conservatives found particularly troubling the effect America's loss of nuclear superiority would have on its extended deterrence posture. They stressed that this loss meant that the United States would no longer have the "excess capability" at the strategic nuclear level to either control nuclear escalation or to deter, for example, the Soviet use of tactical nuclear weapons in Europe.[15] As a result, the lack of America's nuclear superiority would have a corrosive impact on its international commitments, as America's allies would begin to question whether the United States would willingly risk a full-scale nuclear war in response to a regional crisis.[16] For this reason, conservatives insisted that inferiority (or even parity) was "incompatible with extended deterrence duties because of the self-deterrent inherent in such a strategic context."[17] In pointing out this deficiency, this argument mirrored the concern Strausz-Hupé expressed almost fifteen years earlier, namely, that nuclear superiority was vital to the credibility of America's global commitments.

EXPAND U.S. INFLUENCE

Although each administration pursued this goal with different means, maintaining and expanding American influence around the world was a central goal of every president during the Cold War. In the years immediately following World War II, there was a broad consensus regarding the importance of both strengthening the close ties that had developed between the United States and Western Europe and improving America's relationship with the Third World. Yet, as decolonization began and the number of anticolonial, nationalist movements began to rise, the postwar consensus regarding the Third World gradually began to dissolve. By the time Ronald Reagan took office in 1981, the gap between liberals and conservatives had widened significantly, with each espousing radically different opinions regarding the wisdom and ability of the United States to expand its influence in the Third World.

Early Cold War Period

In the aftermath of World War II, there was a general understanding that America's choice of isolationism prior to the war had been strategically unsound and that, given its status as a superpower, such an approach was no longer appropriate. Nor indeed was there major disagreement over the notion that the United States had vital interests, not only in war-ravaged Europe, but throughout the world. The outbreak of the Korean War left little doubt that America's interests were global. This postwar consensus, however, began to fall apart with the push for decolonization and the rise of governments throughout Asia, the Middle East, and Africa that espoused anti-Western, Marxist, or nationalist ideologies. The critical question became how best to expand American influence in a Third World largely dominated by outwardly anti-American governments.

For most liberals, the moral and political value of ending European colonialism, in and of itself, was a major enhancement to long-term American security. By supporting decolonization, liberals hoped that the United States would be seen as a potential friend and ally. Additionally, since most of these new states lacked both the technical expertise and economic infrastructure to function effectively, liberals also urged the United States to provide significant economic assistance and strongly opposed imposing political or economic conditions on such aid. Such conditions amounted, in their view, to little more than "neocolonialism" and would undermine America's appeal in the Third World. Finally, American liberals tended to downplay the importance of Marxist or anti-Western statements by the rulers of these newly independent states, insisting that such statements reflected little more than an effort to either strengthen their nationalist credentials or to attract additional aid from either the Soviet Union or the West. In short, liberals argued that only by "winning over" the rulers and people of the former colonies could the United States measurably increase its support and influence in the Third World.[18]

While most recognized that decolonization was both necessary and inevitable, conservative strategists were significantly more skeptical about the ability of Western aid to, in essence, buy the friendship of the Third World and were extremely concerned about the anti-Western, pro-Marxist tendencies of many postcolonial governments. For conservatives, expanding influence around the world was an important goal, but only in the context of improving the likelihood of a Western victory in the Cold War. According to Burnham, only by supporting its allies and retaining "the solidarity of the non-communist sections of the world" could the United States succeed in destroying communist power.[19] Conservatives saw that, by developing and strengthening a global, anticommunist system of alliances (both formal and informal), the United States could gain two important strategic advantages over the Soviet Union. First, improved relations with key Third World nations would provide a significant enhancement to the West's overall power by allowing the free world to combine its resources to resist Soviet pressure.[20] Second, and even more important in the view of most conservatives, expanded U.S. influence would have a major impact on the crucial ideological battle between democracy and communism. This focus on the ideological struggle represents the most important difference between liberal and conservative views on expanding American global influence. For example, as a result of their emphasis on the ideological dimension of the Cold War, conservatives supported economic assistance but insisted that Western aid be offered only to those states willing to stand with the United States against communist expansionism.[21] By discrediting Soviet ideology, conservatives hoped to diminish the appeal of communism and thereby deprive the Soviets of one of their most important strategic weapons.

Middle Cold War Period

The divide between liberal and conservative views became steadily more pronounced throughout the 1960s with the rise of "national liberation movements" and the deepening social divide over the Vietnam War. America's policy of expanding its influence in the Third World by supporting, in some cases, anticommunist authoritarian regimes had become increasingly controversial. American liberals were highly critical of any effort to gain friends based on a shared opposition to communism, arguing that such an approach ultimately undermined America's appeal around the world, as it caused the United States to ally itself with unpopular and repressive regimes.[22] In the view of many liberals, the damage done to American ideals by supporting Francisco Franco, the shah of Iran, and Chiang Kai-shek posed a far greater risk to American security than the possible rise of anti-Western or Marxist governments in the Third World. Liberals also continued to urge greater economic aid to the Third World and preferred to have the UN oversee the political and economic development of the postcolonial world, rather than have the West impose its own conditions on how aid should be used.[23] Ultimately, liberals argued that expanding U.S. global influence was only possible by winning over "the people" of the Third World by offering unconditional support for revolutionary governments and by downplaying the ideological element of the Cold War.

Unsurprisingly, conservatives took an entirely different approach to expanding American influence around the world. Continuing to focus on the superpower struggle, they argued that the only reasonable basis for an enduring security partnership with the Third World was anticommunism.[24] While acknowledging that authoritarian or military regimes in the Third World were not in America's long-term interest, most conservatives argued that quiet pressure on these regimes to gradually introduce democratic reforms was preferable to abandoning them and allowing pro-Soviet rulers to come to power. While recognizing the need to show "reasonable deference to local sensitivities,"[25] Strausz-Hupé and others urged the United States to use economic aid to promote regional cooperation and greater economic integration with the West.

Still, conservatives cautioned that neither economic aid nor political support could be counted on to win over the Third World. At best, such efforts could only buy time for Third World nations to develop the institutions and economic infrastructure that would orient them toward the West. In the meantime, conservatives argued, only the willingness to use America's superior power to protect its friends and allies could enhance U.S. international influence. Noting that "foreign peoples believe the United States is weaker than the Soviet Union, and is bound to fall still further behind in the years ahead,"[26] Goldwater argued that seizing the strategic offensive against the Soviets was the most reliable way to reassure the world of America's commitment to freedom and thereby win the "war of ideas" with the Soviet Union and expand U.S. influence.

Late Cold War Period

Throughout the early and middle periods of the Cold War, the debate between liberals and conservatives on expanding U.S. influence worldwide revolved around how the United States could best achieve this goal. While this debate was often heated and contentious, there remained a significant area of common ground, rooted in the shared understanding that the United States could and should enhance its standing throughout the world, especially within the Third World. This common ground steadily disappeared in the wake of the highly divisive debates over Vietnam and détente, in large part due to the pronounced leftward shift among American liberals. The new debate was not over *how* to expand American influence, but *whether* the United States should even be pursuing such influence around the world.

For many American liberals, the U.S. intervention and defeat in Vietnam raised fundamental questions about both the morality and effectiveness of American foreign policy. The war served as a rallying cry for liberals and contributed to the rise of the more extreme elements of the democratic Left, culminating in the Democratic Party's nomination of George McGovern in the 1972 presidential election. As a result of this change in American liberalism, a number of new arguments were put forward opposing the expansion of U.S. influence in the Third World. For some, such as George Kennan, the only reasonable response to the decline in American prestige was to become an isolationist, gradually withdrawing from existing commitments (except for Western Europe, Japan, and Israel).[27] Given the decadence and self-absorption of Western society, they argued that "we have nothing to teach the world" and thus have no business attempting to expand influence abroad.[28] For others, the primary obstacles impeding U.S. efforts to enhance its international prestige were the changes in the international system that had rendered the United States unable to exert any meaningful influence abroad. They argued that the reduced importance of military power and the rise of more assertive and independent Third World states meant that neither the United States nor the USSR was capable of controlling or shaping events in the developing world.[29] Finally, a number of liberals (and a few conservatives[30]) argued that previous U.S. efforts had been counterproductive, as they had worsened American security and undermined its broader national goals. They claimed, for example, that American support for the shah of Iran and the positioning of American military bases throughout the world served only to heighten Soviet concerns and inhibit superpower cooperation.[31] In their view, reaching a meaningful détente with the Soviet Union was significantly more valuable than any improvement in U.S. relations with the Third World.

Unlike their liberal counterparts, however, most conservative strategists did not substantially alter their position on the wisdom or value of expanding U.S. international influence in light of Vietnam. Although many questioned how quickly or effectively the United States could rebuild its shattered reputation, few challenged the basic necessity of enhancing American power and prestige. In attempting to justify this goal, however, those within the conservative camp used two slightly different, but mutually reinforcing, arguments. For some, the primary reason for expanding U.S. influence was as a tool for advancing American ideals and fighting the ideological Cold War. While neoconservatives have often been closely identified with the ideological dimension of the superpower conflict, as already demonstrated, conservatives had made similar arguments throughout the 1950s and 1960s. Thus, while well-known neocon Norman Podhoretz argued that the United States needed to focus its efforts on defeating the idea of communism in the Third World,[32] traditional conservatives such as Gerhart Niemeyer also pointed out the need to defend Western values and prestige in the developing world.[33] Conservatives understood that the United States, as the leading power of the Western world, had a responsibility to defend and advance certain core principles. Indeed, they criticized the Nixon administration's failure to recognize that efforts to expand America's influence rested, in part, on the international belief in America's "moral mission in the world."[34] While understanding that tradeoffs between values were inevitable, conservatives believed that, on the whole, a foreign policy based on Western values of freedom and democracy was not only in America's interest, but in the interest of the rest of the world as well.

Other conservatives, while mindful of the ideological element, focused primarily on the material benefits resulting from greater U.S. influence and the inherent dangers of an American withdrawal. Once again, while this notion is often linked to traditional, geopolitically minded conservatives, this view was widely shared among neoconservative strategists as well. Thus, while Brian Crozier pointed out the geopolitical value of assisting those Third World states most vulnerable to Soviet pressure,[35] well-known neoconservatives such as Jeane Kirkpatrick expressed similar sentiments.[36] Both conservatives and neocons argued that America's influential role as leader of the free world facilitated the mutually beneficial economic and political relations that sustained Western prosperity and secured Western democracy. Concerned about the steady erosion of American influence in both Europe and the Third World, they urged the United States to reassert its leadership within NATO and make clear to undecided nations that they could rely on American support.[37] The growing perception of American weakness, combined with the internal domestic turmoil of the period, had led to a strengthened "neutralism" movement within Europe and doubts in the Third World about America's reliability as an international partner. Only by being strong and vigilant could the United States retain its leadership role in the West and thereby preserve its political, social, and economic systems.[38]

In short, while some conservatives tended to focus on one or the other of these two arguments, there was broad consensus within the conservative movement that both arguments helped to justify the need for an assertive effort to expand American influence and power worldwide.

MAINTAIN DIALOGUE WITH USSR

The new global reality in the aftermath of World War II was that there were two genuine superpowers with fundamentally different national interests and goals. It was therefore widely recognized that the interactions between the United States and USSR would be the single most important force determining the stability of the international system. As in the case of maintaining deterrence and expanding U.S. influence abroad, the early Cold War saw a generally widespread acceptance of the "ground rules" that guided American diplomacy toward the Soviet Union. However, by the mid-1950s, these rules had become part of the much broader debate between liberals and conservatives regarding the proper conduct of American foreign policy.[39] The split between the two sides became evident by the 1960s and continued to widen throughout the Cold War, with each side taking fundamentally different approaches to U.S.-Soviet diplomacy.

Early Cold War Period

As was the case of the previous two goals discussed, the early days of the Cold War saw a relatively solid consensus that maintaining dialogue with the Soviet Union was an important goal of U.S. foreign policy, even if such dialogue did not result in a specific agreement. In fact, the understanding that this was a central task of American foreign policy was so widespread that the topic was treated as a "given" in most discussions of international strategy and was rarely a major element of any strategic writer's work.

At the same time, however, the notion that international agreements between the United States and the USSR were the most important goals was scarcely even considered. Soviet violations of the Yalta Agreement, communist repression in Eastern Europe, and the outbreak of the Korean War made the notion of serious negotiations between the superpowers virtually unthinkable to any strategist, liberal or conservative. Nevertheless, the growth of the superpowers' nuclear arsenals, the death of Stalin in 1953, and the 1955 Geneva Summit began to raise hopes that a "final settlement" of issues between the Americans and the Soviets was both necessary and possible.

By the middle of the 1950s, American liberals themselves were deeply divided between what could be described as the "Acheson wing" and the "Stevenson wing" of the Democratic Party. Whereas Acheson and his supporters were more supportive of a hard line against the Soviet Union and less inclined to endorse U.S.-USSR negotiations, the Stevenson wing urged greater U.S. flexibility in its dealings with the Soviets and urged stronger efforts to work with the Soviet Union, through the United Nations, on a comprehensive disarmament agreement.[40]

Conservatives, on the other hand, were significantly more unified in their assessment of the value of U.S.-Soviet negotiations. While accepting the need for regular diplomatic contact with the Soviets, several conservatives expressed deep suspicions regarding the strategic value of a negotiated settlement or disarmament agreement and outlined three major concerns about the West's tendency to equate the routine practice of diplomacy with the drafting and signing of international agreements. First, conservatives noted that the history of disarmament negotiations demonstrated that neither a genuine desire to disarm nor even a signed agreement was sufficient to achieve actual disarmament, as nations frequently violated such agreements when doing so suited their interests.[41] In light of the Soviet Union's ideological goals and history, conservatives were convinced that it would violate any deal that interfered with its ability either to maintain control of its subjects or to expand its global control.

Second, conservatives cautioned that treaties only reflect and codify the *existing* power balance and thus cannot survive significant changes in national power.[42] Given the fluid nature of technological developments and the major impact these developments can have on the international balance of power, conservatives doubted that any treaty could remain both relevant and effective for any extended period of time.

Finally, conservatives cautioned that the two superpowers had fundamentally different approaches to international negotiations and that these differences made a comprehensive settlement with the Soviets extraordinarily unlikely. Whereas the free world saw negotiations as a good-faith bargaining process aimed at finding common interests, conservatives argued that the Soviets viewed them as merely another battleground in their struggle against the capitalist world and were interested in negotiations only to the extent that they provided an opportunity to influence world opinion and sow division among the nations of the West.[43]

Middle Cold War Period

Throughout the 1960s, successful diplomacy with the Soviet Union was increasingly seen, particularly by the foreign policy establishment, as synonymous with the negotiation and signing of bilateral or multilateral arms control agreements. The successful completion of the Limited Test Ban Treaty in 1963 only served to reinforce this idea. This notion, along with the growing partisan division within American society, further widened the split between conservative and liberal strategists, with each side viewing U.S.-Soviet dialogue in radically different ways.

For liberals, the fundamental problem plaguing the U.S.-Soviet relationship was the nuclear arms race, and thus the central task of superpower diplomacy was to slow down and eventually halt the further expansion of the U.S. and Soviet nuclear arsenals. Well-regarded liberal spokesmen such as Kennan and Sen. William Fulbright argued that much of the distrust and mutual hostility between the superpowers was rooted in the mutual fears sparked by the continued buildup of nuclear weaponry. Because the arms race was so dangerous and destabilizing, liberals argued that progress toward disarmament offered the best hope for ensuring humanity's survival *and* preserving the American way of life.[44] At the same time, however, they recognized that a negotiated settlement had proven very difficult to achieve, a fact they attributed to each side's deeply held misperceptions of the other. Thus, arms control agreements had two essential functions: controlling the arms race and reassuring each superpower of the other's intentions. At the core of liberal thinking, then, was the theory that, because tension was rooted in misperception and not the result of fundamentally differing national interests, the basis for a comprehensive agreement existed. The challenge was merely to uncover it.

Conservatives, on the other hand, rejected this entire line of reasoning and set forth a significantly different approach to U.S.-Soviet dialogue. The conservative view revolved around Strausz-Hupé's argument that there were three core tasks of diplomacy: representation, intelligence, and negotiation. He argued that the first two tasks were far more important in the superpower relationship than was the third.[45] Forcefully representing American resolve during a crisis, for example, was vital to preventing misunderstandings or miscalculations that could lead to war, as was providing senior policymakers with information to improve their understanding of current thinking within the communist bloc. He and other conservatives argued that, for several reasons, negotiations were unlikely to produce much in the way of meaningful improvements.

First, and most important, they argued that the ability of arms control to enhance security was severely limited, since, as long as nations have conflicting interests, arms will be a critical component of national power.[46] Neither the destructive power of nuclear weapons nor the ideals expressed in the Charter of the United Nations could alter this reality. As a result, arms control and disarmament could never be the primary focus of the superpower relationship. Second, they reiterated Burnham's observation that treaties last only as long as they conform to the existing power relationship and thus could not serve as the basis of a long-term settlement.[47] Finally, they stressed that there remained no sign that the Soviets were willing to forgo their efforts to incite world revolution and were serious about reaching and honoring a mutually beneficial agreement.[48] Committed as the Soviets were to their ideological goals, conservatives understood that no treaty or agreement could end the struggle between the two competing systems. Rather, the Soviets viewed such agreements as tools to undermine the will of the West, not as means of resolving the superpower rivalry.

In short, conservatives believed that U.S.-Soviet tension was the result not of misperceptions or mistrust, but rather of fundamentally incompatible national interests that could not be resolved via arms control agreements. As a result, they viewed intelligence collection and the clear and forceful representation of American policy and resolve as the more important elements of the U.S.-Soviet dialogue.

Late Cold War Period

In most respects, the debate over U.S.-Soviet dialogue did not change significantly between the late-1960s and the beginning of the Reagan administration. Many of the arguments made during the arms control debates of the 1970s amounted to amplifications of the points made during the more generic disarmament debates of the previous decade. The rise of détente and the signing of the Strategic Arms Limitation Treaty (SALT) Interim Agreement, rather than settling the issue, only served to spark continued debate between detractors and supporters. In fact, this debate would continue throughout the Reagan years, with relatively little change in the fundamental points of either side. Supporters saw their drive for arms control as a way of managing and controlling the superpower conflict, while allowing the West to redirect its resources toward resolving its own domestic problems. For détente's (largely) conservative opponents, however, this effort to make arms control (and particularly the SALT process) the centerpiece of the superpower relationship was rooted in misplaced hopes that the Soviets genuinely desired to preserve the status quo.

For liberals, arms control negotiations continued to represent the most important element of the U.S.-Soviet dialogue and thus remained a critical American goal. While recognizing the difficulty inherent in negotiating arms control agreements (and, for that reason, continuing to call for unilateral disarmament measures), they continued to stress that the nuclear arms race represented the greatest single threat to world peace and thus that controlling it was the most important task for American diplomacy. They argued that arms control was central, regardless of whether or not it modified Soviet behavior or attitudes.[49] Moreover, liberals increasingly argued that the actual content of the agreement was irrelevant. Since, as discussed, they felt that nuclear superiority was a meaningless concept that offered no advantage, it made little difference "who got more" out of a specific agreement. The purpose of arms control was not to so much to balance each side's nuclear forces as it was to "reduce the element of ambiguity in U.S.-Soviet relations and to clarify intentions in such a way as to build confidence and political support in both societies."[50] With each successful arms control agreement, liberals hoped to increase the costs of either side taking provocative actions and to build a foundation for long-term cooperation between the superpowers.

For conservatives, these hopes for a negotiated "final settlement" between the superpowers amounted to little more than wishful thinking and represented a major strategic weakness of the United States.[51] They argued that their liberal counterparts failed to understand that the two superpowers had fundamentally different goals in the arms control process. Whereas the United States hoped to use the SALT negotiations to "reduce the weight of nuclear arms . . . as a factor in world politics" and to slow the Soviet buildup, the Soviet Union saw them as a means "to extend its gains in relative posture while encouraging maximum restraint upon U.S. programs" and to push American public and congressional opinion to accept "unequal compromises unfavorable to the United States."[52]

Given these widely divergent goals, conservatives saw no objective basis for a meaningful and lasting agreement. Rejecting the idea that the very existence of an arms control agreement would reduce U.S.-Soviet tension, they instead continued to insist that any agreement needed to support broader American goals and advance America's global interests. For example, an agreement that imposed equal limits on both sides could enhance crisis stability and change the dangerous Soviet perception that the correlation of forces had permanently shifted in their favor.[53] While acknowledging that, in theory, such an agreement could be drafted, conservatives believed that most Western officials (and the foreign policy establishment as a whole) had become so invested in the negotiating process that they were no longer willing to resist Soviet demands.[54] Rather than focusing on negotiations, conservatives throughout the 1970s continued to argue that the central purpose of U.S.-Soviet dialogue should be the gathering of information and the clear representation of American policy and resolve.

REVERSE SOVIET EXPANSIONISM

The first three goals discussed—preserving deterrence, expanding U.S. influence, and maintaining U.S.-Soviet dialogue—can best be described as goals of necessity. While the manner in which these goals were pursued would vary, the structure of the international system, the fact of Soviet power, and the existence of nuclear weapons made their pursuit largely unavoidable. The final two goals discussed in this chapter—reversing Soviet expansionism and undermining the Soviet Union— represented goals of choice. Until the Reagan administration, these goals had never been pursued and, indeed, had been considered and rejected by previous administrations. For this reason, these two goals, which were more broadly known as "liberation" or "rollback," were extremely controversial. They also represent the most effective means of differentiating between conservative and liberal grand strategy during the Cold War.

Early Cold War Period

The years following World War II represent, in many ways, the high point of liberation thought. Called upon to take up its role as a global superpower and facing a fundamentally different world, the United States desperately needed an organizing principle and defining goal around which to build a new grand strategy. International strategists responded to this period of "strategic flux" with a flurry of creativity, putting forth several competing strategic concepts. Some saw strengthening the infant United Nations as the central purpose of American foreign policy, while others proposed a more traditional, balance-of-power effort akin to Britain's role in the nineteenth and early twentieth centuries. And while (as discussed in chapter 3) containment became the choice of the foreign policy mainstream, the strategic thinking that went into rollback served as the basis for the continued development of a distinctly conservative approach to Cold War strategy.

For much of the foreign policy establishment, the idea that the United States should seek to reverse Soviet gains, specifically in Eastern Europe, was far too risky to be given serious consideration. The Soviet Union's detonation of its own nuclear device in 1949 and the military stalemate in Korea left few interested in under-taking any policy that might provoke a direct military clash with the Soviet Union. Many, in an effort to reassure the Soviets, argued against "a policy of threatening Soviet interests in what has become the settled sphere of Soviet power," such as Eastern Europe.[55] Even Kennan, who had been an early proponent of covert roll-back operations, had decided by 1953 that such operations were hopeless and dan-gerous, and urged that they be halted.[56] Despite his campaign calls for the rollback of communist power, President Eisenhower never pursued the idea vigorously and explicitly rejected the rollback approach presented to him as part of Project Solarium.[57] As a result, containment would represent the most aggressive, forward-leaning strategy the United States would pursue until Reagan entered office.

As discussed in chapter 3, conservatives rejected the fundamental logic of con-tainment, viewing it as a deeply flawed strategic concept with no realistic hope of long-term success. Instead, they argued that the United States must make victory over the Soviet bloc the explicit goal of its foreign policy. Seeing the Soviets as a relentlessly expansionist power, conservatives recognized the strategic and interna-tional political value of forcing the Soviets onto the defensive, reversing their ter-ritorial gains, and ultimately driving communists from power in Soviet client states.[58] In addition, conservatives worried that a policy aimed solely at preserving the status quo would permit the Soviets to consolidate their already sizable empire and greatly enhance their future ability to pursue global domination.[59] During the early years of the Cold War, conservatives viewed Eastern Europe, especially Germany, as the primary target for American liberation efforts. Not only did con-servatives argue that the numerous uprisings in Eastern Europe offered the United States the chance to build upon the clearest examples of popular opposition to communist rule, but they also stressed that the successful rollback of Soviet power in Eastern Europe would represent a major setback for the Soviets' ability to threaten Western Europe, either militarily or politically. At the same time, however, conservatives also called for the rollback of Soviet control in northern Iran, Afghanistan, Manchuria, and on the Korean peninsula.[60] While such calls were certainly much less common during this period of the Cold War, they would steadily increase over time, as the superpower rivalry moved into the Third World.

Middle Cold War Period

By the 1960s, liberation had been thoroughly rejected by mainstream strategic thinkers, who insisted that such a policy was unlikely to succeed and could only lead to a nuclear war between the superpowers. Despite Soviet advances in the developing world, the foreign policy elite largely remained focused on containing Soviet expansion while seeking to reach a lasting détente with the Eastern bloc. In fact, on the rare occasions that the concept of rollback was mentioned at all, it was attacked as an example of the type of foreign policy that was simply too extreme for foreign policy professionals to consider seriously. Ignoring the criticism they received from their liberal counterparts, conservatives continued to develop a comprehensive rollback theory, steadily expanding its focus beyond Eastern Europe into the Third World.

For American liberals, the central challenge of the 1960s was finding some way to prevent Soviet expansion (in the face of steadily rising Soviet power) while reaching some form of long-term resolution to the Cold War. Given the vast nuclear arsenals on each side, they saw no possible advantage in exerting significant pressure on the Soviet Union and saw grave danger in threatening what were widely seen as critical Soviet interests, particularly in Eastern Europe. Instead, they argued that what was needed was a mutual understanding regarding the "rules of the game" as a way of preventing a military conflict. Nor was this view shared only by the more left-leaning members of the Democratic Party (the "Stevenson wing"). In fact, anticommunist liberals, such as Acheson, had also taken the view that restoring and ensuring equilibrium between the superpowers was the single most important task of American foreign policy.[61]

Many liberals also held the view that the ideological element of Soviet policy had largely dissipated and claimed, therefore, that attempting to base American foreign policy on anticommunism was impossible and unwise.[62] Such a policy could only inhibit East-West dialogue and complicate efforts to achieve détente. Some even questioned whether those living in the Soviet bloc, particularly in Eastern Europe, would even willingly choose to disassociate themselves from Soviet rule.[63] They argued, for example, that the communist regimes in Eastern Europe were widely accepted (if not loved) by the general population and had proved their legitimacy by providing significant improvements in the overall standard of living. Overall, liberal (and even mainstream) foreign policy strategists argued that the key goal of U.S. foreign policy was to slow or halt, not to reverse, Soviet gains in the Third World while improving relations between East and West.

Conservatives of the period, on the other hand, continued to view the rollback of Soviet power as a critical goal in the much broader effort to win the Cold War. The strategic advantages of successfully rolling back Soviet control were clear to most conservatives. In addition to the obvious improvements to the military and economic balance of power that a successful rollback would have for the West, conservatives also saw important moral and (in particular) ideological gains from liberating portions of the Soviet empire and demonstrating that global Marxist revolution was neither inevitable nor irreversible. While some continued to focus on Eastern Europe as others turned their attention to the Third World, conservative strategists as a whole urged the United States to take the initiative and seek the liberation of all those living under Soviet domination. Some, such as Strausz-Hupé, challenged the frequently expressed view of the foreign policy mainstream that any effort to roll back Soviet control of Eastern Europe would result in a superpower nuclear exchange. Instead, he argued that while the growth of nuclear arsenals on both sides had resulted in a form of "mutual deterrence" at the military level, it made possible a "psychopolitical offensive" against the Soviets' "peace zone" in Eastern Europe.[64] In his judgment (and that of most conservatives), the Soviets would never resort to either conventional or nuclear war with the United States (particularly in light of America's strategic superiority) in response to Western political warfare against the communist regimes in Eastern Europe. The key component to such a political campaign was making clear to the Soviets, the Eastern Europeans, and the rest of the world that the West would never acknowledge the legitimacy of Soviet control there nor would it cease its efforts to detach Eastern Europe from the Soviet bloc.[65]

While Strausz-Hupé and his supporters argued that Eastern Europe needed to remain the focus of America's liberation efforts, other conservatives, particularly Goldwater, saw the expansion of Soviet influence in the Third World as both a rapidly worsening threat and a better opportunity to reverse Soviet expansion. While Soviet expansion in the developing world threatened to deny the West the crucial natural resources required to maintain its economic health, most pro-Soviet regimes in the Third World were extremely unpopular and had (unlike the communist regimes of Eastern Europe) only a tenuous hold on power. As such, they represented excellent targets for the careful and selective use of American power. While most conservatives saw the elimination of the Fidel Castro regime in Cuba as particularly important, due to Cuba's proximity to the United States, Goldwater stood apart by also recognizing the need for a broader moral principle to guide anticommunist strategy in the Third World. He and other like-minded conservatives urged the United States to make clear to the world that it would support any anticommunist revolt against a communist government and would oppose any communist revolt in a pro-Western regime.[66] And while this principle, which served as one of the major tenets of the Goldwater presidential campaign, died off following his defeat in 1964, one can see in this approach the roots of the Reagan Doctrine.

Late Cold War Period

While a number of events during the late 1960s, particularly the 1968 "Prague Spring" uprising, led a few Western strategists to consider the problem of continued Soviet domination in Eastern Europe, in many respects the 1970s represented a nadir in the debate between liberation and containment. By marginalizing liberation-minded conservatives, Goldwater's massive defeat in the 1964 presidential election greatly contributed to the declining popularity of rollback theory. In addition, the steady rising of détente-style thinking had begun shifting the terms of foreign policy debate steadily leftward, leaving the few remaining conservative strategists even further outside the foreign policy mainstream. But despite the declining popularity of rollback, the 1970s saw a small number of conservatives and neoconservatives offer subtle refinements to the liberation approach, highlighting the strategic and moral advantages of a sustained policy of seeking freedom for those living under Soviet control.

As noted in chapter 3, the 1970s saw the rapid rise of détente as the central strategic concept for Western liberals. The same hope that fueled their desire to see greater U.S.-Soviet dialogue and compromise also led them to unconditionally reject any Western policy aiming to undermine Soviet control over either Eastern Europe or communist client states in the Third World.[67] While most liberals rarely bothered to openly challenge their conservative counterparts' arguments in favor of liberation, when they did their objections to rollback generally relied on three distinct arguments.

First, they argued that any Western effort to incite trouble in either the Third World or Eastern Europe would undermine prospects for a U.S.-Soviet détente, which they viewed as the most important American goal.[68] In their view, no reversal of Soviet expansion was nearly as valuable as establishing a more open, cooperative relationship with Moscow. Second, they argued (particularly in discussions of Eastern Europe) that encouraging upheaval or even offering moral support to people living under Soviet control was inherently immoral, as it would only exacerbate their suffering and increase the likelihood of direct Soviet military intervention without offering them any legitimate hope of improving their situation.[69]

For most of the foreign policy mainstream, the pro-Soviet regimes were to be considered permanent fixtures of the international community. Finally, and most disturbingly, some liberals argued that many Soviet client states were already largely free and thus did not require assistance from the West. Many of these strategists, who had long questioned the real extent of Soviet control in the Third World, argued that much of Eastern Europe was already free to manage its internal affairs without Soviet influence.[70] Overall, American liberals largely ignored the argument for liberation, viewing it as a fringe movement no longer worthy of serious intellectual consideration.

As mentioned earlier, the 1970s were an inhospitable climate for discussions of rollback and thus resulted in a significant reduction in the number of conservative strategists openly discussing and advocating such a policy.[71] Greatly disillusioned by the march toward détente and the overall societal reluctance to pursue an openly anti-Soviet policy, some conservatives who had previously urged a rollback strategy began to view containment as the best American strategy currently available. Yet a few conservatives continued to argue that liberation, both in Eastern Europe and in the Third World, was the surest way to improve Western security. Mindful of the serious weaknesses becoming increasingly evident within the Soviet bloc, conservatives continued to argue that reversing the Brezhnev Doctrine *was* possible, even in Eastern Europe.[72] They also rejected the claim of most mainstream strategists that a closer, more organic relationship between the USSR and Eastern Europe was in America's interest, as it would transform the Soviet Union from a revolutionary to a "satisfied" power.[73] Given the centrality of ideology to Soviet behavior, conservatives insisted that the USSR could never become a satisfied, status quo power and thus that Western support was a necessary condition for the liberation of the Soviet empire. At the same time, conservatives noted how fragile the Soviets' position in the Third World was. The Soviets' aggressive efforts to expand their reach in the developing world had left them vulnerable to an aggressive counterattack. Conservatives therefore urged the United States to find a suitable target in the Third World, with one even noting that "Grenada (the Soviet Union's subsatellite, via Cuba) cries out for the rollback treatment."[74] Roughly eighteen months later, the Reagan administration would, of course, take this advice and overthrow Grenada's Marxist government.

In addition to these more strategic arguments, both conservatives and neoconservatives also increasingly highlighted the superior morality of this goal, arguing that failing to seek the freedom of those living under communist rule was an affront to basic Western morality. For example, while deeply critical of the 1975 Helsinki Agreement for its acceptance of Soviet domination of Eastern Europe, conservatives noted that even this flawed agreement recognized the moral and political right to national self-determination, a right that the Soviet Union had systematically denied its subjects. By refusing to stand up for this right, conservatives believed the West was betraying its own moral beliefs and squandering a potential political advantage.[75] They further noted that Soviet ideology mattered, especially in the Third World, and that the damage communism could inflict on the developing world was staggering.[76] Already plagued by economic backwardness and political immaturity, the nations of the Third World could ill afford the political repression and economic catastrophe that would result from a communist dictatorship.

By making it clear that the West would accept neither the Soviet Union's imperialism in Eastern Europe nor its subversion of the Third World, America could force the Soviets onto the defensive, while regaining the political credibility it had lost since the fall of South Vietnam.[77] What was needed, they argued, was the use of American power (both military and nonmilitary) "to overwhelm and defeat tyranny in every arena where freedom is now threatened."[78] Thus, by the end of the 1970s, conservatives had set forth a series of mutually supporting strategic and moral arguments for aggressively seeking to reverse Soviet expansionism.

UNDERMINE THE SOVIET UNION

The final, and certainly most controversial, goal of the Reagan administration was to undermine and destroy the Soviet regime. In many respects, it represented little more than the logical extension of the goal to reverse Soviet expansionism previously discussed. Just as conservatives saw the installation of communist governments in Eastern Europe and the Third World as inherently illegitimate, so too did they view the continued rule of the Communist Party of the Soviet Union as a threat to both American interests and basic democratic values. Discussions of eliminating the Soviet threat by undermining the Soviet state were, unsurprisingly, rejected and ignored by most mainstream strategists. Yet it represented a major element of most conservative foreign policy thought, which saw the destruction of the Soviet Union as the key to victory in the Cold War.

Early Cold War Period

For much of the foreign policy elite in the early days of the Cold War, the possibility that the Soviets would, some day, lose control of their own internal population was a very real one. The massive damage resulting from World War II, which was actually far higher than most Western estimates, had devastated popular morale and destroyed much of the Soviet economy. This destruction, plus the broad recognition that the Soviets' ruling ideology was increasingly incompatible with the effective functioning of a modern state, made many anticipate some form of change in the Soviet regime. Indeed, the strategic reasoning behind containment was that, if given enough time, the inherent weaknesses of the Soviet Union would eventually force substantial changes in the internal and external policies of the Soviet leadership. The crux of the liberal-conservative debate, then, was whether or not the West should take actions designed to accelerate this process.

It should hardly be surprising that, in rejecting efforts to extend liberation to the Soviet Union, Western liberals relied upon many of the same arguments they used against reversing Soviet expansionism. First and foremost, they cited the inherent danger of this approach, particularly if pursued with military means. Warning that the United States "must not succumb to demands for an anti-Soviet crusade,"[79] American liberals argued instead that such efforts would only strengthen the so-called hard-liners within the Soviet leadership and make internal reform less likely. Second, since many liberals agreed with Kennan that the gradual mellowing of Soviet behavior was inevitable, they believed U.S. actions aimed at weakening the Soviet state could disrupt this gradual process and increase the likelihood of war.

Finally, there was a sense, even among dedicated anticommunist liberals, that the Soviet state had some redeeming intellectual characteristics and thus should not be destroyed. Schlesinger himself argued that communist goals derive from "a respectable intellectual lineage saturated in nineteenth-century values of optimism, rationalism and detailed historical inquiry" and that "Soviet totalitarianism lays greater initial claim on democratic sympathies than does fascism," while praising Lenin for giving the Bolshevik Revolution "a character of sacrificial dedication to the good of humanity."[80] While one certainly cannot question Schlesinger's opposition to communism, the fact that such a well-regarded individual had anything supportive to say about the Soviet regime certainly weakened the willingness of some liberals to see the end of the great "Soviet experiment."

Reflecting Burnham's argument that a defensive policy can never win, conservatives argued that the United States needed to aim for victory in the Cold War and that a true victory ultimately required the destruction of the Soviet Union. Conservatives took issue with the argument of some of their liberal colleagues that communist rule had provided some meaningful benefits to the people of the Soviet Union. Instead, they argued that Soviet rule had been a disaster for the Russian people, who had been socially, politically, and economically better off under the czar. Dismissing the popular view that the Soviet Union was a legitimate state and therefore entitled to the same mutual respect as any other member of the international community, conservatives argued that the Soviets' history of subversion, aggression, and expansionism demonstrated that the USSR was little more than a conspiratorial movement using the power of the Russian state to pursue a goal of world empire.[81] As such, its very existence posed a threat to the United States and the rest of the world. Since the Cold War amounted to a war of survival and since the Soviet leadership showed no signs of relenting in its pursuit of world domination, conservatives saw that the only option for the West was to seek the destruction of communist power in the Soviet Union.

While mindful of the significant weaknesses inherent in the Soviet regime, conservatives believed that, absent sustained Western efforts to exacerbate these difficulties, they were not severe enough to compel the Soviet leadership to make significant internal or external reform. Rejecting containment's "wait-and-see" approach, Burnham argued that, without the strong leadership that could only come from serious external support, mass resistance movements within the Soviet Union were highly unlikely to emerge or succeed.[82] Just as demonstrating the West's solidarity with the people of Eastern Europe was critical to rolling back Soviet expansionism, conservatives insisted that political support for the freedom of the various nations within the Soviet Union was vital to undermining the Soviet system. In fact, contrary to the claims of many of their opponents, most conservatives strongly believed that political, not military, action was the best option for achieving the liberation of the Soviet people.[83] While recognizing that, in the short term, sustained pressure on Soviet weaknesses could result in greater repression, conservatives believed that such pressure would, in the long term, accelerate the breakdown of the Soviet political and economic system and ultimately lead to a fundamental change in the Soviet regime.

Middle Cold War Period

As the hope for "peaceful coexistence" increased within the West, much of the foreign policy elite took a more relaxed view of the Soviet threat, instead focusing their attention on the perceived dangers of upheavals in the Third World or the nuclear arms race. As a result, they saw no real need for liberation and were thus significantly less tolerant of conservative strategists who continued to argue for a rollback strategy. The smear campaign waged against Goldwater during the 1964 presidential campaign was but one example of growing liberal hostility toward any foreign policy that did not conform to "mainstream" views.[84] The idea that the United States should seek to win the Cold War or defeat the Soviet Union was no longer an acceptable point of view. Western liberals insisted that détente and sustained U.S.-Soviet cooperation offered a better approach to advancing American interests. Viewing liberation as "a dangerous promise without substance," they instead argued that the United States needed to make its long-term goals "universal security against military aggression through universal disarmament under adequately enforced world law" and the "achievement of universal human betterment through worldwide co-operation in economic and social development."[85] Rather than challenge or confront the Soviet leadership, they argued that Americans needed to recognize that Soviet leaders largely shared their desire to help protect, support, and improve the lives of their own people.[86] To the extent that there were disagreements between the two superpowers, they believed such disagreements were the result of misperceptions, which could be eliminated by more intense dialogue and renewed efforts at cooperation. But this cooperation was only possible if the United States made it clear that it was "not out to eradicate communism from the face of the earth."[87] Thus, the fundamental focus of the liberal foreign policy elite was not on changing the Soviet system, but rather on finding common ground with the Soviet leadership.

Conservatives, on the other hand, continued to argue that the ultimate U.S. goal in the Cold War could only be victory and that this victory required the destruction of communist rule in the Soviet Union. In a forceful call to arms, conservative strategists insisted that the West's goal must be "to turn the tide of battle against the Communists, to induce them to overextend themselves, to exploit the weakness of their system, to paralyze their will, and to bring about their final collapse."[88] Building on the arguments of their predecessors, conservatives developed two distinct, but reinforcing, arguments in support of undermining the Soviet state. Some made a "survival-based" argument, namely, that the destruction of communist power was the only way to ensure the survival of the Western political and economic system. Others developed a "morality-based" argument, stressing that the West had a moral duty to aid the destruction of the Soviet Union and the liberation of the various nationalities there.

For many conservatives, the existence of communist rule and the steady expansion of Soviet power posed a fundamental, existential threat to the Western world.

They argued that, at its core, the Cold War was neither a purely geopolitical struggle for influence nor a clash of different economic systems. If it were, traditional methods of statecraft, such as negotiations, would have been sufficient to manage the rivalry. Instead, the key unresolved issue between the United States and the USSR was political and specifically the inherent incompatibility of democracy, which strived for individual and national freedom, and totalitarianism, which sought only conflict and conquest.[89] Reflecting their belief in the centrality of Soviet ideology to its behavior, conservatives saw little hope that the Cold War could eventually fade away. Because it was caused by the defining characteristics of each side's political system, the conflict could only be resolved by the destruction of either communist rule or Western civilization.[90] While recognizing the dangers of pursuing such a goal, conservatives argued that it was the only method of ensuring the survival of Western civilization.

While acknowledging the fundamental threat posed by communist power, other conservatives saw liberation as a moral imperative and focused on the moral benefits that would result from the destruction of the Soviet system. The fact that major conservative strategists of this period did focus on the moral dimension of the Cold War is important to highlight, as it demonstrates the remarkable continuity between conservative and neoconservative thought. Given that neoconservatives have been both praised and criticized for their willingness to insert moral principles into strategic thought, it is critical to recognize that traditional conservatives had made similar arguments many years before the emergence of the neoconservatives. In fact, the rise of the Goldwater movement and the Young Americans for Freedom can be traced back to conservative outrage at Eisenhower's refusal to support the 1956 uprising in Hungary, which conservatives viewed as a betrayal of basic American values.[91] Mindful of the inherent immorality of the Soviet system and its international behavior, conservatives argued that there had to be a moral basis for American foreign policy and that the only proper moral aim for the United States was the eventual destruction of the Soviet regime.[92]

Other conservatives made a slightly different, but reinforcing, argument by stressing that the key U.S. moral objective was a world with the greatest possible degree of freedom, justice, peace, and prosperity. Since the existence of the Soviet system made such a world impossible, the destruction of Soviet power had to become a central U.S. goal.[93] Thus, throughout this period, conservatives cited both reasons of survival and reasons of morality to support their goal of undermining and destroying the Soviet Union.

Late Cold War Period

With the Western world focusing increasingly on the prospects of a U.S.-USSR détente, it should hardly be surprising that there was little interest in rollback among much of the liberal foreign policy community. Throughout the 1970s (and well into the 1980s), liberal strategists argued vehemently against rollback efforts, claiming that undermining the Soviet Union was not in America's long-term interest. Many argued that the United States had, for too long, seen the Soviet challenge as a zero-sum game. Instead, they argued that America's long-term goal of international security could only be achieved by accepting Soviet equality and supporting its efforts to achieve a level of global influence commensurate with its superpower status.[94] In their view, the worldwide social and political upheaval of the 1960s and 1970s indicated that the entire international system was in danger of descending into anarchy and instability. Since only some form of U.S.-Soviet entente could prevent such a catastrophe, efforts to weaken or destroy the USSR were counterproductive.[95] Whether this catastrophic threat to international security was environmental degradation, global economic problems, or the arms race, liberals argued that only by working together could the United States and Soviet Union adequately address these emerging threats.

While the early period of the Cold War represents the golden age of liberation strategy, the late period of the Cold War saw relatively little new thinking on the issue of liberating the Soviet Union. As already noted, while some conservatives had given up on extending rollback to the Soviet Union altogether, many other conservatives supported the idea but questioned the willingness of the West to follow through on such an ambitious effort.[96] To some degree, the lack of *new* thought on the issue of liberating the Soviet Union during this period is understandable. After all, it is difficult to underestimate the demoralizing effect that the turmoil of the 1970s and the rise of détente had on much of the conservative movement. The pronounced leftward shift in U.S. foreign policy (and Western society in general) had pushed most conservative ideas far from the political mainstream and given them little, if any, policy relevance. Furthermore, in the view of most conservatives, détente was so dangerous that their primary focus became reinstituting the marginally acceptable containment policy, which conservatives saw as the best approach obtainable in light of the current world situation and political climate.

In addition to the fact that conservatives during the 1970s were preoccupied with undermining détente rather than the Soviet Union, the lack of new thought on this issue also reflected a much simpler reality: the basic conservative argument on this issue had already been largely developed by earlier figures. In short, they continued to argue that the Soviets remained committed to world domination and that only by decisively defeating the Soviet regime could the West advance its moral and strategic goals. As a result, one can find Goldwater continuing to urge the United States to unleash its economic and technological superiority to "reestablish confidence in the power of freedom . . . to overwhelm and defeat tyranny," even within the Soviet Union.[97] Crozier, himself a student of Burnham, was perhaps the most outspoken supporter of rollback, echoing his mentor's position when he argued that the long-term goal of the United States remained the destruction of the Soviet system and the political freedom of the various nationalities within the Soviet Union.[98] To achieve this goal, he called for a "New Forward Policy, the ultimate aim of which can be nothing less than the destabilization and, in time, the collapse of the Soviet empire, including the system itself."[99] Conservatives paid particular attention to rolling back the ideological base of the Soviet Union, urging the West to wage an "official crusade" dedicated "absolutely to the total atomization of the Marxist myth" and the complete discrediting of communism as a political theory.[100]

While traditional conservatives largely dominated the development of this argument, neoconservatives also contributed to this effort. Richard Pipes, for example, noted that the United States needed to recognize the ideological nature of Soviet goals and to "compel the Soviet Union to turn inward—from conquest to reform," understanding that any meaningful reform could only undermine the bases of the Soviet system.[101] Thus, despite the dampening effects of détente, conservative foreign policy strategies of the 1970s continued to reflect an intellectual continuity with the work of James Burnham, Robert Strausz-Hupé, and Barry Goldwater, whose goals would ultimately be embraced by the Reagan administration.

CONCLUSION

This discussion has demonstrated how the central goals of Reagan's grand strategy gradually evolved from their roots in the early days of the Cold War into the coherent whole that had emerged by the end of the 1970s. In some cases, such as the efforts to reverse Soviet expansionism and undermine the Soviet regime (the "goals of choice"), these goals were proposed, developed, and endorsed almost exclusively by conservative strategists. In other cases, such as the widely accepted "goals of necessity," conservatives supported the goals but argued for a fundamentally different understanding of their practical meaning.

Thus, whereas liberals tended to equate nuclear deterrence with MAD and U.S.-Soviet dialogue with arms control, conservatives saw nuclear superiority and unyielding pursuit of American interests as the focal points of these national goals. Throughout conservative writings on these five goals, however, runs a common thread: an unwavering commitment to an American victory in the Cold War. The Reagan administration shared this commitment and made extensive use of all the major tools of national power to achieve its far-reaching goals.

Tools

The previous two chapters have reviewed the beliefs and goals of the Reagan administration and analyzed the link between these elements of grand strategy and conservative strategic thought. Both chapters demonstrated that the key elements of Reagan's grand strategy were rooted in a fundamentally different, conservative approach to foreign policy, one not widely shared by the administration's mainstream and liberal critics. This chapter will conduct a similar analysis on the major military, economic, informational, diplomatic, and intelligence tools used by the Reagan administration. The fact that the administration *used* these tools is unremarkable, as they represent the major means by which any nation seeks to achieve its goals. Rather, what distinguished the Reagan approach from earlier efforts was the *manner* in which these tools were used. This chapter will demonstrate that the Reagan administration's use of these tools was consistent with the larger body of conservative strategic thought.

MILITARY BUILDUP

Historically, the ability to fight and win wars has been an important factor in the ability of any state to preserve its existence and expand its international influence. However, in the aftermath of World War II and the development of the atomic bomb, understanding the role and value of military power became increasingly difficult. For some, the destructiveness of nuclear weaponry had undermined the credibility of military action and the value of military power. Yet in the view of others (including many conservatives), the new era had not fundamentally changed the importance of the military instrument, which remained a critical tool for deterring aggression, preventing blackmail, and advancing American national interests.

At the same time, though, it must be stressed that most conservatives did *not* see military power as the only important element of national power. In fact, the inherently supporting nature of military power is a common theme that appears throughout the history of conservative strategic thought. For conservatives, military strength provided the base upon which to build a much broader, more comprehensive national strategy.

Early Cold War Period

As discussed earlier, in the immediate postwar era, there was widespread understanding among most conservatives and anticommunist liberals that superior power was critical to the West's ability to deal effectively with the Soviet threat. Yet, while they agreed on the need for superior military power, liberals and conservatives saw that power serving fundamentally different purposes. For many anticommunist liberals, U.S. military power was a much more limited tool, useful only as a means of implementing their preferred policy of containment and convincing the Soviets that they had no hope of destroying the West.[1] Having already rejected the notion of winning the Cold War, they paid little attention either to the broader value of military superiority or to the strategic options it offered the West. Greatly influenced by Brodie's belief that, in the nuclear age, the military's only purpose was to prevent war, Western liberals rejected the idea that America's military superiority could be used to coerce concessions from the Soviet Union or to enhance America's global influence.

Conservatives, on the other hand, even at a time when the United States possessed a monopoly on atomic weapons, viewed the West's military strength as a *supporting* element of national power, but one that could contribute to achieving far more ambitious goals. In the view of Burnham (and most other conservatives), the military tool was, first and foremost, a *defensive* component of the West's grand strategy, useful primarily to prevent communist encroachment in Western Europe and the Third World.[2]

However, contrary to the claims of their critics, conservatives understood that the primary purpose of superior military power was not to reverse by force communist control of Eastern Europe or to invade the Soviet Union. Rather, they argued that an unrivaled U.S. military would provide the West two important strategic advantages. First, by achieving and maintaining military superiority, the United States could, in essence, "beat the Soviets at their own game." By remaining significantly ahead of a Soviet regime based on force and violence, one in which "the value of power far outweighs the power of values," America would demonstrate the futility of the Soviets' global challenge to its power and devalue the Soviets' only real strategic asset.[3] Second, conservatives argued that American superiority would not only deter Soviet aggression, but would also enhance America's influence with its friends and allies and, most importantly, "buy time" for the West to use its superior political, economic, and spiritual resources to achieve its ultimate goal: the rollback of Soviet expansionism and the destruction of communist power.[4] By denying the Soviets the ability to engage in significant military expansion (particularly into Western Europe), the United States could more easily target key Soviet economic and political weaknesses and thereby destroy the Soviet regime.

In this early period, then, one can see the beginnings of a recurrent theme in conservative strategic thought: military superiority was a necessary, but not sufficient, condition for a Western victory in the Cold War.

Middle Cold War Period

By the 1960s, the gap between liberals and conservatives on the value of military power had begun to widen, with each side viewing military power in fundamentally different ways. For many liberals, Soviet aggression had become virtually unthinkable, particularly in such key areas as Western Europe, despite the West's conventional inferiority. As a result, the "Soviet threat" was becoming a steadily less important one. Instead, they viewed the arms race itself as the primary threat to both U.S. security and better relations with the Soviet Union.[5] In the view of many liberals, the destructive power of modern weaponry had made the military instrument of national power increasingly unusable, while radically increasing the costs and risks of accidental war. In light of these changing views of the threat, liberals throughout this period became increasingly skeptical about the real value of military power and called for more robust efforts at achieving a general disarmament.[6] While still reluctantly accepting the need for a deterrent force of nuclear weapons, liberals were especially critical of significant conventional forces, which they felt were too expensive, had little deterrent value, and provided no meaningful increase in Western security.[7] The fact that U.S. conventional forces were, by the end of the decade, still unable to achieve victory in Vietnam merely served to reinforce this skepticism about the value of military superiority.

Despite the enormous changes in the international system since the end of World War II, the conservative view of military power during this period was largely consistent with that of their predecessors: military power was a critical, but supporting, tool in the pursuit of broader political goals. Unlike their liberal counterparts, conservatives argued that all elements of military power, including conventional and tactical nuclear forces, could contribute to achieving America's broader national goals. In outlining his strategy for victory over communism, Goldwater reiterated Burnham's view that military power should undertake the defensive task of deterring Soviet aggression while the United States waged political warfare aimed at the Soviets' destruction.[8]

Yet, in addition to its value in deterring actual military aggression, conservatives during this period also began to stress the ability of superior military power to deter Soviet political coercion and blackmail. By developing and maintaining superior nuclear and conventional forces, conservatives insisted the United States could eliminate the ability of the Soviet Union to intimidate or threaten America or its allies.[9] Since these attempts to intimidate the noncommunist world were central to the Soviets' expansionist efforts, Western military power could have a profound impact on the broader political struggle between the two superpowers.

At the same time, however, some conservatives increasingly saw other uses for Western military power, particularly in response to unrest in the developing world. In light of the sustained Soviet campaign of aggression in the Third World, many conservatives noted that a robust conventional capability offered important strategic options for the West. If the United States was serious about taking the strategic offensive, expanding its influence in the Third World, and developing an "independent rather than reactive" foreign policy, Strausz-Hupé argued that the ability to use force was essential.[10] Indeed, he cautioned that "to abjure the use of force under all circumstances except self-defense in a contest with a revolutionary power is a fateful decision," since the most effective deterrent to revolution is the willingness to use superior power.[11] As a way of defending itself against Soviet efforts to spark a worldwide communist revolution and discrediting Marxist ideology, conservatives urged the West to use military power to reverse communist expansion, focusing in particular on Cuba and (to a lesser degree) Albania.[12] While their calls for such actions were largely ignored (particularly after the Bay of Pigs fiasco), this support for a more aggressive use of military power in the Third World would continue throughout the 1970s and helped form the intellectual basis for the Reagan administration's actions in Beirut, Grenada, and Libya.

Still, even in these calls for the more aggressive use of military power, conservatives continued to emphasize that force alone could not win the Cold War and that the "actions of arms must always be considered in combination with political, educational, and organizational measures aimed at the isolation and total political discreditation of the enemy."[13]

Late Cold War Period

The liberal-conservative divide steadily widened throughout the 1970s, as the two sides' views gradually hardened to represent fundamentally opposing views on the importance of military power. In many respects, much of the debate over the value of military power reflected the disagreement between the two camps over the importance of nuclear superiority, which was discussed in chapter 4. Because liberals had decided that the destructiveness of nuclear weaponry rendered nuclear superiority meaningless and that changes in the international system had made the military tool of statecraft unusable, they were obviously less willing to support the development of robust conventional or nuclear forces. At the same time, conservatives who continued to see value in military power urged the West to take seriously the danger of Soviet aggression and reestablish military superiority via a sustained buildup of allied defenses.

Most leading liberals of this period assessed the various proposals to develop or enhance Western military power on the basis of their impact on détente and their ability to slow or halt the arms race. Since they continued to believe that military power was rapidly declining in political importance, the only purpose nuclear or conventional forces could possibly serve was deterrence.[14] As a result, only those programs (which were few and far between) deemed unlikely to either worsen U.S.-Soviet ties or accelerate the arms race were considered even minimally acceptable. Indeed, liberals were virtually unanimous on the need for the United States to show unilateral restraint in its efforts to update its military forces or improve its defensive capabilities. Sen. Edward Kennedy, for example, went so far as to call for the United States to provide a "full public disclosure of nuclear weapons doctrines and programs" (even absent a similar disclosure by the Soviets).[15] He also demanded that the United States not build any weapon system that could either be seen as a rejection of Mutual Assured Destruction or was intended to serve as a bargaining chip for future arms control treaties.[16] Rather, the United States needed to limit its development of modernized nuclear (and conventional) forces and focus instead on obtaining an arms control agreement with the Soviets.[17] In short, guided by the belief that military power was strategically meaningless, most liberal strategic thinkers argued that the United States needed to ensure that nothing it developed could reasonably be expected to challenge the power equilibrium that most liberals believed existed between East and West.

For conservatives, the Soviets' nuclear and conventional buildup, which had begun in the 1960s, raised troubling questions about Soviet intentions and convinced them of the need for a similarly robust Western effort to enhance its military power. In the view of many conservatives, America's conventional and nuclear inferiority (combined with the aftereffects of Vietnam) had rendered the West dangerously vulnerable to Soviet psychological manipulation and political pressure. Reversing that inferiority, restoring the West's ability to deter Soviet aggression, and rebuilding the ability of the United States to act decisively in the Third World were the key goals of conservatives throughout the 1970s. To do so, conservatives argued that the United States needed first to redress the massive Soviet military advantage by acting quickly to restore its nuclear deterrent and rebuild its conventional forces.[18] By improving America's military forces, conservatives hoped to deny the Soviet Union any plausible scenario in which it sought to emerge from a nuclear or conventional war more powerful than the United States, and to thus eliminate the danger of Soviet coercion. In addition, while America's experience in Vietnam had made military intervention almost impossible to contemplate, conservatives continued to build upon Strausz-Hupé's argument that the West needed to be prepared to act decisively, particularly in the Third World.

Nevertheless, during this phase of the Cold War, as in earlier periods, conservatives continued to highlight the inherently political nature of the West's struggle with the Soviet Union and, therefore, the necessarily *supporting* role that military power played in their Cold War grand strategy. Thus, conservatives saw the rebuilding of U.S. military power as a critical element in overcoming the psychological and political barriers to the coordinated use of American power. Understanding that the U.S. defeat in Vietnam had greatly undermined the rest of the world's confidence in America's willingness to counter Soviet pressure, conservatives recognized the need to reverse this perception of American weakness. They argued that a sustained military buildup was critical to overcoming "an attitude toward nuclear weapons which leaves us increasingly vulnerable to subtle forms of psychological and political blackmail" and to reassure America's friends and allies that it had not given up hope of winning the Cold War.[19] The primary purpose of an arms buildup, then, was to demonstrate to the Soviets and the world that the West would not be intimidated by communist pressure nor deterred from acting in areas of its vital national interests.[20] Thus, conservatives throughout the Cold War based their view of military power's role in American grand strategy in largely Clausewitzian terms, seeing it as a tool for achieving political ends.

ECONOMIC WARFARE

The strategic use of America's vast economic power to achieve broad political objectives is a topic frequently overlooked by the foreign policy community. Much writing on America's foreign economic policy (both during and after the Cold War) tended to assume that the primary goal of such policies was, for example, to foster domestic economic growth or, at its most ambitious, to improve America's relations with the rest of the world. To the extent that more aggressive actions were considered, such discussions generally focused on the efficacy of trade sanctions and similar instruments as symbols of U.S. displeasure. Rarely was the possibility considered that economic tools could serve as powerful weapons to be wielded against the enemies of the West. Indeed, the liberal-conservative debate on the West's economic policy toward the Soviet bloc hinged on whether and how economic power could effectively advance America's interests.

As a result, throughout the Cold War, the appropriate level of Western economic interaction with the Soviet bloc was a deeply contentious issue, with each side motivated by different overarching theories regarding the impact such trade would have on the broader strategic competition between the United States and the USSR. For some, strict sanctions, heavily restricted economic relations with the communist world, and the economic burden of the arms race offered the greatest hope for a Western victory in the Cold War. Others insisted that greater economic integration and arms reductions offered the United States the greatest opportunity to exert leverage and influence over Soviet actions. The gradual ascendance of the latter theory would result in the steady relaxation of Western export controls, the loosening of trade restrictions, and the renunciation of the arms race as a tool of economic warfare, decisions conservatives strongly opposed and which the Reagan administration would quickly reverse.

Early Cold War Period

In response to the violent repression of Eastern Europe and the Soviet support to North Korean forces in the Korean War, President Truman imposed wide-ranging economic sanctions and trade restrictions against the Soviet Union and its allies.

Despite some resistance within his own administration, he was largely able to retain these economic restrictions throughout his tenure in office.[21] However, much of the liberal and mainstream establishment viewed these restrictions as ineffective and, in fact, counterproductive. In their view, the Soviet Union and its allies constituted a self-sufficient society that was, therefore, largely immune to most forms of economic pressure.[22]

More importantly, however, much of the liberal establishment felt that the expansion of East-West trade relations would generate goodwill toward the United States within the Soviet bloc, demonstrate the Soviets' material weakness, and enhance the West's negotiating leverage over the Soviets. According to this approach, Western trade would improve standards of living within the Soviet bloc, which would increase popular pressure on the Soviet leadership to pursue a more conciliatory policy toward the West and reform it political institutions. This theory was ultimately endorsed in Eisenhower's Project Solarium and would serve as the basis for the efforts of Eisenhower and his successors to "reduce radically the restrictions on East-West trade."[23]

Conservatives, on the other hand, took the view that the fundamental purpose of U.S. economic policy toward the communist world was to exacerbate, not relieve, the Soviets' economic difficulties, as part of a larger effort to weaken and eventually destroy the Soviet state. Whereas much of the establishment believed that a more prosperous Soviet Union would be more likely to seek genuine accommodation with the West, conservatives believed that a stronger Soviet economy could only result in a more aggressive and dangerous global rival. Criticizing those who sought to expand East-West trade, Burnham argued that the Soviets viewed trade as a zero-sum struggle for power, not an effort to find mutual advantage, which forms the basis of trade among capitalist states.[24] Instead, conservatives urged the nations of the West to harness the power of their own economies by reducing trade barriers between capitalist nations and particularly by supporting the nascent efforts to create a unified European economy. A stronger, more unified Europe would be better able to resist Soviet intimidation and would be able to contribute more to the military defense of Europe.[25]

Conservatives also hoped that a more united Western economy would make a common policy toward East-West trade more likely and thus increase the chances that the United States could convince its allies to impose severe limits on Western economic contact with the communist bloc. In the view of most conservatives, such restrictions, by carefully targeting key Soviet vulnerabilities, would work to America's strategic advantage. By exacerbating bottlenecks in the Soviet economy, trade restrictions would force the Soviet leadership to make more difficult decisions regarding resource allocation and, potentially, compel it to abandon its expansionist efforts. In addition, by worsening the Soviets' economic problems, they would undermine popular support for the Soviet regime and intensify nationalist opposition to Soviet rule. While not popular within the foreign policy establishment, this view of trade controls as a key weapon to use in the West's struggle with the Soviet Union would emerge as a central element of conservative Cold War strategy.

Middle Cold War Period

By the late 1950s and early 1960s, both East-West trade and the arms race had become highly contentious issues within the United States. Many liberals felt that Eisenhower's efforts to reduce trade barriers between the superpowers had not gone far enough and instead supported a significant expansion of economic ties between the United States and USSR. Liberals such as James Warburg argued for the full normalization of trade with the Soviet bloc, insisting that existing restrictions imposed far greater burdens on a market economy than on a command-style economy.[26] At the same time, they expressed increasing concern over the acceleration of the arms race, which they felt was not only strategically meaningless but also economically counterproductive. Deeply concerned about the economic strain caused by the arms race, some argued that the United States had no realistic hope of winning an arms race with the communist world, which had a much greater manpower supply, ample access to raw materials, and the ability to "channel the energies of their people into military preparations at the expense of civilian needs and comforts."[27] Others, while more optimistic about the ability of the United States to compete in the arms race, argued that using the arms race as a tool of economic warfare would make a negotiated political settlement with the USSR less feasible.[28] At its core, the general liberal approach to economic warfare was to deny its usability and to view it instead as a threat to broader efforts to improve relations with the Soviet Union.

Conservatives, on the other hand, argued vehemently against any expansion of trade with the Soviet bloc and urged the West to use its economic prosperity as a weapon to undermine the Soviet regime. While recognizing the potential for mutually beneficial trade, conservatives argued that the West needed to prohibit any East-West trade in strategically useful goods. In the view of most conservatives, "strategic trade" included any item that could facilitate industrial development or improve the technology base of the Soviet bloc.[29] Understanding the importance of allied support for these restrictions, conservatives highlighted the need for improved Western coordination on export controls, stressing that tighter restrictions would "remove from the Communist enterprise the material supplements it needs to keep its staggering economy in motion."[30] Recognizing the continued weakness of the Soviet economy, conservatives saw economic pressure as a tool for compelling the Soviets to curtail their aggressive efforts to expand their influence in the Third World. By forcing the Soviet leadership to make difficult economic choices, conservatives sought to use this economic offensive to undermine the cohesion of the Soviet bloc, complicate Soviet decision making, reduce the ability of the Soviets to foment international conflict, and convince them that global hegemony was an unachievable goal.[31]

Conservatives also urged the West to withhold all trade credits, thereby forcing the Soviets to expend their scare supply of hard currency, and to forbid the flow of capital or capital goods into the Soviet bloc, in order to prevent the Soviets from easing production bottlenecks and enhancing the reliability of their economic system. For example, conservatives (led by the Young Americans for Freedom) mobilized to oppose the building of a Firestone synthetic rubber plant in Romania, arguing that the material would not only have direct utility for Warsaw Pact forces, but would also provide critically needed technical knowledge to the communist bloc.[32] While conservatives were largely successful during this period in preventing either the large-scale expansion of East-West trade or the extension of Western government credits to the Soviet Union and its satellites, by the end of the 1960s the popular desire for détente and the opposition to the Vietnam War made it progressively more difficult to sustain public support for such policies.

Finally, in addition to their calls for tighter restrictions on East-West trade and their opposition to Western trade credits, conservatives during this period increasingly saw the arms race itself as an important element of their Cold War economic strategy. Recognizing both the inherent economic weaknesses of the Soviet regime and the West's comparative advantage in economic productivity, they urged the West to accelerate—not relax—the arms race. While the primary reasons conservatives supported the arms race were (as discussed earlier) to discourage Soviet adventurism and enhance the West's ability to go on the strategic offensive, there was also an important economic component to their calls for a military buildup. Conservatives argued that a sustained arms race would allow the United States to "undermine [the Soviets'] ability to do world mischief, cut [their] flexibility, and prod the discontents of [their] subjects."[33] They also noted that America's technological strength and innovation provided the United States the ability to render obsolete large amounts of Soviet hardware and significantly drive up Soviet military costs, making it possible to "grind the Soviet revolutionary dynamism to a halt."[34] As in the case of trade and credit restrictions, however, by the end of the 1960s popular fatigue with East-West tension and the Vietnam War had undercut the conservative position on the arms race and opened the door to the arms control efforts that characterized détente.

Late Cold War Period

Given that expanded East-West economic ties were one of the cornerstones of détente, it should hardly be surprising that foreign policy strategists' view of détente closely corresponded to their views on improved economic relations between the United States and USSR. Throughout the 1970s (and well into the 1980s), liberal and conservative analysts struggled with one key question regarding East-West economic cooperation: what effect would Western aid, credit, and trade have on the behavior of the Soviet Union and its allies? Or, put another way, would Western efforts to exacerbate the Soviets' economic difficulties provide any meaningful benefit to Western security? The debate between liberals and conservative on this topic would be heated and prolonged, and serves as one of the most revealing examples of the two sides' fundamentally different strategic approaches.

Most liberals argued that expanding East-West trade, particularly by increasing trade credits and reducing U.S. restrictions on technology exports to the Soviet bloc, offered a number of important strategic advantages for the West. Organizations such as the Trilateral Commission argued that improved economic relations would lead to a reduction in international tension, a decline in the likelihood of East-West conflict, and a greater propensity within the Soviet leadership to seek other areas of cooperation with the West. These conclusions were based on the belief that "highly developed economic relations between countries can help reduce the incentives to develop and exploit tensions."[35] Believing that much of the Soviets' internal repression and hostility toward the West was rooted in its perception of capitalist hostility, liberals also argued that improved trade relations would demonstrate Western goodwill, thereby strengthening the "peace camp" within the Soviet leadership and increasing the pressure on Soviet rulers to seek "greater accommodation with the United States and its allies."[36] By bringing the Soviets into the global economic system, the foreign policy establishment believed that the Soviets would become increasingly dependent on Western economic support and would, therefore, "develop a stake in the smooth functioning of the international economic order of capitalism."[37]

In addition, liberals argued that relaxed rules on East-West trade would also improve the lives of Eastern Europeans. They insisted that, by expanding economic contacts directly with Eastern Europe, the United States and its allies would "encourage greater autonomy . . . loosen ties between Moscow and some of its Warsaw Pact allies, and . . . facilitate some broadening of contacts between Eastern and Western Europe."[38] Thus, for liberal strategists, the expansion of East-West trade would serve as a moderating influence on Soviet behavior, promote reform within the Soviet bloc, and make a lasting, negotiated settlement between the superpowers easier to achieve.

Conservatives, on the other hand, saw the expansion of East-West trade, and particularly the 1972 decision to permit the Export-Import Bank to extend U.S. government-backed credit to the Soviet Union, as a major strategic mistake that posed a serious threat to the United States and its allies. Building on the arguments conservatives had made throughout the Cold War, most conservatives argued that increased economic ties to the Soviet Union would not only strengthen the Soviets' ability to cause or exacerbate international tension, but also would reduce their incentive to consider internal reform. They argued that trade with the West had already provided significant assistance to the Soviets' expansionist efforts and insisted that expanding East-West trade would simply enable the Soviets to divert more money to military expenditures and improve their ability to challenge Western influence worldwide.[39] Throughout the latter days of the Cold War, conservatives argued that only massive internal and external failures, such as those caused by the collapse of the Soviet economy, could convince the Soviet leadership that reform was necessary.[40] Indeed, many conservatives saw no fundamental difference between "strategic goods" (such as computers and other high-technology items) and "nonstrategic goods" (such as raw materials and agricultural products), arguing that any trade with the Soviet Union would help it overcome bottlenecks in its production process and free up resources to assist in Soviet expansionism.[41] While recognizing that the political climate of the 1970s rendered such sweeping restrictions infeasible, these conservatives would continue to push for stricter limitations on East-West trade throughout the decade and well into the Reagan years.

In addition to concerns regarding the support East-West trade provided to the Soviets' military capabilities, conservatives argued that expanding trade relations and extending credit to the Soviet bloc had failed to have any meaningful impact on Soviet international behavior and had, in fact, created a new Western vulnerability to Soviet pressure. Casting aside mainstream theories about the power of trade to create converging national interests, conservatives pointed out that "neither relaxations of U.S. export controls nor promises of increased trade and credit appear to have had a noticeably moderating effect on Soviet policy in Africa, the Middle East, or Asia, or on the continuous Soviet military buildup."[42] In fact, the reduction of limitations on East-West trade coincided with a rapid expansion of Soviet activity, particularly in the Third World, as the Soviet leadership took advantage of America's defeat in Vietnam to back more vigorously pro-Soviet dictatorships around the world.

Conservatives further noted the huge increase in Eastern bloc governments' debt to Western companies throughout the 1970s (and the very real danger of these governments defaulting on their debts) and argued that these debts had led to precisely the "reverse leverage" that they had repeatedly cited as one of the dangers posed by East-West trade.[43] Rather than giving America a new source of leverage over the actions of the communist bloc, these credits had caused Western businesses, fearful of losing the millions of dollars they had invested in the Soviet Union and Eastern Europe, to pressure Western governments to be more flexible and responsive to Soviet economic and political demands. This expansion of trade had also opened up new opportunities for the Soviets to weaken Western unity by "[m]ultiplying and tightening the links connecting Western Europe to the Soviet Union and its dependencies" and thereby undermining the willingness of Western Europe to support an aggressive anti-Soviet policy.[44] Finally, they argued that, contrary to the claims of its supporters, expanded trade with Eastern Europe had undermined popular resistance to Soviet domination and weakened opposition to increased defense spending within the Warsaw Pact.[45]

Thus, for conservative opponents of détente, enhanced East-West trade posed a serious threat to the United States and represented a missed opportunity for the United States to use its considerable economic power to target a key Soviet vulnerability and undermine the Soviet system. Rather than continue to pursue these failed policies, conservatives urged the West to recognize the valuable weapon its economic strength could be and to use it to compel the Soviets to engage in serious reform.[46]

POLITICAL WARFARE

Given that the Cold War was, at its core, a struggle between two fundamentally different political theories, it was natural that political warfare played a central role in

Cold War strategic thought. Yet the phrase "political warfare" itself was seldom used by most mainstream strategists, who too often mistakenly focused almost exclusively on negotiations, while viewing public diplomacy and rhetoric as minor, supporting elements of national power. Conservatives disagreed with this limited view of the political dimension of the Cold War struggle and argued that diplomacy involved more than merely negotiations. As Strausz-Hupé pointed out, diplomacy also consists of a representation function and an intelligence function, both of which he argued were significantly more important to the United States than negotiations with the Soviet bloc.[47] In many ways, the liberal-conservative debate over Cold War diplomacy reflected fundamentally different views over which element of diplomacy was most important to the West.

Early Cold War Period

While the Soviets' brutal repression in Eastern Europe and their blatant violations of the Yalta Agreement provoked widespread concern across the political spectrum about their reliability as negotiating partners, the liberal-conservative divide on the role of political warfare emerged surprisingly early in the Cold War. By the end of the 1940s, less than five years after the end of World War II, liberal strategists were increasingly arguing for renewed efforts to reach a negotiated settlement with the Soviets and had largely rejected the notion of a sustained international political campaign against Soviet ideology and behavior. Insisting that the purpose of foreign policy is "to produce real changes in a real world," many Cold War liberals argued that, while the United States may disagree with the character or morality of the Soviet regime, speaking out publicly against Soviet behavior was counterproductive.[48] Although some, such as Kennan, supported the limited use of propaganda, they saw it primarily as a defensive weapon intended to convince the Soviet leadership that their efforts to destroy the West would not only fail, but would also weaken their own system.[49] For much of the Cold War liberal establishment, aggressive assertions of Western economic and political values could only increase superpower tension and weaken "moderates" within the Soviet leadership.

This general opposition to pro-Western propaganda would steadily increase over time and would become a central tenet of liberal views on the political dimension of the Cold War. Instead, liberals saw a key role for negotiations, both as a way of undermining Soviet propaganda and as a way of providing "hope to captive people that their freedom need not come about through a general war that they could probably not survive."[50] They believed that, by actively pursuing a negotiated settlement with Moscow, the United States could disprove Soviet claims that the capitalist West was seeking to launch a new war for global domination and thus expand American influence. But this preference for a negotiated settlement with the Soviets also demonstrated a key difference between liberal and conservative views of the Cold War. In the view of many liberals, victory in the Cold War was impossible, thus the overriding U.S. goal could only be to manage, control, or limit superpower rivalry. Conservatives, on the other hand, believed that victory over the Soviets was not only possible, but necessary to the survival of the West.

As a result, conservatives viewed political warfare as a critical component of the West's Cold War strategy and paid particular attention to the use of public diplomacy and propaganda to represent America's position to the rest of the world. Noting the importance the Soviets placed on propaganda and the ideological battlefield, conservatives urged the West to engage in a serious, sustained, and wide-ranging effort to not only counter Soviet misinformation, but also to take the ideological offensive by attacking communist ideology and using the ideals of the West as strategic assets. In particular, conservatives highlighted the need to provide accurate, honest information that focused on the inherent flaws and political repression of the communist system and the merits of democratic capitalism.[51] To be effective, this information needed to be widely disseminated, both within the Soviet bloc (to the extent possible) and to the "undecided" nations throughout the world, and needed to come from both Western governments and private organizations. In keeping with the tendency of conservatives during this period to focus on the situation in Europe, they highlighted the potential role NATO could play in orchestrating a broad political warfare campaign and urged the West to use such a campaign to break the Soviets' hold over Eastern Europe, particularly East Germany.[52] By engaging in vigorous public diplomacy, conservatives argued that the West could not only prevent further Soviet gains in the Third World, but could greatly weaken the cohesion of the Soviet bloc and, ultimately, undermine the stability of the Soviet state.[53]

While strongly supportive of public diplomacy and other "representational" efforts, conservatives were deeply skeptical of conferences, treaties, or open-ended negotiations with the Soviet Union. As noted in chapter 4, while conservatives were not opposed, in principle, to negotiations with the Soviet Union, they insisted that the West enter any such negotiations from a position of superiority. Arguing that international conferences and treaties could only lead to a lasting agreement when each side shares "a common frame of interest,"[54] conservatives were highly doubtful that the two sides shared any significant interests. They further argued that the Soviets' ideological opposition to any permanent peace with the capitalist world (as well as their long history of treaty violations) made a lasting settlement with the Soviet Union impossible. As a result, they saw little reason to expend significant political energy on disarmament talks or similar efforts. Such negotiations could only increase domestic political pressure to reach an agreement while misleading Western publics into thinking that the Soviets were more moderate and open to genuine compromise than they really were. This skepticism toward superpower negotiations and strong preference for public diplomacy would characterize conservative diplomatic strategy throughout the Cold War.

Middle Cold War Period

For a number of reasons, by the beginning of the 1960s Western liberals had increasingly viewed the management of superpower conflict via arms control as the primary purpose of diplomacy. The apparent stability of the Soviet bloc convinced many liberals that the Soviet Union was likely to remain a fixture on the international scene. As a result, bitter denunciations and "Cold War polemics" were neither useful nor appropriate.[55] In addition, the rapid decolonization of the Third World and the spread of "national liberation movements" in former Western colonies convinced many liberals that Western values, such as individual rights, free markets, and democratic pluralism, were alien to and unwelcome in much of the world, thus making Western propaganda efforts pointless.[56]

This generally hostile view of pro-Western and anti-Soviet public diplomacy, while certainly present during the early 1950s, strengthened throughout the 1960s in response to the wider public support for détente. While President Kennedy generally supported a more aggressive use of Voice of America (VOA) and Radio Free Europe (RFE), there was nevertheless a gradual movement toward toning down broadcast attacks on Soviet behavior, lest they exacerbate superpower tension. This movement became even more pronounced following the Soviet quashing of the 1968 Prague Spring movement, with VOA and (to a lesser degree) RFE becoming more journalistic and pro-détente.[57] Finally, the growing concern about the arms race, and popular fears that it could lead to a full-scale nuclear war, convinced many Cold War liberals that some form of arms control was necessary to ensure the physical survival of the West. The belief that the United States and USSR had developed a mutual interest in arms control led many liberal and mainstream strategists to view negotiations, particularly arms control, as the key first step toward cultivating a broader political settlement to the superpower rivalry.[58]

Building on the arguments of their predecessors, conservatives of the 1960s vehemently rejected this focus on arms control negotiations and instead argued that the political battle between East and West was *the* key struggle of the Cold War. As a result, conservatives considered efforts to manage or control superpower rivalry (such as arms control) dangerous, as they granted the USSR a moral equivalency it did not deserve and weakened the will of the Western public to oppose Soviet policies. In their (ultimately unsuccessful) effort to defeat the Limited Test Ban Treaty, conservatives argued that the agreement was a strategic distraction, drawing the West away from a policy of confronting and resisting Soviet aggression.[59] At the same time, however, it must be stressed that most conservatives did not reject outright all arms control negotiations. Provided the final agreement was both verifiable and in the interests of the West, conservatives generally viewed arms control as a useful, albeit minor, tool.[60] Yet, the focus of conservative strategists was primarily on winning the key, political struggle of the Cold War. Conservatives argued that forceful public and private representational diplomacy, by attacking the ideological and moral legitimacy of communism and exposing the true nature of Soviet rule, was critical to a Western victory in the Cold War.

During this period of the Cold War, conservatives recognized that representational diplomacy needed to achieve two different, but mutually supporting, tasks: winning over allies and undecided countries, and undermining the ideological legitimacy of the Soviet system. Much as in the earlier period, conservatives argued that telling the truth about U.S. and Soviet global intentions and highlighting the moral stakes in the superpower conflict were the most effective means of improving allied cohesion and enhancing America's standing in the Third World.[61] Central to such efforts were such organizations as RFE/RL, VOA, and USIA. Conservatives repeatedly urged the U.S. government to make better strategic use of these assets by making them forceful proponents of American values, ideals, and beliefs.[62] Recognizing that the Soviets had moved aggressively to expand the influence of their ideology, conservatives urged the West to engage fully in the ongoing "war of ideas." Such a war, they insisted, could be won if the United States improved its efforts to "prove and sell [its] set of ideas" while demonstrating the hypocrisy of the Soviet system.[63] In addition, conservatives argued that since the struggle for the minds of man was central to the outcome of the Cold War, the export of U.S. ideology was critical to victory over the Soviets.[64] This belief in the power of American ideology would become a central tenet of the neoconservative movement.

While enhancing America's global influence and strengthening the unity of the West were important for conservatives, so too was the task of weakening the ideological underpinnings of the Soviet bloc. Since communism formed the sole justification for the governments of Eastern Europe and the Soviet Union, they believed the central purpose of America's political war against the Soviets was to discredit Soviet ideology while reassuring the world that it intended to fight and win the Cold War. Conservatives saw a major role for public diplomacy in this effort and called for a full-scale political offensive against communist ideology aimed at demoralizing the Soviet elite and reassuring the domestic opposition within the Soviet empire that the West supported their cause. Specifically, conservatives urged the United States to highlight the reality of Soviet colonialism and to make more effective use of Soviet émigrés and dissidents to show the world the brutality of Soviet rule.[65] They also urged the West to highlight through official speeches and radio broadcasts the political and economic differences between the "Open Society" of the West and the "Closed Society" of the Soviet bloc as a means of weakening Soviet control of its restive populations, especially in Eastern Europe.[66] Conservatives believed that publicizing the West's material and moral superiority could only weaken the morale of the ruling elite in the East and increase popular pressure for the relaxation of totalitarian control. Thus, conservatives argued that honest portrayals of life in the West could only highlight the political and economic failures of the Soviet system and increase pressure on the Soviet leadership to undertake significant reform.

Late Cold War Period

By the early 1970s, support for a negotiated resolution, based on arms control, to the East-West conflict had definitively entered the political mainstream. Political liberals hailed the arrival of détente as a fundamental change in America's view of the Soviet Union, shifting from a relationship rooted in mistrust and conflict to one of mutual respect and cooperation. While understanding that some form of peaceful competition with the Soviet Union was inevitable, most Western liberals also argued that the low-level political warfare that had been a staple of the superpower conflict since the end of World War II was no longer useful or appropriate. In the view of the vast majority of the foreign policy establishment, harsh rhetoric, public denunciations, and other openly political efforts to criticize Soviet actions were counterproductive. Such efforts, they insisted, harmed U.S.-Soviet relations, strengthened anti-Western hard-liners in the Soviet leadership, and ultimately did nothing to improve the situation in Eastern Europe.

This view had, by the early 1970s, steadily eroded the tough, anticommunist message of America's two principal tools of political warfare, VOA and RFE/RL. By 1973 the VOA had become so sensitive to Soviet opinion that it refused to read from Aleksandr Solzhenitsyn's masterpiece, *The Gulag Archipelago*, lest VOA be seen as using the plight of dissidents as a political weapon.[67] So widespread was this opposition to any U.S.-backed broadcast that could be viewed as hostile to the Soviets that such leading liberal figures as Sen. William Fulbright repeatedly tried (and very nearly succeeded) to cut off all funding for RFE and RL. This tendency reached its high point in 1978, when the chairman of the Board for International Broadcasting (which had oversight responsibilities for RFE and RL) proposed providing Soviet and Eastern European officials time on the radio stations to respond to claims they felt were inaccurate.[68] While congressional opposition blocked that specific proposal, the event highlighted the extent to which America's public diplomacy tools had changed from their original role as staunchly anticommunist political weapons into purveyors of inoffensive, sanitized, and largely apolitical cultural journalism.

Western liberals, having successfully marginalized political warfare as fundamentally incompatible with the détente policy of negotiation and compromise, instead urged the United States to downplay the political differences between the two sides and focus its diplomatic energies on controlling the arms race.[69] For many, America's experience in Vietnam convinced them that the dynamics of the arms race, when combined with militant anticommunism, was the greatest threat to world peace and American security. In fact, so convinced were Western liberals of the need to stop the arms race that they argued the actual content of an arms control agreement was largely irrelevant, as was its impact on Soviet behavior or society.[70] What mattered was that these agreements existed and made possible additional negotiations and compromise that could ultimately lead to a broader improvement in East-West relations. Ideally, this network of treaties and compromises would not only halt the arms race, but discredit the hard-line anticommunist ideology that liberals felt also threatened Western security. Thus, for much of the foreign policy mainstream, political warfare was a largely useless tool that could only harm American interests. In their mind, only negotiated agreements could advance America's goals.

Conservatives, on the other hand, continued to make a fundamental distinction between the representation and negotiation functions of diplomacy. While they continued to focus on the representation function throughout the 1970s, it is important to note that some conservatives *did* see a limited role for negotiations, particularly in the area of arms control. Even the Committee on the Present Danger, which was often portrayed as being unalterably opposed to all arms control agreements, explicitly supported genuine, mutually advantageous treaties.[71] Unlike their more liberal counterparts, however, conservatives never saw these negotiations as critical to Western security. As one pointed out, "arms control talks are desirable, but we have lived without them. Their absence could not endanger peace."[72]

In addition, conservatives were much more inclined than their liberal counterparts to set conditions on the types of agreements they would be willing to support. Particularly worrisome for many conservatives was the Soviets' long history of violating treaties and international agreements, a practice deeply rooted in Soviet ideology. Rather than see these agreements as tools for achieving mutual interests, the Soviets saw them as a way to buy themselves "time to strengthen their empire economically and militarily" and as a tool for "psycho-political" warfare against the West.[73] For the Soviet Union, arms control treaties between it and the United States offered the opportunity to weaken Western unity by raising doubts in the minds of America's allies (particularly in Western Europe) about its willingness to defend them. As a result, most conservatives believed that meaningful arms control would not be possible until there was "a basic and fundamental change in the Soviet approach to East-West problems,"[74] specifically a willingness on the part of the Soviets to break from this ideological view of international agreements. Given the Soviets' penchant for ignoring inconvenient elements of its international obligations, many conservatives believed that stringent, intrusive verification was critical to successful arms control agreements.[75] Finally, conservatives rejected the liberal argument that the content of an agreement was largely irrelevant, instead arguing that the agreements were valuable only to the extent that they advanced Western interests and reduced the risk of war.[76] Thus, conservatives of this period argued that the United States should only pursue those treaties that were both in its national interest *and* could be readily verified.

Much more important, in the conservative view, were the representational elements of diplomacy and the use of political warfare as a tool of national power. Much like their predecessors, the conservative strategists of the 1970s saw the outcome of the political war as central to a Western victory in the Cold War and believed that public and private political pressure was critical to advancing America's interests. During the 1970s, conservatives continued to focus on using America's diplomatic and informational arms to attack the USSR, its goals, and its international behavior. At the root of these attacks was the recognition that Soviet actions and beliefs were based on lies and that, as a result, the West could politically defeat the Soviets with a massive, sustained, and worldwide effort to tell the truth about its communist adversaries.[77] In particular, conservatives recommended the West pursue three major "lines of attack" in its political struggle with the Soviet Union. In each case, they argued, these attacks would expose Soviet dishonesty, undermine Soviet cohesion, complicate the Soviets' relationship with its client states (particularly in Eastern Europe), and reduce its attractiveness and influence within the Third World.

First, conservatives called for the United States to highlight the Soviets' unreliability by publicizing the large number of Soviet treaty violations, starting with the 1918 Treaty of Brest-Litovsk, continuing through Potsdam and Yalta, and culminating in the ABM Treaty and the Biological and Toxin Weapons Convention.[78] Conservatives hoped that these violations would not only temper Western enthusiasm for additional arms control treaties with the Soviets but, more importantly, also reduce Soviet international influence by raising serious doubts in the minds of foreign leaders regarding the value of Soviet promises.

Second, conservatives (particularly neoconservatives) saw tremendous value in calling attention to and vigorously defending traditional Western values of free enterprise, democracy, and human rights.[79] Conservatives believed that for too long the West in general (and especially the United States) had refused to defend itself against Soviet denunciations of alleged Western immorality, a decision that had cost the United States dearly in international prestige and influence. Citing Daniel Patrick Moynihan's tenure as U.S. ambassador to the UN as a model, conservatives urged the United States to defend itself strenuously and return the rhetorical fire launched by the USSR and its allies.[80]

Finally, recognizing that much of the Soviet leadership's legitimacy was based on communist ideology, conservatives urged a full-scale ideological assault on the fundamental failures of Marxism in general and the Soviet system in particular.[81] Critical to this effort was highlighting to the world that the Soviet system offered neither economic stability nor political freedom and that the countries of the democratic West were the only real supporters of progress in the Third World.

By incorporating these three major themes in the West's diplomatic and informational efforts, conservatives argued the United States could reverse Soviet political gains and exert significant pressure against one of the Soviets' greatest weaknesses: its political system.

COVERT ACTION

When compared to the other tools of statecraft previously discussed, the emphasis Cold War strategists placed on the use of covert action was surprisingly limited. In addition, at least until the 1970s, there was generally greater consensus among liberal and conservative thinkers about the need for and value of covert operations. As a result, the type of heated discussion and debate that surrounded other contentious issues (such as East-West economic relations) did not emerge on the topic of covert action until the latter days of the Cold War. In short, until the 1970s, covert action was not a particularly controversial issue, nor was the gulf between liberal and conservative views on its use particularly large.

The only major disagreement between the two sides involved the use of covert action on the other side of the Iron Curtain. In the opinion of most liberals, such efforts were unlikely to succeed and could only damage U.S.-Soviet relations. Meanwhile, conservatives argued that such efforts would reassure the captive nations of U.S. support, force the Soviets onto the strategic defensive, and, if properly planned, could succeed in weakening communist rule in Eastern Europe or within the Soviet Union itself.

Early Cold War Period

To some degree, it is understandable that there are very few public discussions or policy writings on the role of covert action in Western strategy from the early days of the Cold War. Given the widespread recognition at that time of the need for secrecy during times of conflict, neither the American press nor most strategic thinkers were particularly inclined to discuss or advocate covert action openly. Nevertheless, recent studies have cast light on how the foreign policy mainstream within the Truman and Eisenhower administrations thought about and used covert action.[82]

In general, there was widespread agreement on the careful, judicious use of covert operations in support of anticommunist governments and groups in the Third World, as evidenced by a number of successful covert actions. In addition to backing pro-Western figures in Iran and Guatemala during the early 1950s, the CIA provided critical support to the Congress for Cultural Freedom, which would serve as a forum for mobilizing intellectuals in opposition to communist ideology.[83] These and other examples of successful covert action demonstrate an understanding on the part of the foreign policy mainstream that these operations were a usable and viable option for policymakers.

At the same time, however, important disagreements between liberals and conservatives gradually emerged regarding the value of covert operations within Eastern Europe and the Soviet Union. The failure of a few of these efforts in the early 1950s convinced a number of liberal strategists that covert action in the Eastern bloc was largely hopeless. In fact, by 1953 Kennan, who had previously supported these efforts, changed his mind and opposed any further effort to conduct operations within Eastern Europe or the Soviet Union.[84] On this point, Burnham (who was serving as a consultant to the CIA on political warfare) and other conservatives vehemently disagreed. Arguing that the communist regimes of Eastern Europe remained extremely unpopular and fragile, conservatives stressed that the United States had both a moral obligation and a strategic interest in providing political and material support to any popular uprisings against the communist governments in the region.[85] While recognizing the inevitable human costs of such uprisings, they argued that these costs were significantly lower than the alternative of allowing the Soviets uncontested domination over Eastern Europe.

Similarly, conservatives argued that "untraditional methods" such as guerrilla warfare and subversion were also capable of undermining the Soviet state and ultimately destroying Soviet power.[86] Reminding the West that communist rule was no more popular to the captive nations within the USSR than it was in Eastern Europe, conservatives urged the United States to take advantage of this widespread unrest. In their view, given that the Soviets had been engaging in efforts to infiltrate and subvert the democracies of the West, the West needed to side with the peoples of the Soviet Union and "organize fifth columns of one kind or another in every country behind the iron curtain, including the Soviet Union."[87] In addition to supporting military aid to governments under siege from Soviet-backed insurgents, Burnham went a step further by also calling for Western aid to anticommunist insurgents fighting Soviet-backed regimes worldwide.[88] Years later, such a policy would, of course, become known as the Reagan Doctrine.

Middle Cold War Period

This distinction between liberal and conservative views of covert action would largely continue through the 1960s. With the Cold War now fully established and popular resistance to discussing covert action fading, both liberals and conservatives became more open and vocal about the potential uses of covert action. And while the general support for these measures continued to be shared across the political spectrum, American liberals were growing increasingly uneasy with the

use of covert action in the Third World. In the wake of the growing decolonization movement, many liberals became more skeptical of the wisdom of supporting pro-Western authoritarian regimes, more open to U.S. support for "national
liberation movements," and more resistant to a foreign policy based on anticommunist ideology. Believing that many Western values, such as capitalism and
democracy, were largely alien to non-Western cultures, liberals began to urge the
West to side with anticolonial revolutions and make clear that the United States
was also a revolutionary power, using all its abilities to advance a "great, unfinished
experiment" in human freedom.[89] As the decade proceeded, liberal strategists
increasingly worried that many of the covert actions undertaken in the Third
World were strategically unsound, unlikely to succeed, and would ultimately result
in reduced U.S. influence around the world. While these strategists were, in general, not particularly effective in changing the thinking of the foreign policy elite
during the 1960s, they would become increasingly important during the 1970s as
their view of covert action would rapidly enter the political mainstream in the
aftermath of Vietnam.

Unsurprisingly, conservatives during this period remained strongly supportive
of covert action and continued to urge greater use of this tool to confront Soviet
expansionism and undermine the bases of the Soviet system. Rejecting the claims
of some that the United States needed to take a more "evenhanded" approach to
communist insurgents in the Third World, conservatives urged the West to provide military aid to support any regime threatened by communist-backed gueril-
las.[90] While such operations had been conducted repeatedly in the past (witness
Truman's assistance to Greece in the early days of the Cold War), they had grown
increasingly controversial in light of the push to decolonize the Third World. With
regard to operations behind the Iron Curtain, conservatives continued to argue
that the regimes in Eastern Europe were deeply unpopular, an assessment strengthened by the 1956 uprising in Hungary.

As a result, while recognizing that the United States could not create revolutionary movements in either Eastern Europe or the Soviet Union, conservatives
believed that it could and should provide moral and material support to these
movements once established.[91] They argued, however, that such support should
not come solely from the U.S. government. Instead, they called for a truly national
effort, involving trade unions, private foundations, educational institutions, and
civic groups, to support democratic forces within the Soviet bloc.[92] This approach,
while ignored at the time, would eventually be implemented by the Reagan

administration, which worked closely with a number of such organizations, such as the American Federation of Labor and Congress of Industrial Organizations (AFL-CIO), to assist the Solidarity movement.

Finally, drawing on the successful covert actions of the previous decade, conservatives urged the West to reverse Soviet expansionism by providing more support to anticommunist movements in Soviet client states, such as Cuba.[93] Such operations, while controversial and risky, offered tremendous payoffs if successful, as they would disprove the Soviets' prediction that a communist world was inevitable, significantly damage Soviet international prestige, and send a powerful signal to America's allies that the United States would remain active in the Third World. Most importantly, however, conservatives argued that these types of operations would force the Soviet Union onto the strategic defensive, compelling it to waste scarce resources propping up these regimes, and enable the West to "reverse the psychological equation" to favor the United States.[94]

Late Cold War Period

While liberal and conservative views on covert action had begun to drift apart by the mid-1960s, the disillusionment and bitter political division resulting from the Vietnam War widened this gap. Accusations that the CIA and other Western intelligence agencies had engaged in unauthorized secret wars, rogue assassination plots, illegal domestic espionage, and other questionable activities led many liberal strategists to question the morality of covert action. At the same time, they argued that rising anti-American sentiment in the Third World was the direct result of American overt and (particularly) covert support for pro-Western regimes, such as Augusto Pinochet's Chile and the shah's Iran.

Believing such actions were increasingly proving counterproductive, a number of important liberal thinkers, such as Anthony Lake and Marshall Shulman, argued that such covert actions in support of an anticommunist foreign policy were both immoral and unnecessary.[95] In addition to such operations being inherently undemocratic, opponents insisted that, with the rise of détente, they were rapidly becoming a strategic liability, as they could only disrupt East-West accord and revive the Cold War. As a result, many called for the United States to accept, as one of its guiding principles, the "non-interference by force in processes of internal change."[96] By renouncing the use of covert action and similar means, they argued that the United States could avoid finding itself on the "wrong side of history" and improve its relations with the Eastern bloc and the Third World.

For conservative thinkers, on the other hand, the rise of Soviet power and influence (particularly in the Third World) and the growing political constraints on the use of U.S. military power made covert action even more important than in the past. Seeing these actions as critical to winning the West's political struggle with Moscow, conservatives urged the United States to make greater use of covert operations. While acknowledging that some previous operations were ill-advised and better oversight of such activities was needed, they argued that covert operations remained an important tool of foreign policy and that the United States needed to take a more balanced view of its use.[97] Given the fragility of communist rule, both in Eastern Europe and the Third World, conservatives argued that covert campaigns to undermine these regimes would not only force the Soviets to defend their territorial gains, but could actually reverse communist expansion.

Conservatives also saw an opportunity to use these activities to strengthen the Western alliance. Some went so far as to urge the development of a NATO-run "Department of Unconventional War," which would coordinate allied policy and direct allied actions against Soviet-backed subversion worldwide.[98] Mindful of the conventional military weakness of most NATO allies, conservatives believed that supporting these covert operations against the Soviets was a way for Western Europe to make a meaningful contribution to Western security while providing the United States with the political support it required to remain actively engaged in the Third World.

Throughout the 1970s, despite the post-Vietnam opposition within Western society to such actions, conservatives continued to call for vigorous support to America's allies in the developing world, such as a significant expansion of covert assistance to pro-Western forces in Africa and Southeast Asia.[99] Indeed, by the end of the decade, support for the robust use of covert action had become a political position occupied almost exclusively by conservatives.

CONCLUSION

As mentioned at the beginning of this chapter, the fact that these tools were used by the Reagan administration to implement its grand strategy is hardly surprising or remarkable. Every president has, with varying degrees of success, sought to make use of these fundamental elements of U.S. power to pursue America's national interests, however defined. What is noteworthy, however, is the fact that, as in the case of its core beliefs and overarching goals, the Reagan administration's use of the tools of statecraft closely mirrors the thinking of conservative Cold War grand strategists. The administration's emphasis on achieving Western military supe-riority, its use of economic warfare, its approach to the international political strug-gle against the Soviets, and its support for covert action reflects over thirty years of conservative thought aimed at delivering a Western victory in the Cold War.

6

The Role of Reagan
and His Advisors

The preceding chapters have defined grand strategy, outlined the Reagan administration's "strategy of victory," and discussed the intellectual roots of the administration's strategic beliefs, goals, and tools. Yet there remains a final question to be answered regarding this strategy: How was it created and implemented? How could so many ideas that had been rejected by the foreign policy elite find their way into national policy? What can explain the fundamental shift in American grand strategy during the 1980s?

In order to answer these questions, Reagan's management style must be analyzed, since the development and implementation of the strategy was itself a direct outgrowth of Reagan's approach to decision making and his preferred method of organization. This chapter will briefly outline Reagan's management style, explain how this style affected the development and implementation of the administration's strategy, highlight the central role that Reagan himself played in the process of strategy development, and delineate the roles of Reagan's advisors in implementing this strategy.

REAGAN'S MANAGEMENT STYLE
AND ITS IMPACT ON
ADMINISTRATION STRATEGY

Handling the almost-overwhelming job of president of the United States is, to say the least, a daunting task. Unlike any other job, presidents daily make decisions on a whole host of issues far beyond the scope of any one individual's expertise. Indeed, the scope of issues relating to foreign relations alone is too broad for any single person to master completely. When combined with the even broader array of domestic issues requiring the president's attention and his need to address the electoral and political realities of his time (such as seeking reelection or strength-ening his political party), the need for a system to manage the multitude of deci-sions the president must make becomes obvious. In light of the vast number of systems that various presidents have used to guide their decision making through-out American history, it seems self-evident that each system will, invariably, reflect the particular president's preferred approach.[1]

While analyzing all major elements of presidential decision making is far beyond the scope of this work, assessing a president's management style regarding the three core elements of grand strategy (beliefs, goals, and tools) is of particular importance in identifying the sources of the administration's grand strategy. Thus, first it is crit-ical to identify how the central beliefs of an administration are developed. Does the president have an understandable set of beliefs about the nature of the international system and his adversary? Are these beliefs shared by the rest of his administration?[2] Second, it is necessary to identify how an administration's foreign policy goals are set. Does the president enter office with a clear vision of where he wants to lead the country? Does the president seek to create something new, or is he content with addressing foreign policy issues on an *ad hoc* basis? Third, it is important to under-stand how such decisions are implemented. Does the president have a set idea about how to achieve national goals, or does he seek recommendations from a broad array of advisors? Does he frequently "reach into" the bureaucracy to guide the imple-mentation? By analyzing these aspects of Reagan's management style, certain con-clusions can be made about the respective roles of Reagan and his advisors in the development and implementation of the administration's grand strategy.

In Reagan's case, the fact that he entered office with a very clear idea of what he believed and where he wanted to lead the United States has been established with thunderous unanimity. Every one of Reagan's key advisors has repeatedly made clear that it was Reagan himself who dictated, from the outset, his admin-istration's underlying beliefs and core goals.[3] He was, contrary to the claims of his critics, quite knowledgeable, well-read, and interested in foreign policy matters. He was also very familiar with the thoughts and writings of many of the key strate-gists discussed in this book. For example, in 1983, as he bestowed the Presidential Medal of Freedom on Burnham, Reagan remarked, "I owe him a personal debt, because throughout the years traveling the mash-potato circuit I have quoted [him] widely."[4] Indeed, as a longtime reader of *National Review*, Reagan was unquestionably familiar with Burnham's writings. Likewise, Reagan had certainly read at least some of Strausz-Hupé's writings, having quoted his work in a speech in 1969, met with him (and other Soviet scholars) during his 1980 presidential campaign, and appointed him ambassador to Turkey in 1981.[5] Similarly, Reagan noted in his diary that he had frequently read and corresponded with Brian Crozier, finally meeting him face-to-face in 1985.[6]

Indeed, for a man who was supposedly so ignorant of foreign affairs, it is startling how much of his political career can be linked to his foreign policy views.[7] The very real problem of communist infiltration of Hollywood largely defined his first real "political" position, the presidency of the Screen Actors Guild, and gave him an appreciation of the Soviets' relentless ambition. His involvement with the Crusade for Freedom, an organization started in 1950 that called for the rollback of the Soviet empire, demonstrated his early commitment to defeating Soviet power.[8] His strong support for Barry Goldwater during the 1964 presidential contest was based, in part, on his support for Goldwater's beliefs and determination to reverse Soviet expansion. Reagan's effort to challenge Gerald Ford for the presidential nomination in 1976 was largely based on his rejection of the Ford foreign policy, while many of his radio commentaries from the late 1970s detailed the beliefs and goals his administration would subsequently pursue. His senior advisors during his victorious 1980 campaign also understood, and made clear to his administration's national security team, that the beliefs and goals Reagan had espoused his entire adult life were the ones his administration would follow.[9] In short, while most of his advisors shared his beliefs and goals, it was Reagan himself who was the ultimate source of these components of his administration's grand strategy.

While Reagan was, undoubtedly, the principal source of his administration's beliefs and goals, his involvement in the development and use of its tools is less definitive. As both supporters and critics have widely reported, Reagan's management style focused on conveying "the big picture," while seeking broad input from his senior advisors on how best to implement his vision.[10] It was at this level that the infamous battles among the State Department, Defense Department, the NSC, and the CIA were waged. As several participants have acknowledged, the internal struggles over foreign policy within the Reagan administration were not over what it believed or which goals to pursue, but rather how best to achieve these goals.[11] Thus, for example, while Reagan made clear to his subordinates that he wanted to attack the Soviets' economic weaknesses by cutting off the trade of strategic technologies to Moscow, he left the details of identifying such technologies to experts at the NSC and in the Departments of Defense, State, and Commerce. While critics derided this approach as causing Reagan to be overly reliant on his subordinates, it actually provided Reagan the flexibility necessary to change tactics in pursuit of his goals. This ability to adapt to changing circumstances was particularly important, as it prevented Reagan from being overly committed to a specific path to victory. As one advisor stated, because of the difficulty in accurately predicting how effective a specific tool would be, Reagan "could never be certain any one element would work, but gladly utilized them all, flooding the end zone with excellent receivers."[12] For this reason, excessive presidential focus on any single tool was strategically unwise and, in fact, counterproductive, as it could only draw Reagan's attention away from "the big picture."

At the same time, there are at least two key tools over which Reagan clearly asserted ownership and for which he felt personally responsible. The first, and most well-known, was SDI. Reagan, a man who was never comfortable claiming personal credit for the successes of his administration, was uncharacteristically assertive in highlighting his own personal commitment to the idea of strategic defense.[13] Reagan's refusal to use SDI as a "bargaining chip" at the Reykjavik Summit, despite tremendous pressure from the State Department, some of his own advisors, and Gorbachev himself, can only be explained by Reagan's deep, personal belief in the need to move away from the immorality and strategic folly of MAD.

Similarly, Reagan took great personal interest in his administration's political warfare efforts as well, specifically the important impact of his own speeches. Understanding how powerful the tool of rhetoric could be, Reagan cared deeply about the words attributed to him and thus spent a great deal of time revising and rewriting his speeches to ensure they accurately represented his thinking.[14] What his critics saw as merely the rhetorical flourishes of a former actor were actually, in Reagan's view, one component of the plan he had for winning the Cold War.

As noted, Reagan's management style was specifically designed to ensure that his beliefs and goals controlled the development of his administration's strategy, while encouraging debate and discussion over its implementation. The primary source of his administration's strategy having been identified as Reagan himself, the next section will demonstrate how the strategy's beliefs, goals, and tools can be found in Reagan's own thoughts and writings.

BELIEFS
Rejection of Containment and Détente
For Reagan, both containment and détente were deeply flawed approaches to U.S.-Soviet relations that offered little hope for meaningful advancement of

America's national security interests. While his public comments on the underlying theory of containment are quite limited, it is clear that Reagan believed containment, while the "default" approach that many administrations had pursued, was entirely too defensive and passive to serve as a unifying concept of American foreign policy.

Nor did he believe, based on his own knowledge of Soviet weaknesses, that containment was even necessary any longer. As he noted in his famous 1981 speech at the University of Notre Dame, "the West won't contain communism, it will transcend communism. It won't bother to denounce it, it will dismiss it as some bizarre chapter of human history whose last pages are even now being written."[15] In Reagan's view, containment offered only guidelines on how to *react* to Soviet expansion but provided no strategic direction or final outcome capable of guiding America's actions. He grasped, long before becoming president, that the United States needed to pursue a positive goal, and he understood that, given the Soviets' absolute aims, the only acceptable outcome was an American victory and a Soviet defeat. As he told his future national security advisor Richard Allen in January 1977, his idea of U.S. policy toward the Soviet Union was simple: "We win and they lose."[16]

While his criticisms of containment were relatively subtle, his opposition to détente was well known long before his election. In fact, while his comment at his first presidential press conference that he believed détente had been little more than a "one-way street" favoring the Soviets drew a great deal of public and media attention, he had been making similar statements for years. Throughout the 1970s, he argued that the Soviets were taking advantage of the West's internal division, lack of resolve, and dedication to détente to accelerate its expansionist efforts.[17] Indeed, his decision to challenge Ford for the 1976 Republican presidential nomination was primarily a reaction to Ford's continued support for Nixon's détente policies. While recognizing and supporting the widespread desire to stabilize superpower relations and reduce the risk of war, he argued that détente was proving to be counterproductive. Rather than encouraging Soviet moderation, it was only emboldening the Soviets to take even more aggressive actions, particularly in the Third World. Echoing the criticisms earlier conservatives (particularly Goldwater) had launched against "peaceful coexistence," he argued that the Soviets viewed détente not as a way of reducing tensions with the United States, but rather as a more effective strategy for pursuing their long-term goal of expansion and global domination while sapping America's will to resist.[18]

Major Role of Communist Ideology in
Soviet Foreign Policy

In Reagan's view, the defining characteristic of the Soviet Union was its relentless dedication to communist ideology. From his earliest days in politics, Reagan recognized that much of the power and prestige accorded the Soviet Union (particularly in the Third World) was rooted in its claim of the historical inevitability of communism. As a result, he set out to demonstrate both the barbarity of communist rule and the intellectual bankruptcy of communist ideology. As he repeatedly pointed out to his friends and colleagues over the years, Reagan received his first real lesson in communist tactics during his period as president of the Screen Actors Guild, when he successfully thwarted several efforts by communists to take over the motion picture industry.[19] Highlighting the threat communism posed to self-determination around the world, he noted in a 1957 letter to the then vice president Richard Nixon that, of all the political and economic systems throughout the world, "only 'Communism' is dedicated to imposing its 'way and belief' on all the world."[20] Sharing the view of many conservatives, he argued that communist ideology posed a fundamental threat to basic human values: "Communists are not bound by our morality. They say any crime . . . is moral if it advances the cause of socialism."[21] Echoing Whittaker Chambers's view that Soviet communism represented an absolutist "rival faith" to the West, Reagan noted that every Soviet leader since Lenin had dedicated himself to the goal of imposing communism on the world.[22]

Nor did his view of communism's role in Soviet behavior change during his time in office. While much has been made of Reagan's relationship with Gorbachev, with many pundits claiming that his views on communism softened as a result of the Soviet leader's reform efforts, there is remarkably little evidence to support such a claim. Rather, Reagan's own words indicate that, to the contrary, he continued to condemn the immorality of communism and recognize its central role in Soviet foreign policy. In 1986 he noted that the Soviet Union "is bent on an expansionist policy in an effort to make the whole world into a single Communist state."[23] Even after the signing of the Intermediate-Range Nuclear Forces Treaty (which many saw as "proof" that the Soviets had changed), Reagan continued to reassure his supporters that "I'm still the Ronald Reagan I was and the evil empire is still just that."[24] These comments demonstrate that Reagan's view of the nature of the Soviet regime never changed significantly. While he recognized the opportunities for progress on East-West relations that emerged from

Gorbachev's reform efforts, he clearly never lost sight of the ideological struggle that, in his view (and the view of many other conservatives), was at the heart of the Cold War.

Centrality of Superior Power in Dealing with the Soviet Threat

Reagan also understood, based on both his reading of human history and his understanding of communist ideology, that national power was critical to any effort to halt or reverse expansionist powers. Drawing from the failures of Britain, France, and the United States prior to World War II, he recognized the need to confront aggression with overwhelming power. As one of his closest advisors noted, Reagan emphasized, from the outset of his administration, the importance of having "sufficient power that you're not forced to accept someone else's view of the world," but rather having "sufficient power to impose your view" on an adversary.[25] Recognizing that much of communist theory was rooted in the use of power, he believed that it was absolutely essential that the United States only deal with the Soviet Union from a position of strength.[26]

This position of superior power would, in Reagan's view, provide two important benefits to the West. First, and most importantly, superiority would make the Soviet goal of a communist world impossible to achieve. And while military power played a major role in this effort, Reagan recognized that other, nonmaterial factors were also critical to achieving true superiority. As he noted in the late 1970s, "only by mustering a superiority, beginning with a superiority of the spirit, can we stop the thunder of hobnailed boots on their march to world empire."[27] He also recognized another, practical value of American superiority: its impact on the will of the enemy.

Reagan noted that there were, in essence, two approaches one could take to attempt to influence an adversary's behavior. The one advocated by most of his critics and much of the foreign policy establishment called for the United States to recognize the "legitimate" goals of the Soviet Union and reach some form of mutual accommodation. The other, urged by Reagan and his conservative allies, was to engage in a policy of sustained confrontation with the Soviets "based on the belief (supported so far by all evidence) that in an all out race our system is stronger, and eventually the enemy gives up the race as a hopeless cause."[28] This approach would characterize the approach Reagan ultimately took upon entering the White House.

Recognition of Soviet Weaknesses

While Reagan understood well the dangers communist ideology and the Soviet military posed for human freedom, he also believed that the Soviet system had many vulnerabilities that Western policies could exacerbate. For Reagan, the weakness and absurdity of the communist system were common topics of letters, conversations, and speeches. He noted that, throughout his life, he "had always believed that, as an economic system, Communism was doomed."[29] Even during the 1970s, when popular opinion held that the Soviet economy was rapidly gaining on the West, Reagan attacked the very notion of successful communist economics. "Nothing proves the failure of Marxism more than the Soviet Union's inability to produce weapons for its military ambitions and at the same time provide for [its] people's everyday needs."[30] This deeply skeptical view of the Soviets' economic situation was reinforced in early 1982 when Reagan received two detailed CIA briefings on the Soviet arms buildup and the Soviet economic situation. The mismatch between Soviet military planning and the fragile economic base available for supporting such a buildup further convinced him that the serious vulnerabilities existed within the Soviet economic system.[31]

But while the Soviets' material weaknesses were important, Reagan also believed that the Soviets faced serious political and spiritual deficiencies that could be used to the West's advantage. In fact, given Reagan's belief in the essentially ideological nature of the Cold War, these weaknesses were probably even more important to him than the material ones. Perhaps the best summary of Reagan's view of the political absurdity of communism came in a speech he gave during his 1980 campaign:

> The greatest fallacy of the Lenin-Marxist philosophy is that it is the "wave of the future." Everything about it is as primitive as tribal rule; compulsion in place of free initiative; coercion in place of law; piracy in place of trade, and empire-building for the benefit of a chosen few at the expense of the many. We have seen nothing like it since feudalism.[32]

In Reagan's mind, communism was not a historical inevitability, but rather an abomination that was ultimately unsustainable. In addition to communism's clear political failings, Reagan also felt deeply that the loss of spiritual freedom was one of the Soviet Union's most significant vulnerabilities. Calling the inability of the Russian people to worship as they please "the most important human right being violated in the Soviet Union,"[33] he often expressed hope that the pent-up desire for freedom of religion could spark internal change within the communist bloc. For Reagan, these hopes were reinforced by the reaction of the Polish people to the visit of Pope John Paul II in 1981. Following the visit, Reagan expressed hope that "religion may very well turn out to be the Soviets' Achilles' heel."[34]

Superiority of Democracy and Capitalism

Much has been made of Reagan's optimistic view of America's future, rooted in a firm belief in the inherent political, economic, and spiritual superiority of Western systems based on free markets, individual rights, and democracy. For Reagan, this superiority was not merely a fact, but a necessary condition for a functioning democracy. In his view, every form of government was rooted in a single characteristic that, if lost, threatens the stability of the state. For democracies, he argued, the defining characteristic is virtue, while for dictatorships the key characteristic is fear.[35]

This belief in the superiority of the democratic West, and this notion of preserving American virtue, was central to his foreign policy vision. To demonstrate the higher moral standards that democracies set for themselves, he frequently invoked such programs as the post–World War II Marshall Plan as examples of American generosity and often quoted a former Australian prime minister who highlighted the many sacrifices the United States had made throughout its history for the benefit of others.[36] While recognizing that, in many cases (such as the Marshall Plan), this generosity also advanced American national interests, he nevertheless understood that this fact did not diminish its inherently moral quality.

Much like the neoconservatives, Reagan believed that democratization and the expansion of human freedom needed to be central elements of any sustained, long-term American foreign policy. In fact, one of the key elements of the foreign policy he unveiled during his 1980 campaign was to demonstrate, particularly to the Third World, the inherent superiority of the Western system of democratic capitalism and the strength of American ideals.[37] Yet Reagan did not limit his interest in expanding democracy abroad to the Third World alone. He often noted that he "would like nothing better than to see the Russian people living in freedom and dignity instead of being trapped in a backwash of history as they are."[38] This belief in the power of American ideals is critical to understanding the foreign policy goals that Reagan set for his administration.

GOALS

Preserve Deterrence

Like every president since the bombing of Hiroshima, upon taking office Reagan needed to come to terms with the necessity of nuclear deterrence. Despite his deep personal revulsion of nuclear weapons, he understood the importance of this task. Unlike his predecessors, however, Reagan never accepted the conventional wisdom regarding proper nuclear strategy and instead set out to alter the fundamental thinking underlying American nuclear doctrine, Mutual Assured Destruction. For a number of reasons, Reagan had long considered MAD strategically absurd and morally dubious.[39] He was appalled by the notion that, in times of crisis, a suicidal bout of mass slaughter was the only strategy available to the United States in response to either a nuclear strike or major conventional defeat in Europe. He was also concerned that, since the Soviets themselves had repeatedly rejected MAD and espoused a war-fighting strategy, clinging to this concept could be highly dangerous during a crisis.[40] Equally important was the fact that MAD required the permanent presence of nuclear weapons, something Reagan deeply resented. Throughout his life, he had often spoken of his desire to see the elimination of nuclear weapons.[41] While he understood the difficulties in verifiably eliminating all nuclear weapons, it seems clear that Reagan also saw the renunciation of MAD as a useful step in this direction.

At the same time, given the Soviets' massive conventional superiority (particularly in Europe), Reagan understood the need for some form of extended nuclear deterrence. Echoing the work of Strausz-Hupé and Nitze, he recognized the need for a "margin of safety" and noted that the United States needed "to be so strong that no other nation will dare violate the peace."[42] He did not believe, as many of his critics did, that international stability required the United States to eschew military superiority, but rather felt that only unquestionable American power could, in the long run, deter Soviet adventurism. Reagan believed that only by restoring this "margin of safety" could the United States pursue its other, more far-reaching goals. This understanding of the requirement for some type of deterrence, yet also the need to move away from MAD, would lead to one of Reagan's most well-known efforts: the Strategic Defense Initiative.

Expand U.S. Influence

As discussed in an earlier chapter, the 1970s witnessed a heated debate between liberals and conservatives over whether and how to reverse the post-Vietnam decline in American power and prestige. For Reagan, as well as many other con-servatives, the problem was not (as many of their opponents claimed) that the United States had nothing to offer the world or that it had squandered its moral authority by backing unpopular regimes. Instead, he argued that it was the fail-ure of the United States to stand behind its friends and allies that had diminished America's standing in the world. In Reagan's view, America's support of South Vietnam had not been a case of the United States backing the wrong side of a civil war, but rather "a noble cause" consistent with American morality.[43] He argued that many of America's Third World allies had been steadfast supporters of U.S. policy and taken significant risks to resist Soviet expansionism. He saw abandoning these allies (such as in South Vietnam and Iran) in their time of need as a gross violation of democracy's moral code and a grave strategic error.

Based on this view, Reagan believed that rebuilding U.S. credibility was cen-tral to any effort to expand American influence. Echoing the arguments of both traditional conservatives and neoconservatives, Reagan posited that the widespread international perception of American retreat from the world had convinced many friends and allies that they had no choice but to reach some form of accommo-dation with the communist world. He noted, for example, that the United States' withdrawal from South Vietnam had undermined America's relationship with sev-eral other Asian nations, which were then forced to open negotiations with China and postwar Vietnam.[44] Such an accommodation could only endanger Western security in the long run. Instead, he insisted that only by reassuring America's friends and allies that the United States would stand firm against Soviet encroach-ment could the United States hope to rebuild its international reputation and expand its influence. While recognizing that such a view was quite unpopular among many Americans during the late 1970s, he understood that only a renewed effort to restore U.S. leadership of the free world would convince America's allies to take the political risks required to resist Soviet expansionism.[45]

Maintain Dialogue with USSR

Of all Reagan's major foreign policy goals, his desire to maintain communications with the Soviet Union is perhaps the least understood, particularly among his more outspoken critics. Despite overwhelming evidence to the contrary, many continue to claim that Reagan had little interest in discussions with the Soviet leadership and that it was only the arrival of Gorbachev on the world scene that spurred Reagan to pursue East-West dialogue seriously.

While it is certainly true that Reagan had only modest interest in the formalized arms control negotiations that much of the foreign policy establishment considered the most important form of dialogue, it is also indisputable that Reagan was committed to maintaining superpower discussions. Early in his presidency, he sent his first personal letter to Brezhnev, stating clearly that the United States would never accept the Brezhnev Doctrine but also urging the Soviet leader to seek meaningful dialogue with the United States.[46] Reagan would continue this effort at personal dialogue with various Soviet leaders throughout his presidency, using his letters to forcefully represent American policy while making clear his desire to find areas of practical cooperation. One can see in his views a striking similarity to Strausz-Hupé's "three pillars of diplomacy," with Reagan paying particular attention to the "representation" element.

While committed to continuing superpower dialogue, however, Reagan also recognized that discussions with the Soviet Union were fundamentally different from those with any other nation. Based on his belief that power was central to Soviet thinking, Reagan understood that superpower diplomacy amounted to a struggle for political power based on relatively simple cost-benefit calculations. As he noted in a letter to one of his supporters, diplomatic discussions with the Soviets were "really a case of presenting a choice in which they face alternatives they must consider on the basis of cost."[47] Thus, Reagan rejected the popular notion that the United States and Soviet Union had a large number of mutually agreeable goals that could be achieved if each side negotiated in good faith and demonstrated flexibility. Rather, he saw relatively few common goals (avoiding a nuclear exchange being the most important one) for the two sides and thus believed that the scope of useful superpower negotiation was quite limited, as were the likely benefits of such negotiations.

Reverse Soviet Expansionism

As noted in chapter 2, the Reagan administration's desire to reverse Soviet expansion and undermine the Soviet state were the two truly defining elements of its grand strategy. These two goals, which represented the most important strategic innovation of the Cold War, were central elements of Reagan's personal foreign policy philosophy. Representing both moral and strategic thought, Reagan's goal of rolling back Soviet expansionism represented the logical outgrowth of his deeply held beliefs in the power of human freedom and the centrality of communist ideology in Soviet foreign policy. At the moral level, Reagan saw the destruction of communist domination and the expansion of human freedom as intrinsically moral acts, stating during the 1980 campaign that the United States should support those "who want to be free of Soviet and Cuban domination."[48] Throughout his political career, Reagan remained committed to the "captive nations" of Eastern Europe, whom the United States had all but abandoned following World War II. Even the 1980 Republican platform, which was largely written by Reagan's campaign staff, notes that one of his administration's goals would be to "pursue positive, non-military means to roll back the growth of communism."[49] In his mind, "peace and freedom for the enslaved people behind the 'iron curtain'" were the only morally appropriate U.S. goals for these nations and those in the Third World suffering under communist rule.[50]

While there was certainly an important strand of moral reasoning in Reagan's pursuit of rollback, he also understood the strategic benefits of reversing Soviet expansion. Recognizing that their claims of the historical inevitability of worldwide communist expansion were central to the Soviets' expansionism and their own domestic legitimacy, Reagan made disproving the Brezhnev Doctrine one of the central goals of his administration.[51] Unlike many of his critics, he saw that communism's claim to be the "wave of the future" represented the only possible justification the Soviet leadership could offer their people for Soviet material poverty and political repression. By reversing history's allegedly unstoppable march toward a communist world, Reagan saw an opportunity to strike a devastating blow to the international perception of Soviet power, as well as demoralize the Soviet elite and challenge the regime's internal stability. This dedication to disproving communist ideology would exert a powerful influence over Reagan's use of military power and covert action.

Undermine the Soviet Union

Yet, in Reagan's mind, it was not enough "merely" to reverse Soviet expansionism. Given the inherent incompatibility between Western democracy and Soviet communism, Reagan believed that only by eliminating communist rule within the USSR itself (and thereby destroying the Soviet state) could the West truly be secure. As Reagan noted in his autobiography, given his understanding of communism's numerous failures, "I wondered how we as a nation could use these cracks in the Soviet system to accelerate the process of collapse."[52] Throughout his political career, Reagan made reference to his desire to see the end of communist rule and the emergence of democratic freedom within the Soviet Union. During the 1980 campaign, he reassured one supporter that the United States must "keep alive the idea that the conquered nations—the captive nations—of the Soviet Union must regain their freedom."[53] As this statement demonstrates, Reagan believed that America's efforts to expand political and economic freedom needed to extend not only to the captive nations of Eastern Europe, but also to those nations within the Soviet Union itself. Reagan's desire to pursue this goal as a central element of his grand strategy was well known to his closest advisors, who shared his belief that "it was possible and desirable to roll back Soviet advances and basically defeat the Soviet Union."[54] Although revolutionary in view of the conventional wisdom of the time, this goal was actually a quite common theme of many conservative strategists.

While it would be easy to ascribe this goal as a simple outgrowth of Reagan's idealism and belief in the power of freedom, it is also important to recognize the shrewd strategic analysis that went into Reagan's pursuit of undermining the Soviet system. Reagan clearly understood (contrary to the accusations of his critics) that the United States could not achieve the destruction of the Soviet Union through military conquest. Instead, it seems clear that his goal was to force the Soviet leadership into making an extraordinarily difficult decision: either attempt to reform the Soviet system in order to better compete with the United States or continue their efforts to keep up with the resurgent military, economic, and political power of the West. As he noted in a 1975 radio address, "What do we envision as the eventual outcome? Either that [the Soviets] will see the fallacy of their way and give up their goal or their system will collapse."[55]

The brilliance of this effort lies in the fact that Reagan understood that either decision would necessarily lead to the erosion of Communist Party control. Without substantial political and economic reform, Reagan recognized that the Soviet Union would rapidly lose ground under the relentless pressure of American power and become unable to assist the "forces of history" in spreading communism around the world. But Reagan also knew that no Soviet reform effort could succeed without reducing the role communist ideology played in Soviet policy, thereby undermining the leadership's only justification for political repression. As Gorbachev would later state, Reagan's goal was "to take the Soviet Union to the edge of the abyss and then induce the regime to take 'one step forward.'"[56]

TOOLS
Military Buildup
For Reagan, the precipitous decline in military spending that occurred throughout the 1970s was a catastrophic strategic blunder that undermined Western security

and increased the likelihood of superpower conflict. Echoing the arguments conservatives had been making since the 1960s, Reagan stressed that a robust and capable military had both operational and political-psychological effects. He argued, for example, that while U.S. military superiority played a major role in the outcome of the Cuban Missile Crisis, by 1973 the strength of the Soviet military had grown to the point that the Soviet threat to intervene in the Arab-Israeli war forced the Israelis to halt their operations against Egypt.[57] America's ability to influence and shape international events, in his view, had declined as a result of the significant reductions in military spending and general loss of America's self-confidence following the U.S. withdrawal from Vietnam. In response, America's global influence began to wane, as friends and allies throughout the world "reluctantly conclude[d] that America [was] unwilling or unable to fulfill its obligations as the leader of the free world" and sought to reach their own separate accommodation with the Soviets.[58] Reagan believed that only by strengthening America's military capability and resolve could the United States effectively counter the expansion of Soviet influence and regain the strategic initiative.

Yet Reagan also saw that a significant military buildup (particularly in strategic weapons) was critical to maintaining deterrence and preventing a war between the superpowers. Rejecting the counsel of the foreign policy mainstream who insisted that the U.S.-Soviet military balance was politically meaningless, Reagan insisted U.S. superiority was crucial to international peace, arguing that "war comes not when the forces of freedom are strong, but when they are weak."[59] In Reagan's view, superior power, not negotiations or compromise, was the most certain and reliable path to peace. As he argued in 1978, "if the object of the SALT II talks is to reduce the possibility of war, what better way is there than to stay so far ahead in weaponry that Russia's imperialistic desires will be inhibited?"[60] Given his faith in the economic strength and technological prowess of the West, he had little doubt that the United States and its allies could, with relative ease, overcome and ultimately reverse the Soviets' military advantage. No other Reagan administration program demonstrated this belief in the innate power of the West better than SDI.

Of all the military program and initiatives the Reagan administration developed, none was as closely identified with Reagan as SDI. In fact, the administration's decision to pursue SDI was the direct result of Reagan's personal commitment to the concept of strategic defense and was taken despite the strenuous objections of many officials in both the State Department and the Defense Department.[61] While some of his more shrill critics insisted that Reagan drew the

idea of strategic defense from one of his old movies, in fact Reagan had been interested in the idea of missile defense since at least 1967, when he was briefed on
America's ABM efforts as part of a tour of Lawrence Livermore Laboratories
arranged by Edward Teller.[62] In Reagan's view, history had repeatedly demonstrated that the development of a new offensive weapon inevitably sparked the
development of a countersystem. Given his personal hatred for nuclear weapons,
Reagan hoped that this historical trend would ultimately provide an opportunity
for both sides to develop highly reliable defenses, escape from the immorality of
MAD, and ultimately make possible the eventual elimination of nuclear weapons.

While Reagan's dedication to SDI certainly had an important "idealistic" component, he also recognized, understood, and embraced the strategic value SDI
had in his quest to roll back Soviet expansion and undermine the Soviet state.
Shortly after Reagan's 1983 speech announcing the creation of SDI, the CIA
informed Reagan that the Soviets would feel compelled to match the U.S. effort
in strategic defense but would find it increasingly difficult to do so, given the
growing frailty of the Soviet economy.[63] This fact, along with the much broader
program of economic warfare Reagan endorsed, demonstrates that his refusal to
compromise or trade away SDI stemmed not merely from his idealistic hopes of
a nuclear-free world, but also a shrewd understanding of the power the program
had to render useless the Soviets' advantage in strategic missiles, weaken the Soviet
economy, and thereby undermine the Soviet state.

Economic Warfare

While somewhat less outspoken (particularly during the 1960s) in his views on the
dangers of extensive East-West trade, Reagan's views on the proper use of American
economic power were remarkably consistent with those of leading conservative
strategists. In one of his earliest public speeches on the topic, delivered in 1963,
Reagan outlined his opposition to the mainstream view that expanded trade with
the communist bloc advanced the interests of the West. Instead, he argued in
terms strikingly similar to those of Strausz-Hupé and Goldwater:

> If we truly believe that our way of life is best aren't the Russians more likely
> to recognize that fact and modify their stand if we let their economy come
> unhinged so that the contrast is apparent? Inhuman though it may sound,
> shouldn't we throw the whole burden of feeding the satellites on their slave
> masters who are having trouble feeding themselves?[64]

As successive American presidents moved steadily toward a policy of détente, Reagan became increasingly convinced that the dominant theory of East-West trade was hopelessly flawed and strategically unsound. As Reagan pointed out in his autobiography, "in theory, expanding trade was supposed to make the Soviets more moderate, but . . . it had simply allowed them to spend fewer resources on agriculture and consumer goods and more on armaments."[65] Expanding trade and extending credit had not, as its proponents expected, changed the Soviet leadership's mind about the value of free market capitalism, nor had it exposed the people of the Soviet Union to the benefits of individual freedom. Rather, it had merely strengthened Soviet control over Eastern Europe and the peoples of the Soviet Union and created a more efficient, powerful, and dangerous adversary.[66] Throughout the mid- and late-1970s, Reagan would make the real effects of East-West trade one of the central themes in his criticism of détente.

In Reagan's writings (both before and during his presidency), one can also see support for each of the key elements of his administration's program of economic warfare against the Soviet Union. Recognizing how dependent the Soviet Union was on Western capital goods and financing, Reagan understood the strategic value of cutting off the flow of credit to the communist bloc.[67] Long critical of the Nixon administration's decision to permit the Kama River truck plant to be built with Western technology, Reagan called for much tighter restrictions on the types of material that could safely be exported to Eastern Europe and the Soviet Union.[68] Even his thinking on the need for a defense buildup, while primarily rooted in his concern about America's declining military capability, had an important economic component. By making clear to the Soviets that the United States was "going to spend whatever it took to stay ahead of them in the arms race," Reagan sought to use the economic superiority of the West as a weapon against the Soviet Union.[69]

There was, however, at least one area where Reagan's views diverged slightly from those of some conservatives. His decision to lift the grain embargo against the Soviet Union (which President Carter had imposed following the Soviet invasion of Afghanistan) was heavily criticized by some conservatives at the time as a betrayal of his goal of rollback.[70] As he noted in a letter to a supporter, however, lifting the grain embargo had a strategic purpose—namely, to drain the Soviets' extremely limited hard currency assets and thus reduce their ability to purchase advanced technology or capital goods.[71] Overall, however, Reagan's thinking on the strategic use of economic power closely mirrored that of Burnham, Strausz-Hupé, Goldwater, and other conservative strategists.

Political Warfare

While Reagan certainly recognized the importance of both military power and economic warfare in America's struggle against the Soviet Union, he clearly saw the political battleground of the Cold War as the decisive one. From the time he first entered the national political spotlight, giving his nationally televised speech in support of presidential candidate Goldwater in 1964, Reagan had repeatedly stressed that victory in the Cold War was possible, provided the West regained its spiritual strength and recognized the inherent power of its own ideals.[72] Throughout the 1960s and 1970s (and well into his presidency), Reagan's writing and thinking placed an extraordinary emphasis on accurately representing America's intentions and ideals to the world. As America's foreign policy elite increasingly viewed sustaining détente and encouraging arms control as the central tasks of managing the Cold War, Reagan became increasingly vocal in his skepticism about the enduring value of negotiations with the Soviets. In doing so, Reagan demonstrated that his thinking on diplomacy and political warfare largely reflected that of his fellow conservatives, particularly Strausz-Hupé.

For his entire adult life, both before and during his political career, expressing himself and his ideas was one of Reagan's most important tasks. As noted earlier in this chapter, Reagan spent a significant amount of time ensuring that his speeches reflected his own views. This tendency was particularly pronounced in his foreign policy addresses, which he understood to be a key element of his political offensive against the Soviet Union. In his repeated rhetorical attacks on Soviet conduct and immorality, as well as his efforts to restore faith in the democratic capitalism of the West, Reagan made clear the primacy he gave to the representational element of diplomacy. Since his early days in Hollywood, Reagan had been outspoken in his denunciation of communist ideology, calling it "a predatory system of absolute, authoritarian rule that had an insatiable appetite for expansion"[73] and "the most dangerous enemy that has ever faced mankind in his long climb from the swamp to the stars."[74]

Reagan's commitment to representational diplomacy can also be seen in his strong support for strengthening America's public diplomacy. Having begun his own show business career in radio, he understood the power it had to influence and inform those behind the Iron Curtain. It is therefore no accident that, during his 1980 campaign, he promised to use Voice of America and Radio Free Europe/Radio Liberty to "take the lead in pointing out to third world nations the superiority of our system" and to "call attention to those nations that once were poor but now enjoy a standard of living far above that of their neighbors who put their faith in communism."[75]

At the same time, it is important to stress that, contrary to the claims of many of his critics, he did see a role (albeit a limited one) for negotiations with the Soviet Union. Many of his biographers have noted that Reagan was deeply influenced by *The Treaty Trap*, a book written by an old friend, which argued that nations only obey treaties when doing so is in their interest.[76] The long history of Soviet violations of arms control treaties served only to reinforce Reagan's view of the limited utility of these agreements. As a result, Reagan believed that the elaborate arms control schemes advocated by détente enthusiasts throughout the 1970s were ultimately doomed to fail. Only agreements rooted in a realistic understanding of each side's strategic interests had any hope of lasting. Nonetheless, he repeatedly stressed, both before and immediately after entering office, that he "would like nothing better than to see the two great superpowers, the U.S. and the Soviet [Union] agree to a real and effective reduction of armaments . . . one that would increase not decrease our hopes for lasting peace."[77] In his view, "continued negotiations with the Soviet [Union] is essential" and the United States must never be afraid to negotiate, provided it retains a clear understanding of its interests and its adversary.[78] Contrary to the claims of some critics, Reagan's willingness to negotiate a mutually advantageous arms control agreement with Moscow was present from the outset of his administration. In fact, within the first few months in office, Reagan publicly stressed that he was willing to "negotiate as long as necessary to reduce the number of nuclear weapons" but that the Soviets' refusal to embrace arms reduction made such an agreement impossible.[79]

Yet Reagan never made the mistake of thinking that the Cold War could ever be settled via negotiations or that the fundamental differences between the two sides could be resolved by frequent summits or mutual professions of peaceful intentions. For him, negotiations were not a means of escaping superpower confrontation, but merely another tool for waging a political war against the Soviet Union.

Covert Action

Of the four tools used by his administration to confront Soviet power, Reagan had the least to say publicly about covert action. This relative quiet should hardly be surprising. For most of his adult life, these sorts of activities were rarely discussed in public. Politicians across the political spectrum understood the sensitivities of discussing covert action and generally refrained from openly commenting on or advocating these activities. Only after the highly publicized congressional investigations of the intelligence community during the 1970s (such as the Church Committee) did a more open discussion of covert action become fairly common. As a result, it is much more difficult to identify from Reagan's own writings his personal views of the utility and purpose of covert action. Nevertheless, the views he did express on the use of intelligence and covert action largely mirror those of conservative strategists.

Reagan's first serious involvement with the intelligence community occurred in January 1975, when President Ford named him a member of the President's Commission on CIA Activities within the United States, better known as the Rockefeller Commission. This commission, which preceded the more well-known and controversial Church Committee, reviewed a number of questionable CIA activities, including the illegal opening of private mail to and from the Soviet Union and the monitoring of the political activities of domestic political groups.[80] As a member of the commission, Reagan was granted extensive access to agency files and was briefed on a number of ongoing CIA operations. While CIA critics accused the Rockefeller Commission of being a "whitewash," it offered a number of reasonable and constructive recommendations for improving the oversight and performance of the intelligence community. While critical of the CIA's serious mistakes, Reagan nevertheless pushed American intelligence to become even more active abroad and repeatedly urged caution in considering more extensive and onerous regulations of the CIA's overseas operations.[81]

Later, during the 1980 presidential contest, Reagan campaigned on the idea that the CIA should be "unleashed" and allowed to be more active in conducting covert action abroad. His selection of (and unwavering support for) William Casey, a staunch advocate of covert action, as DCI further demonstrated his intention to pursue a more proactive and aggressive program of covert action against Soviet interests worldwide.[82] In Reagan's endorsement of covert action, especially in the Third World and in Poland, one can see striking similarities between his views and those of Burnham, Frank Rockwell Barnett, and Strausz-Hupé.

But no strategic plan, no matter how carefully thought out, matters unless it is diligently and faithfully implemented. As already noted, while Reagan was unquestionably the primary source of his administration's grand strategy, he could not have accomplished as much as he did without the loyal support of his key advisors. These individuals, and their subordinates, were the ones primarily responsible for using their respective tools of statecraft in a manner consistent

with the beliefs and goals that Reagan set forth. The rest of this chapter will identify those individuals and organizations that played important roles in the use of
each of the administration's principal tools.

IMPLEMENTING THE STRATEGY

One of the more interesting and unusual facts about the Reagan foreign policy
team was the stability of its composition. With the exception of the national security advisor slot, there was remarkable consistency among most of the key cabinet-
level positions. William Casey and Caspar Weinberger served from the outset of
the administration until May 1987 and November 1987, respectively, while
George Shultz was named secretary of state in July 1982 and served until the end
of Reagan's second term. Jeane Kirkpatrick's tenure as U.S. ambassador to the
United Nations lasted roughly four years, the longest tenure at the position since
the 1960s, as did Edwin Meese's position as counselor to the president.

Each of these individuals, as well as Reagan's first two national security advisors (Richard V. Allen and William Clark) were either longtime, loyal aides to
Reagan or (in the case of Shultz and Kirkpatrick) highly regarded individuals who
strongly supported the president's vision. Meese, who led the Reagan transition
effort, including the search for cabinet officials, noted that support for rolling
back Soviet expansion was, in essence, a precondition for anyone being offered a
senior-level foreign policy position.[83] While there were certainly a number of vigorous disagreements among these officials over the implementation of this strategy, it is notable that these personnel have stressed that the famous battles within
the administration were primarily over the use of various tools, not over the underlying beliefs or major goals of the strategy. Contrary to much of the conventional
history, for example, Weinberger and Shultz actually agreed on a large majority of
issues. Their most important area of disagreement regarding U.S.-Soviet relations
was over the timing and content of arms control proposals, which were themselves only one piece of the political warfare effort, which was but one component
of the overall strategy.[84] Similarly, their disputes over pipeline sanctions and
Central America, while heated, were not over the fundamental strategic approach,
but rather over how best to implement Reagan's plan. Ultimately, however, such
disputes were quite uncommon at the senior level, since this rather remarkable
collection of foreign policy advisors generally recognized that their job was to use
these tools to achieve Reagan's strategic goals.[85]

This discussion raises an obvious question: if there was general agreement among Reagan's chief advisors on the key elements of American grand strategy, why have so many former Reagan administration officials complained of obstructionism, bureaucratic subterfuge, and outright insubordination in the implementation of Reagan's decisions? A number of factors can help explain this discrepancy. First, as has been noted, the divisions within the administration that did exist, such as on arms control, were significant and received a great deal of media and public attention.

Second, it is important to note that much of the opposition to Reagan's decisions occurred well below the cabinet level. In any presidential administration, lower-level officials (whether political appointees or not) are not necessarily chosen based on their close ties to the president and do not necessarily agree with the president on every issue. Unlike cabinet members, these officials receive little to no "face time" with the president and are not privy to the closely held, senior-level discussions that can serve to restrain the actions of cabinet secretaries. As a result, these officials will frequently seek to develop policies that *they* believe appropriate, particularly in the absence of direct guidance from the senior leaders of their departments.

Third, Reagan's grand strategy was a radical departure from traditional American Cold War strategy and actively opposed by the vast majority of the foreign policy elite. It is, therefore, unsurprising that lower-level officials (particularly career civil servants who see themselves as members of the elite) would view his proposed changes to American policy as dangerous and see their own job as "reining in" an administration "blinded by ideology" and led by an "amiable dunce." As theoretically appealing as it may be to imagine that career bureaucrats are apolitical, history has shown that presidents whose political views are widely shared by the bureaucracy have a far easier time getting their programs implemented than those whose views are widely opposed.

Finally, one can never underestimate the impact that routine, bureaucratic turf wars can have on the day-to-day implementation of *any* policy effort, much less one as radically different as the Reagan strategy. Battles over which department (or part of a department) would be in charge of a given program were inevitable, leading to delays and obstructionism in the implementation of presidential decisions.

These four factors, when combined with the reality that only a very small percentage of interagency disputes ever get resolved at the cabinet level, go far in explaining why the policies that were made crystal clear to Reagan's senior advisors were so frequently sabotaged at the lower levels.

Military Buildup

It should be blindingly obvious that the vast majority of the planning, managing, directing, and decision making regarding the significant increase in the U.S. defense budget Reagan sought (and obtained) was the work of Weinberger and his staff. A serious increase in the defense budget was one of Reagan's key campaign promises, as an extensive modernization of the American military was long overdue. Weinberger was relentless in pushing for this increase, despite the opposition of some of Reagan's domestic policy advisors and budget personnel, who repeatedly fought to cut back some of Weinberger's budget requests.[86] On this issue, however, there was broad agreement among Reagan's key foreign policy advisors. All of them recognized that rebuilding America's military strength was absolutely necessary for the country to have any hope of winning the Cold War. This consensus, however, did not extend into the other two key pieces of the military component—namely, the Strategic Defense Initiative and the administration's greater assertiveness in the use of military power.

As noted, the creation of SDI was the direct outcome of Reagan's own personal disgust for nuclear weapons, his own belief in the immorality of MAD, and his faith in the power of American technology. Given the extremely closely held manner in which SDI was developed (neither Weinberger, Shultz, nor any of their subordinates knew about this effort until a few days before Reagan's nationally televised speech) and the president's clear personal commitment to this program, opposition to the program itself was largely muted. However, as it became increasingly clear that SDI would play an important role in the arms control debate, the battle lines became much more starkly defined. For Weinberger, Meese, and Casey, SDI represented an opportunity to undermine one of the key bases of Soviet power, to move away from MAD, and (later) to complicate further the Soviets' difficult economic circumstances.[87] For National Security Advisor Robert McFarlane and Shultz, SDI represented instead a "bargaining chip" that could be useful in convincing the Soviets to accept steep cuts in the superpowers' nuclear arsenals.[88] Shultz also worried about the impact that aggressively pursuing SDI could have on U.S.-Soviet negotiations, fearing that it could create "huge, perhaps insuperable, problems."[89] In this case, the strongest supporters of SDI were much closer to Reagan's real view of the program, a fact that should have been obvious to anyone working closely with Reagan long before it was made public in the collapse of the Reykjavik Summit, where Reagan solidified the position that SDI would never be a bargaining chip.

Weinberger and his staff were also critically important to operationalizing the final element of the buildup, a greater assertiveness in using military power. Under his watch, the military implemented more aggressive concepts, such as the Maritime Strategy, which represented a greater willingness to challenge Soviet military power. At the same time, however, the Defense Department leadership repeatedly felt the need to restrain those who called for even more aggressive actions. Early in the Reagan administration, Weinberger argued strenuously against Haig's suggestion that the United States invade Cuba to eliminate the Castro regime.[90] While there was broad support among Reagan's key advisors for the 1981 operations against Libya and the 1983 invasion of Grenada, Weinberger often found himself arguing against State Department proposals for more aggressive uses of force, particularly in Lebanon.[91]

However, Weinberger and his staff were hardly the only ones playing an important role in this area. One of the critical defense efforts of Reagan's first term, the INF deployment to Europe, was also an important signal to the Soviets that the United States would not allow them to intimidate its allies. While much work was done to encourage this deployment through military-to-military channels, the ultimate keys to the successful positioning of these weapons were the sustained diplomatic campaign and the major public diplomacy effort largely led by the State Department and the NSC staff, respectively. In short, while the bulk of the work involved in implementing this component of the strategy fell to Weinberger and his staff, they received important support and assistance from others within the administration.

Economic Warfare

Given the nature and scope of the economic challenge that Reagan sought to pose to the Soviets, any successful use of economic warfare required a well-designed, coordinated, and broad effort that spanned a number of bureaucracies. The program of economic warfare that the administration pursued cut across several agencies' formal responsibilities, placing a premium on interagency cooperation. As a result, much of the work to implement Reagan's program of economic warfare was done by the NSC staff under the guidance of Richard Allen and (later) William Clark, though with a great deal of assistance from the Defense Department (specifically Richard Perle and Stephen Bryen) and CIA Director Casey.

Indeed, Reagan's critical decision to expand the pipeline sanctions to licensees and subsidiaries of American firms was made at the urging of the NSC, DOD, and CIA, over the objections of the State Department. This decision, while deeply resented by the allies, ultimately forced the West to reassess its economic relations with Moscow and develop a much tougher line on East-West trade. At the same time, the State Department deserves much of the credit for crafting the final deal, which ended the unilateral sanctions in exchange for strengthening COCOM restrictions and cutting off trade credits to Moscow. This compromise was largely developed under the leadership of Under Secretary of State James Buckley, but the NSC staff, particularly Norman Bailey and Roger Robinson, provided critical assistance. Reagan approved this deal in October 1982, largely over the objections of the Defense Department, which felt it did not go far enough. This episode highlights a common feature of Reagan's decision making: an absolute willingness to take a tough stand, despite the fierce opposition of the so-called moderates, while being equally ready to ignore the concerns of the hard-liners when he felt he had accomplished his key goals.

Implementing a new, more security-minded export control policy was, to say the least, a difficult undertaking for the Reagan administration. Despite Reagan's clear personal commitment to cutting off the flow of advanced technology to the Soviet Union, it was extremely difficult to ensure that his wishes were followed. Domestic pressure to permit exports was significant, with much of the business community urging a more relaxed set of restrictions. While the official administrative responsibility for reviewing export licenses fell to the State Department, it was the Defense Department that ultimately played the dominant role in determining what technologies could safely be exported.[92]

At the outset, however, there was little consensus even within the DOD over who should be in charge of reviewing these exports. After a sustained bureaucratic struggle between Perle and Under Secretary for Research and Engineering Richard DeLauer, who preferred a less stringent approach, Deputy Secretary Frank Carlucci ultimately sided with Perle.[93] This decision resulted in the creation of the Defense Technology Security Administration (DTSA), which was led by Perle's deputy, Stephen Bryen. While Perle and Bryen nominally reported to Under Secretary of Defense for Policy Fred Iklé, Iklé largely delegated this work to them, giving Perle and Bryen tremendous freedom to set departmental, and hence national, policy on export controls.[94]

Political Warfare

Reagan himself was directly involved in some elements of his administration's political warfare campaign against the Soviets. And as important as his speeches were to this effort, his vision of his administration's political warfare campaign was significantly broader and required sustained, senior-level oversight and good interagency coordination. Under NSDD-77, the national security advisor was responsible for exercising this coordination and oversight as the chairman of the Special Planning Group (SPG) for public diplomacy. NSDD-77 also directed the creation of four subcommittees, each of which oversaw key elements of the overall public diplomacy effort. The committees consisted of

- the Public Affairs Committee, cochaired by the White House communications director and the deputy national security advisor, which was "responsible for the planning and coordination of major speeches on national security subjects" and other public communications;
- the International Information Committee, chaired by the deputy director of USIA, which would mainly oversee USIA activities but was also responsible for managing Project Truth;
- the International Political Committee, chaired by the State Department, which was responsible for coordinating "aid, training and organizational support" for national democracy-building efforts, to include Project Democracy; and
- the International Broadcasting Committee, chaired by the NSC staff, which was responsible for the diplomatic and technical planning required to modernize America's radio broadcast capabilities.[95]

This interagency structure proved remarkably successful in ensuring that the administration stayed "on message," providing a focus for America's political warfare efforts, and allowing all key members of the national security team to participate in the political war with Moscow. And, indeed, each made important contributions to support the efforts of Clark and his staff. For example, CIA Director Casey strongly backed this effort and was instrumental in developing the early structure of what eventually became Project Democracy.[96] Kirkpatrick was a strong supporter of this political assault on the Soviet Union, and her unyielding rhetoric at the United Nations played an important role in discrediting Soviet ideology internationally. The State Department, in addition to chairing the committee with the broadest mandate, was generally supportive of these efforts, though Shultz and some of his allies within the White House (particularly White House chief of staff James Baker and his deputy, Michael Deaver) did not approve of some of the harsh rhetoric used to attack the Soviets' human rights record.[97] The Defense Department also strongly backed these efforts and worked to improve its own psychological operations capability, which had declined throughout the 1970s.[98] Even the USIA (not normally considered a major player in national security discussions) made a valuable contribution by launching Project Truth. While there were certainly disagreements among the various bureaucracies over the implementation of the president's guidance, the administration's successes in such areas as support of the Polish freedom movement, the INF deployment, and SDI demonstrated the strategic impact that political warfare could have.

The final key component of the administration's political warfare campaign was, without a doubt, the most contentious and divisive issue in the Reagan administration: arms control. It was in this area that, once again, Reagan himself ultimately was forced to intervene to ensure that his views, rather than those of his advisors, controlled America's actions. While most conventional histories give the bulk of the credit to Shultz's influence, the truth is significantly more complicated. First, it must be stressed that everyone on Reagan's national security team understood that arms control was *one* tool for achieving America's objectives. Even Weinberger, who is commonly portrayed as vehemently opposed to arms control, shared Reagan's commitment to achieving an agreement, provided it enhanced America's security.[99]

Second, and equally important, none of Reagan's senior foreign policy advisors believed that any agreement, regardless of content, was a step in the right direction. Shultz, as leader of the "pro-negotiation" side of the administration, agreed with Reagan's view that arms control agreements were but one element of America's relationship with Moscow and that arms control could never resolve the underlying differences between the two sides. Thus, the struggle was not over whether the United States should pursue arms control, but rather over the much more detailed question of what the terms of such an agreement should be.

The impact and importance of the "Weinberger camp" can be seen in the outcome of the two most important arms control–related issues of the Reagan administration: the INF Treaty and the administration's embrace of the "broad interpretation" of the ABM Treaty. Contrary to the conventional view that the signing of the INF Treaty represented a defeat for the so-called hard-liners, in truth the content of this agreement largely vindicates their positions. For example, despite Haig's vehement opposition and Shultz's plea for greater flexibility, it was the Defense Department–developed "zero option" that Reagan endorsed and the INF Treaty ultimately codified.[100] It is impossible to imagine that this treaty could ever have taken the shape it did without the active input of the hard-liners.

Similarly, Reagan's announcement of SDI led to a heated debate within the administration over whether and how the United States could pursue strategic defenses in a manner consistent with the ABM Treaty. While Weinberger made clear that he preferred withdrawing from the treaty (particularly in light of the Soviets' repeated violations), he and his allies were ultimately successful in getting Reagan's approval of the "broad interpretation" of the ABM Treaty rather than the narrow one Shultz and his supporters had advocated.[101] Embracing the "broad interpretation" permitted the administration to investigate and even develop a broad array of potential defensive technologies and thus complicated the Soviets' efforts to keep up with American technological innovation. Given how important SDI was to Reagan's strategy, his decision to back the broad interpretation was crucial to his strategy's success. Thus, in both these critical cases, a more accurate reading of the administration's actions shows the vital role that the hard-liners played in Reagan's arms control successes.

At the same time, however, it is important to note the successes for which the "Shultz camp" was largely responsible, specifically in the efforts to reach agreement on the INF Treaty. As noted, Reagan supported the "zero option" and was insistent that it represent America's ultimate goal. Yet, because the Soviets had denounced it as unacceptable, it was not particularly popular with some segments of the European population and was causing serious domestic political pressures for many NATO allies. At Shultz's urging, and despite opposition from some of Reagan's advisors, the president did announce in March 1983 an "interim solution" that would have permitted the Americans and Soviets to deploy equal numbers of INF systems.[102] While such a stance was rejected by the Soviets, it proved very popular within Europe and helped counter the perception that the United States was not interested in arms control negotiations. This proposal, as well as the intense diplomacy that maintained alliance unity during this difficult period, helped make it possible for the United States to "buy time" until the Soviets' political and economic failures compelled it to negotiate in good faith. Much of the credit for the skill with which this effort was implemented belongs to the Shultz camp. In the end, as was the case in the pipeline sanctions debate earlier discussed, both camps made important contributions to Reagan's arms control proposals. On substance, Reagan largely agreed with the Weinberger camp, yet he was also flexible enough to side with the Shultz camp when changes were needed. As Shultz himself noted, the battle between the two sides led to gradual movement on INF, "with the timing and content of our moves being just about right."[103] This happy circumstance could only have occurred with both sides aggressively advocating their positions.

Covert Action

Much as in the case of the military buildup, the bulk of the responsibility for implementing Reagan's goals via covert action fell to a single agency—in this case, Casey's CIA. In many ways, Casey was the perfect DCI for Reagan. A former agent of the Office of Strategic Services during World War II and an extremely intelligent man, he embodied the risk-taking, aggressive attitude Reagan admired and needed to implement his strategy. Having served as Reagan's campaign manager, Casey had developed a strong relationship with the president before taking office, and this closeness "opened the door to more operations than would have been the case otherwise."[104] He was vehemently anticommunist and, as his critics have noted, had one overriding interest for his time at the CIA: to wage war against the Soviet Union.[105] While he usually sided with Meese, Allen, Clark, Weinberger, and Kirkpatrick in interagency battles, he did get important support from Shultz on certain issues.

The most well-known of the administration's covert actions were those taken to implement the Reagan Doctrine. In particular, the administration gave crucial support to anticommunist movements in Afghanistan, Angola, and Nicaragua. While aid to the mujahideen in Afghanistan began under Carter, his administration's goal had been not to defeat the Soviets, but merely to harass them.[106] Despite vehement opposition within a CIA bureaucracy fearing the loss of plausible deniability, Casey (with the support of the entire foreign policy team) gradually increased aid to the Afghan rebels in the hope of driving the Soviets out of Afghanistan. All Reagan's key foreign policy advisors also supported the critical 1986 decision to provide the rebels Stinger missiles, despite resistance from both the CIA and military bureaucracies.[107] Likewise, support for arming the Angolan resistance was fairly widespread within the administration and, once congressional concerns were resolved in 1985, significant aid (including Stingers) began to flow to the UNITA movement.[108]

In fact, the only major area in which there was significant internal infighting over implementing the Reagan Doctrine was in Central America, specifically supporting the Nicaraguan contras. On this issue, the much-discussed division between hard-liners and moderates was most evident. For Weinberger, Meese,

Casey, and Kirkpatrick, the logic of the situation was self-evident: support for the Nicaraguan resistance was an important part of the Reagan strategy to roll back the Soviet empire. They believed the United States should take the same attitude toward the Sandinistas as it did toward any inherently illegitimate Soviet-backed government. For Shultz and his allies, however, the administration needed to balance the threat the Sandinistas posed with broader concerns regarding the sustainability of America's support for their opponents. In light of significant congressional hostility to contra aid, they urged Reagan to seek some form of negotiated solution, even if such a solution left a Marxist government in power in Nicaragua.[109] Whereas in previous struggles Reagan himself settled the debate, in this case Congress would also play a major role by cutting off aid to the contras. This issue would, of course, continue to plague the administration and would contribute to the Iran-Contra debacle.

In addition to his key role in implementing the Reagan Doctrine, Casey was also crucial to a number of other important covert actions undertaken by the administration. Responding to the declaration of martial law in Poland, Casey played an important role in supporting the Solidarity movement, funneling money, supplies, and intelligence information to key members of the labor union.[110] His efforts, which enjoyed broad congressional support, included working extremely closely with the AFL-CIO and other interested American organizations, and even briefing Pope John Paul II, who was engaged in an even larger effort to support Solidarity, on the U.S. efforts. Fascinated as he was by challenges to the Soviets' internal stability, he was also deeply involved in other efforts, such as smuggling anticommunist propaganda into Soviet Central Asia. Finally, by all accounts, he was the primary driver for urging the United States to use Vladimir Vetrov's information on Soviet technology theft to wreak further havoc on the Soviet economy.[111] In short, the aggressive and largely successful use of covert action during the Reagan administration was due, in large part, to Casey's dedication, hard work, and vision.

CONCLUSION

This depiction bears little resemblance to the one commonly found in journalistic and academic accounts of the Reagan administration, which tend to overstate the importance of the president's advisors while slighting the role he himself played in his own administration's foreign policy. However, this simplistic view is becoming increasingly outdated as more information becomes available regarding Reagan's own foreign policy views and as greater documentation from the his administration is released. As already demonstrated, Reagan had strongly held and insightful views regarding what America's Soviet policy should be. Given his deep roots in conservative thought more generally, it is unsurprising that his thinking should mirror that of such people as Burnham, Goldwater, Strausz-Hupé, and Niemeyer. Rather, what is surprising is that so much of the current scholarship on Reagan's foreign policy neglects to analyze the clear and important connections between Reagan and the conservative intellectual movement or to recognize that he played the definitive, central role in the development of his administration's grand strategy.

There is a great temptation, when discussing the roles that each of Reagan's key advisors played in implementing his strategy, to claim that one side was clearly in the right, while the other side was secretly trying to implement policies that were contrary to the president's wishes. Such a portrayal is certainly easier, as it allows the analyst to lionize one group while vilifying the other. For this reason, it is a common thread in most journalistic histories of the administration.

But, as is often the case, the truth is much more complex. Neither the Shultz camp nor the Weinberger camp was perfectly attuned to Reagan's mind, nor did either ever succeed in "winning over" Reagan to its point of view on every issue. Even well into his second term (when many traditional accounts claim that the Shultz camp had won the struggle for Reagan's support), Reagan's own diaries demonstrate that he frequently sided with one advisor or another based on how well that side's position reflected his own thinking.[112] Simply put, Reagan was too strong-willed and confident in his own views for any of his advisors to "capture" him. Nor was either side innocent of using bureaucratic maneuvers or well-timed leaks of information to circumvent the decision-making process in an effort to ensure that their preferred policies won. Fortunately for Reagan, these scuffles remained at the tactical level and never posed a serious threat to his overall strategic goals. Ultimately, the fights over arms control and Central America, while making good headlines and interesting tell-alls, were of limited strategic importance. On the whole, the Reagan team worked quite well together, faithfully implementing Reagan's strategy while offering the president their best advice.

The reasons for their success would appear twofold. First, most of these individuals, especially those from his first term, knew, understood, and respected Reagan and his ideas and were committed to his program. Second, they also (for the most part) adhered to Reagan's preferred method of decision making: allowing everyone with a stake to express his or her views, then making a decision. It was only when these two conditions broke down during Reagan's second term, as individuals (particularly on the NSC staff) who had no real understanding of Reagan's goals and who consistently short-circuited the decision-making process became more influential, that the Reagan administration committed its greatest strategic blunder: the Iran-Contra scandal.

Conclusions

The preceding chapters have proposed a working definition of grand strategy, used that definition to identify the Reagan administration's grand strategy, and demonstrated the degree to which the key components of this strategy correspond to the beliefs, goals, and tools conservative strategists had advocated since the early days of the Cold War. In addition, this study has also identified Ronald Reagan himself as the ultimate source of the grand strategy his administration pursued and has pointed out the critical role that a select group of close advisors played in ensuring this strategy was implemented. These findings raise a number of interesting questions regarding the conventional history of the Reagan administration and, more generally, the nature of grand strategy and the role of the individual in international affairs. This final chapter will explore the broader implications of these findings and will attempt to draw some conclusions about the practical challenges of developing and implementing grand strategy, particularly in a post-9/11 world.

RETHINKING THE HISTORY OF THE REAGAN ADMINISTRATION

As discussed earlier, much of the conventional history regarding Reagan, his role in directing his administration's foreign policy, and the credit he deserves for America's victory in the Cold War has proven steadily less plausible as historians have obtained greater access to Reagan's personal and presidential papers. The fact that a rethinking of Reagan is long overdue should hardly be surprising; many presidents are more accurately and fairly judged only after most of the political passions and partisan rancor surrounding them fade.[1] While some of the political battles of the 1980s are still being fought, the time has come for a more fair-minded assessment of Reagan and his foreign policy team. It now seems reasonable to reach a number of conclusions about the Reagan years that would have seemed overstated only a few years ago.

First, it is difficult to overstate how revolutionary the Reagan approach to American grand strategy truly was. Rarely in American history has a president so totally focused the power of the United States on such a lofty and seemingly unachievable goal. While Woodrow Wilson certainly hoped to transform the international system in the aftermath of World War I, he was either unable or unwilling to harness America's national power to achieve this end. Similarly, while Franklin Roosevelt was certainly eager to wield America's vast economic and military power, his ultimate war aims seemed little more than a slightly altered version of the prewar status quo. Alone among the Cold War presidents, Reagan sought to end the struggle by fundamentally altering the international landscape and eliminating the greatest single threat to American security. The fact that he did so in the face of heated, often hysterical opposition from both political adversaries and the foreign policy establishment makes his success all the more remarkable.

A second key conclusion that can be drawn from the historical record is the remarkable consistency and quality of Reagan's foreign policy thought. The record now clearly demonstrates that, contrary to the claims of many who insist that he "saw the light" and radically softened his view of the Soviet Union, Reagan never ceased his intense criticism of the Soviet regime, nor did his views of America's goals appreciably change over the course of his presidency.[2] Here again, one should not be surprised at the consistency of Reagan's views. Reagan was an extremely smart man who was confident in his own judgment. He had also spent a significant portion of his adult life thinking about American foreign policy and, as even his closest advisors have acknowledged, could be extraordinarily stubborn when convinced that he was right. Nothing in Reagan's own writings supports the "Reagan reversal" theory, nor do those who worked most closely with him make such a claim. The persistence of this theory reflects little more than the intellectual pride and persistent bias of journalists and much of the foreign policy elite. Forced to explain how a man widely "stereotyped as a likable and decent man who was lacking in intellectual candlepower"[3] could have achieved so much, the only rationalization they can come up with is that Reagan must have "grown" in office and embraced the policy positions the elite had been advocating all along. Apparently, the possibility that they themselves had simply been wrong cannot be considered.[4] As the previous chapter shows, Reagan understood the Soviets' political and economic vulnerabilities far better than his critics and developed the brilliantly effective strategy his administration would use to target those weaknesses and ultimately win the Cold War.

A final conclusion that flows naturally from this analysis of the Reagan administration's strategy involves the relative credit Reagan and Gorbachev deserve for end of the Cold War. Once again, much of the conventional history grossly misrepresents the causes of the Soviet collapse by portraying it as the result of Gorbachev's farsightedness and wisdom. In this view, it was Gorbachev who sought to end the Cold War by instituting a broad program of political and economic reform while reaching out to and reassuring the West of the Soviets' peaceful intentions. Indeed, much of the conventional wisdom criticizes Reagan for allegedly failing to move fast enough in supporting Gorbachev (due primarily to his own hard-line beliefs and those of his advisors). A number of stubborn facts tend to discredit the conventional story and instead put credit where it rightly belongs: with Ronald Reagan himself.

First, the very existence of the strategy, as outlined in NSDD-75 and its supporting documents, supports the conclusion that it played the pivotal role in the collapse of the Soviet empire. While, theoretically, one could dismiss as mere coincidence the fact that this strategy immediately preceded the end of the Cold War, such a conclusion strains logical thought. Second, it is important to point out that Gorbachev's efforts were not designed to end competition with the West, but rather to strengthen the Soviet Union and expand its global power. Following his rise to power in 1985, he increased the Soviet defense budget by roughly 45 percent over five years, while vastly expanding his nation's covert offensive biological warfare program (in direct violation of the Biological and Toxin Weapons Convention); neither of these actions bespeaks peaceful or "moderate" intentions.[5] He never sought either the dissolution of Soviet domination over Eastern Europe or the destruction of communist rule in the Soviet Union proper. As long as such conditions held, however, some form of Cold War was inevitable.

Finally, while Reagan recognized early on that Gorbachev was different, he never made the mistake of trusting him, nor did he ever change his view of the inherent immorality of communism (an ideology that Gorbachev has never renounced) or his goal of defeating the Soviet Union. As was demonstrated in the previous chapter, Reagan's view of communism was deeply rooted in an accurate understanding of its real goals. He would never abandon those views merely because Gorbachev was successful in presenting himself as a more moderate, humane version of his predecessors.

INHERENT RISKS AND UNCERTAINTIES OF THE REAGAN STRATEGY

In discussing and analyzing the Reagan administration's strategy from the safety of the post–Cold War era, one runs the danger of assuming that the collapse of the Soviet position in Eastern Europe and the disintegration of the Soviet Union itself were inevitable. To make such an assumption, however, is to commit the same intellectual error that lies at the heart of Marxist ideology: believing that the "laws of history" dictate the outcome of human endeavors. Such a fallacy is both alluring and dangerous, as it reassures the statesman that, eventually, the "good guys are going to win," while simultaneously absolving him of any responsibility to assist the "good guys" in their efforts. History follows no laws, and thus every grand strategy (no matter how well developed and planned it may be) bears certain risks and challenges. The intrinsic uncertainty involved in the clash of two opposing strategic plans renders the outcome and its costs unknowable until the struggle is resolved. In order to better understand the nature of the Reagan strategy, as well as for the sake of historical accuracy, it is therefore important to outline and discuss the risks of the Reagan approach.

Certainly the most obvious risk, and the one that critics used most frequently to attack the administration, was the danger that pursuing a policy of confrontation with Moscow would result in a full-scale superpower war, one likely to end in a nuclear exchange. On the surface, there are some reasons to acknowledge that this danger was a real one. First, and most obviously, the sweeping nature of Reagan's goals increased this danger. By seeking to exacerbate Soviet weaknesses with the intent of destroying the Soviet state, Reagan risked placing the Soviets in a position in which they judged that war was less risky than peace. Second, the Soviets had become steadily more aggressive since the end of the Vietnam War, increasing the danger that the Soviet leadership could miscalculate Western resolve and overreach, leading to an unanticipated Western reaction. Finally, compounding this danger was the fact that the Soviet leadership did not understand that the foreign policy of Ronald Reagan would bear little resemblance to the realist, balance-of-power machinations of the Nixon-Kissinger years.[6] Many have claimed, for example, that NATO's 1983 Able Archer exercise was nearly misinterpreted by the Soviets as a sign that the United States was about to start a war in Europe. And while these breathless claims now appear to have been overstated,[7] there is no question that a more aggressive American strategy *could* have so rattled the Soviet Politburo that it *may* have started a third world war.

Yet, this (marginally) increased danger of war must be balanced against two other dangers: the danger that American weakness could invite a Soviet overreach, resulting in war, *and* the danger a perpetual Cold War held that some other miscalculation, technical malfunction, or mental breakdown of either sides' leadership could result in an accidental war. On balance, the Reagan administration judged (rightly in the author's view) that seeking to win the Cold War offered a lower chance of conflict in the long term than did attempting to manage it indefinitely.

There were, however, other risks inherent in the strategy, chief among them the risk that the Soviets would figure a way out of the strategic trap the Reagan administration had set for them. Some have argued that, for example, the Soviets could have saved themselves if they had reduced the crushing burden of their military expenditures, been less insistent about overcoming SDI, or reduced their massive outlays of aid to their Third World clients.[8] These specific claims, however, are highly questionable and rest on the inaccurate assessment that the root cause of the Soviet collapse was economic in nature. In truth, as argued in earlier chapters, the economic weaknesses of communism were the direct result of its irrational political system. If a reduction in military expenditures may have partially alleviated the Soviets' economic problems, why then did the Soviets not pursue such a course?

The answer is obvious: such a radical political decision was not possible given the highly ideological worldview espoused by Gorbachev and his predecessors. To permanently escape Reagan's trap, the Soviet leadership would have been required to jettison their commitment to Marxist ideology, thereby destroying the only justification for the Soviet regime. Otherwise, the best they could do was to pursue the course they eventually took: attempt to "muddle through" by tinkering with marginal improvements in the Soviet bureaucracy while attempting to sway Western public opinion into taking a softer line toward the Soviet Union. Indeed, such an effort very nearly succeeded, as evidenced by James Baker's efforts during George H. W. Bush's administration to prop up the failing Soviet government.[9]

The final, and certainly most significant, risk revolves around the question of how sustainable this strategy really was. As demonstrated in chapter 2, Reagan's strategy was a radical departure from those of his predecessors. And yet there was virtually no way to ensure that Reagan's strategy would continue to be implemented after January 1989. While Vice President George H. W. Bush was loyal to Reagan, it was no secret that he did not share all of Reagan's views, particularly in the area of U.S.-Soviet relations. Individuals who would become Bush's key foreign policy advisors, particularly Baker, did not support the plan outlined in NSDD-75, nor did they see the collapse of the Soviet Union as being in America's interest.[10] Thus, Reagan had only eight years in which to make his strategy work. Had the Soviets not been in so great a political and economic decline, or had the leadership of the United Kingdom, France, Germany, and the Vatican been less willing to support Reagan's efforts, or had the Soviets realized that Reagan's policies would not outlive his administration, this strategy may not have been successful. The George H. W. Bush administration would likely have resorted to a more traditional policy of containment, allowing the Soviets to cling to a central government rooted in Marxist ideology. In such a case, it is not inconceivable that historians of the early twenty-first century would remember the Reagan years as a period of heightened superpower tension that faded after the entry into office of a "more enlightened" American administration and the signing of a new arms control agreement. America's foreign policy would have continued to revolve around managing the U.S.-Soviet relationship, while its defense community continued to agonize over the military challenges stemming from a large-scale Warsaw Pact invasion through the Fulda Gap.

While the findings of the previous chapters provide a better, more complete picture of the Reagan administration, they also provoke some additional, more general conclusions about the necessity and universality of grand strategy, the challenges in its development and implementation, and the role of the individual in foreign policy. In light of the potential for a lengthy "global war on terrorism" (GWOT), the need for a prudent and comprehensive grand strategy becomes evident. The remainder of this chapter will draw out these conclusions and suggest additional areas into which further research should be done.

NECESSITY AND UNIVERSALITY OF GRAND STRATEGY

There are a number of reasons for arguing that some form of grand strategy is an absolute requirement for any president or head of state. Certainly the nature of the international system heavily favors the creation of a grand strategy. The modern international system is extraordinarily complicated. Determining how confrontational he should be in his relations with a potential adversary, how accommodating he should be to a current ally, and how he should balance his country's numerous competing economic, political, electoral, military, and moral interests are but a few of the decisions that a leader cannot make (or at least not well) without some form of grand strategy.

In addition to the pressures the international system exerts toward the development of a grand strategy, so are those of the modern state. Particularly in light of the difficulties inherent in controlling the contemporary bureaucratic state, any national leader who fails to harness and control the vast array of government agencies that nominally serve him faces almost certain ruin. When left to their own devices, such bureaucracies will inevitably dilute presidential authority, circumvent presidential decisions (at least those with which they disagree), and misallocate national resources. Grand strategy is a necessary (though not sufficient) condition for controlling these bureaucracies, as it should provide a clear vision of the beliefs and goals that will guide the use of the nation's tools of statecraft. Finally, leaders (at least in democratic countries) are presumably elected on a platform and are thus personally driven to achieve certain foreign policy objectives, even if only to fulfill their campaign promises. Absent some form of grand strategy, achieving these objectives is likely to prove extraordinarily difficult. For these reasons, developing and ensuring the implementation of grand strategy is one of a leader's central tasks.

Yet the necessity of a grand strategy does not always mean that it takes the form similar to the one the Reagan administration created. While documents roughly analogous to NSDD-75 (though, obviously, with different content) can be found in the archives of the Truman, Eisenhower, Johnson, Carter, and Bush administrations, it does not appear that a written, interagency-approved statement of America's strategy vis-à-vis the Soviet Union was ever created for the Kennedy, Nixon, or Ford administrations.[11] But even in the cases of these three administrations, some form of strategic thought was clearly evident. For example, any effort to identify the Nixon administration's grand strategy would clearly include Kissinger's contention that the world had become pentapolar as one of its core beliefs, the administration's efforts to play the balancing role between the various poles as one of its goals, and Nixon's diplomatic opening with China as one of the tools to achieve his goals. And while a detailed assessment of every Cold War president's grand strategy is far beyond the scope of this study, the central point remains clear: in one form or another, every president has developed and attempted to implement a grand strategy. A similar argument can be made for every head of state of every country in the world.

If every president has a grand strategy, what explains why some strategies fail while others succeed? There are a number of possible reasons, some of which are found in the definition of grand strategy developed in chapter 1—namely, *the planned use of all available tools of statecraft to achieve first-order national goals based on a given understanding or belief regarding the nature of the international system.* Thus, a carefully planned and focused effort, using every element of national power, aimed at clearly expressed goals, and based on an accurate understanding of the international system, has a much greater chance of success than one that is haphazardly implemented, pursues contradictory goals, or is rooted in wishful thinking or unrealistic beliefs about the international system.

At the same time, as pointed out earlier, even a well-made strategy (such as Reagan's) can fail, while a poorly developed one can occasionally succeed. Gorbachev's grand strategy, while deeply flawed, could have succeeded had a different president been in office. It is always possible that one's adversary could be more clever, more prepared, more capable, or even more fortunate, resulting in his victory. Clausewitz noted that "in war, everything is uncertain" and that success in war is "universally bound up with chance."[12] His observations about the uncertainty inherent in war are equally applicable regarding grand strategic conflict.

GRAND STRATEGY AFTER THE COLD WAR

One of the fundamental advantages that Cold War presidents had was a general recognition that America's grand strategy had to be focused on the Soviet Union. In fact, apart from a few isolated rumbles during the Carter administration claiming that the East-West dimension had become less important than the so-called North-South divide, America's grand strategy and its strategy vis-à-vis the Soviet Union were synonymous. Dealing with the international implications of Soviet power had been the central task of Western foreign policymakers since the end of World War II. The importance of a central organizing threat to grand strategy can be seen in the strategic confusion, hesitation, and outright failures that occurred in the ten-year period between the collapse of the Soviet Union in 1991 and the terrorist attacks of September 11, 2001.

As mentioned earlier, George H. W. Bush was never entirely comfortable with the aggressive attacks and ideological offensives that characterized the Reagan administration. His dominant foreign policy advisor, Secretary of State James Baker, did not see the collapse of the Soviet empire as necessarily good for the West, nor did he see the destruction of the Soviet state as something the United States should look upon favorably. The administration's general lack of any real vision of the purposes and goals of American foreign policy could have proven catastrophic at any other time of the Cold War. Fortunately such a vision was not necessary, as much of the administration's dealings with Eastern Europe and the Soviet Union involved responding to the tremendous changes that the previous administration had set in motion. With a few notable exceptions (such as discouraging the Baltic states from pursuing their long-denied and rightful independence), the Bush administration handled these changes about as well as could be hoped. But the absence of a unifying focus for U.S. foreign policy left American grand strategy adrift until the 1991 Gulf War.

The Iraqi invasion of Kuwait was the first sign that the relatively easy and (most importantly) peaceful resolution of the East-West conflict would not be typical of the post–Cold War era. Rather, it signaled to the Bush administration that addressing the threat and use of force outside the context of the East-West struggle would be a central challenge in the post–Cold War world and that America's grand strategy needed to reflect the new realities. It was in light of these events that President Bush outlined his hope for a "new world order" in which superior American power would be used, in concert with major allies, to respond to international aggression. At the same time, and partially to implement this vision, the Defense Department developed its own strategic concept, in which the United States would convince "potential competitors that they need not aspire to a greater role or pursue a more aggressive posture to protect their legitimate interests."[13] The domestic and international outcry resulting from the leak of this strategy, which was criticized (wrongly) as a sign that America intended to remain the sole superpower and would threaten any nation seeking to challenge it, was but the first of several examples of the difficulties in developing a post–Cold War grand strategy: the fundamentally different views of the beliefs and goals that should guide America's foreign policy.

These difficulties persisted through the Bill Clinton administration, which entered office with an entirely different set of guiding beliefs and major goals. The administration's use of diplomacy and military force in areas such as Haiti, Somalia, and the former Yugoslavia provide useful insights into its grand strategy. In Clinton's view, the primary challenge to American national security in the post–Cold War era was not another Desert Storm, but rather dealing with ancient hatreds and ethnic tension that had been suppressed or ignored during the Cold War and were now exploding across the globe. Peace-keeping, peace-making, and nation-building were the tasks that would occupy the West's military forces and diplomatic corps, while America's economic might and technological innovation would help mitigate the (alleged) causes of conflict by spreading prosperity and facilitating international communication and dialogue. Gone was the concern expressed by the previous administration regarding the rise of a rival superpower. In the Clinton administration's view, the rise of Europe and China, the two emerging superpowers, was inevitable. Thus, the proper strategy was not to challenge or oppose their rise, but rather to use multinational institutions and economic integration to alter gradually their perceptions of their interests (particularly in the case of China) in a direction more favorable to the United States. In doing so, the Clinton administration pursued a strategy similar to the one détente supporters urged the United States to follow during the 1970s. Unsurprisingly, many of the same conservatives who rejected the idea of détente with the USSR in the 1970s were equally hostile to the revival of such a concept in the post–Cold War 1990s. Conservatives criticized the Clinton administration as being too deferential to America's allies, too solicitous of China's great power ambitions, and too reluctant to use American power for more traditional national interests.

A great deal more could be said about the two post–Cold War grand strategies that emerged under the administrations of George H. W. Bush and Bill Clinton and the skill with which they were pursued. However, for the purposes of this study, the key point is that these strategies were fundamentally different both from the Reagan administration's approach and from each other. The fact that there were several competing approaches to American grand strategy during this period demonstrates the difficulties inherent in developing a grand strategy absent a clearly understood, obvious main challenger. Domestic political considerations, although present even during the Cold War, become harder to ignore and more influential in the absence of a strategic opponent, while the multitude of potential American goals can cause the president and his national security team to lose focus and begin pursuing ancillary, and even contradictory, goals. This lack of focus and the tendency to view foreign policy as a mere outgrowth of domestic policy makes it especially difficult for the national leadership to anticipate emerging strategic challenges, as evidenced by the fact that neither administration foresaw the rise of international terrorism, specifically the al Qaeda movement, as the next great challenge to American power and ideology.

GRAND STRATEGY AFTER 9/11

To say that the terrorist attacks of September 11, 2001 changed the way America thought about national strategy is to repeat the obvious. Not since Pearl Harbor had America been attacked so directly, nor had Americans civilians ever been so directly targeted as they were that day. In the aftermath of these attacks, a number of strategic thinkers highlighted the lessons America learned during the Cold War and attempted to apply them to the global war on terrorism.[14] They rightly noted, for example, that victory in the GWOT, like victory in the Cold War, required far more than defeating an armed adversary, but also discrediting a hostile, totalitarian ideology. As is the case in the GWOT, America's adversary in the Cold War threatened not merely Western security interests, but also its fundamental social, political, and economic institutions. The extreme ideology that animates al Qaeda can, like communism, be readily used as a means of subversion and is particularly adept at using the openness and freedom inherent in Western society as a shield to protect itself.

As a result, victory in the war on terrorism requires an integrated, wide-ranging effort to prevent terrorist attacks, while engaging in a sophisticated ideological battle to discredit radical Islamist thought. And while there are a number of important differences between the Cold War and the current war on terrorism, much of the Reagan administration's strategy can be readily applied to the GWOT. The next several paragraphs will briefly outline the central elements of an American grand strategy for the post-9/11 world.

Beliefs

The first core belief of a modern grand strategy must be a recognition of the centrality of American power to the international system. Contrary to the predictions of many pundits and the wishes of those who seek to strengthen international institutions such as the United Nations, the world is unipolar and is likely to remain so for the foreseeable future. Only the United States has the resources, capabilities, global reach, and willingness to combat terrorism worldwide. As a result, the locus of decision making for the GWOT will reside not in Turtle Bay, London, Paris, or Beijing, but in Washington. While the United States will certainly require the cooperation of many nations, the indispensable need for American power will necessarily make the GWOT, like the Cold War, a U.S.-centered enterprise.

A second core belief that should guide American strategy is the recognition that, given the open nature of Western societies, only an offensive posture can ultimately lead to a Western victory. In every Western city, there are hundreds of potential targets, any one of which could be attacked to cause panic, terror, and significant casualties. As a result, purely defensive measures such as police patrols, bag checks, border controls, and similar measures simply cannot provide an adequate level of protection while preserving the freedoms upon which Western society is based. Only by forcing terrorists onto the defensive, by actively disrupting terrorist planning, and aggressively targeting terrorist leaders (and their supporters), will the West have any hope of winning its struggle against terrorism.

A third guiding belief upon which America's strategy should be based is the understanding that Islamic radicalism is ultimately rooted in the political failures of the Islamic world. Unfortunately, this belief is not widely acknowledged, either among the ruling elite in the Muslim world or within much of the foreign policy elite in the West. Many argue that only massive increases in economic aid will "drain the swamp" of the angry young men who are turning to terrorism due to the lack of jobs and economic opportunities at home.[15] While it is comforting to believe that the threat of terrorism can be eliminated by merely "throwing money at the problem," in truth the problems are significantly more complex. Although there is no doubt that the lack of economic opportunities contributes to the terrorist problem, these economic shortcomings are fundamentally a result of the corrupt and undemocratic political systems existing throughout much of the Muslim world.

The final belief that should form the basis for America's GWOT strategy is a recognition of the political and moral superiority of democratic government. It is notable that this belief is virtually identical to the one the Reagan administration espoused in its own struggle with the Soviet Union. The reason for this similarity is obvious: in both cases, the driving force behind America's adversary is a philosophy and ideology that utterly rejects democratic governance. And while there is significantly less support for radical Islamism among Western intellectuals than there was for communism, it enjoys far greater support among the Islamic public than communism ever did among the people of Russia and Eastern Europe. It therefore remains critical that the United States make clear that it believes in and will vigorously assert the core values of democracy, such as the notion that all political power derives from the consent of the governed and that individuals possess certain inalienable rights. Faith in the universal attraction and power of these ideals is a crucial component to sustaining the support of the Western public and convincing the population of the Islamic world to turn against radical Islamism.

Goals

Preventing and responding effectively to terrorist attacks is perhaps the most obvious goal of America's GWOT strategy. Given that, for al Qaeda and its associated groups, successfully striking targets in the West is critical to their victory, effectively protecting the homeland is an absolute necessity. Requiring close coordination and cooperation among the law enforcement, intelligence, and "first responder" communities, this goal embodies the largely defensive approach to terrorism that existed prior to 9/11. While the terrorist attacks on the World Trade Center and the Pentagon certainly demonstrated the need to take a more proactive approach, it also highlighted the need for a much more robust set of defensive countermeasures. More aggressive offensive actions against terrorists can never prevent all attacks; as a result, a layered, reliable set of defenses are needed to identify and disrupt terrorist activity in the homeland while minimizing the impact of a successful terrorist attack. The need for an effective consequence management capability is especially important in light of the growing concern that terrorists may successfully use chemical, biological, or nuclear weapons.

Since terrorists must live, organize, train, and plan somewhere, a second key goal is the elimination of support and sanctuary for terrorist organizations. While an obvious example of such an effort was the destruction of the Taliban regime in Afghanistan, there remain a number of nations and individuals that provide Islamic radicals the support required to plan and conduct additional attacks. Although many such support nodes can be found throughout the Muslim world, it is also important to note that many exist in the Western democracies as well. The July 2005 bombings of the London transportation system, for example, were planned and conducted by legal residents of the United Kingdom. According to most accounts, terrorist cells exist in every major country of Western Europe, as well as within the United States itself. Indeed, the arrest of a New York City taxi driver accused of plotting to use weapons of mass destruction illustrates the danger posed by domestic terrorists. Whether provided as a matter of state policy or as a result of individuals acting alone, the United States needs to limit, reduce, and ultimately eliminate the outside support so critical to sustaining terrorist organizations.

A third important goal for America's GWOT strategy must be the capturing or killing of the key leadership figures within al Qaeda and its associated organizations. While much has been made of the fact that radical Islamist groups have become steadily more decentralized in recent years, it is important to recognize that this change has been the direct result of U.S. and allied success in dismantling and marginalizing al Qaeda's central leadership. And while these distributed operations pose a new set of counterterrorist challenges, on the whole this development is a favorable one, as these smaller, more regionally focused organizations are less capable of conducting the sensational attacks al Qaeda needs. Continued targeting of the remaining central leadership is crucial to preventing the regeneration of a more tightly controlled movement and enabling more successful operations against local groups.

A longer-term, but equally important, goal of America's grand strategy to fight terrorism is the discrediting of radical Islamic thought and the encouragement of a more moderate (and far more extensively practiced) version of Islam. This task will certainly prove immensely difficult, as it will require a subtlety and discretion rarely found in either Western political leadership or the national diplomatic corps. Indeed, because of the cultural differences between the West and the Muslim world, it is impossible for the United States or its allies to play the leading role in discrediting radical Islamism. Rather, much of the Western effort to achieve this goal will, by necessity, take the form of quiet but sustained support for legitimate Muslim religious leaders and prodemocracy nongovernmental organizations. Only by making clear to the Muslim world that radical Islamism will inevitably lead to political repression, moral bankruptcy, and economic hardship can the West help eliminate the environment that produces al Qaeda and its ilk.

Closely related to the previous goal, the United States must take the lead in reasserting the cultural and political values of Western civilization. It is, as Reagan understood, simply not enough to demonstrate the flaws and failures of a "rival faith" without highlighting the superiority of religious, cultural, political, and economic freedom. Doing so will serve a number of important strategic purposes. First, by demonstrating the West's commitment to religious freedom, it will reassure the Muslim world that the West has no hostile intent toward the peaceful practice of Islam. Second, by making clear that the West cannot be intimidated or frightened into abandoning its beliefs, it will dishearten violent extremists who believe that the West is too decadent to fight back. Third, demonstrating that the West continues to stand by its cultural and political traditions will strengthen the will of prodemocracy political reform movements, which can be found in virtually every Muslim nation. The success of these movements is critical to eliminating the political corruption that truly fuels Islamic radicalism.

Finally, it will serve as a constant reminder to Western publics that the stakes in this war are as absolute as they were during the Cold War, that losing the war on terrorism will mean nothing less than the wholesale destruction of the political, social, economic, and religious institutions that form the basis of Western civilization. The message the West must send to Islamic extremists is the same one

Reagan himself emphasized in his Westminster speech, that we are a "free people, worthy of freedom, and determined not only to remain so but to help others gain their freedom as well."[16]

Tools

While the threat and use of military power is an important component, as was the case with Reagan's strategy, America's GWOT strategy cannot be primarily a military-led effort. Since the stunningly successful U.S. invasion of Afghanistan, no other nation has so openly and blatantly backed al Qaeda and its associated groups. As a result, there simply are not a particularly large number of viable military targets, nor is there an obvious adversary who can be effectively threatened. Nevertheless, military power has played and will continue to play an important supporting role, particularly in concert with the intelligence community, in capturing or killing key al Qaeda leaders and forcibly cutting off support to terrorist organizations. Operations such as the use of armed unmanned aerial vehicles to kill terrorists along the Pakistan-Afghanistan border and the worldwide use of Special Operations forces against terrorist targets will be critically important to preventing terrorist attacks and acquiring additional intelligence on terrorist organizations. In addition, security assistance, counterterrorist training, and military-to-military contact will play an increasingly important role in strengthening the ability of friendly nations and key regional allies to protect themselves against terrorist attacks and conduct their own counterterrorist operations. Finally, novel approaches such as the Provincial Reconstruction Teams now operating in Afghanistan, which combine diplomacy, intelligence collection, and economic aid, represent another way for military power to contribute to the war on terrorism.

Similarly, whereas economic warfare played an absolutely central role in the Reagan strategy, its value in a modern GWOT strategy is less evident. Certainly efforts to track and cut off terrorist groups' funding sources are important and must continue. Yet the actual amount of money terrorists require to conduct even spectacular attacks is quite small. According to the National Commission on Terrorist Attacks upon the United States, the 9/11 attacks cost between $400,000 and $500,000 to plan and execute, a relatively small sum given the massive damage the attacks caused.[17] Preventing terrorist groups from obtaining this level of funding is virtually impossible. Unlike the Soviet Union, which only had a few options for obtaining the hard currency needed to fund its activities in the Third World, al Qaeda has numerous avenues for obtaining necessary funding, ranging from the voluntary contributions of wealthy supporters to drug smuggling to quasi-legitimate business dealings around the world.

Nevertheless, a few areas hold some promise for effectively using economic tools to attack al Qaeda and its affiliated groups. Much of their current funding still comes from a number of wealthy Middle Eastern donors, particularly Saudis. Identifying these individuals, then either seizing their assets or arresting them could interrupt the flow of resources to these groups. Unsurprisingly, however, doing so will not be easy, as some states in the region (despite their claims to the contrary) still have little interest in fighting Islamic extremism. Even in the states that do, these individuals represent a politically well-connected and influential "fifth column" that is difficult to eradicate, especially in regimes that are already politically unstable.

As with the Cold War, the West's victory in the GWOT will ultimately depend on politically and ideologically defeating Islamic extremism. Political tools will continue to be absolutely critical to this effort—even more so than during the struggle with communism. Unfortunately, to the (very limited) extent that the West has even tried to engage in a political contest with radical Islamism, its efforts have been halting, misguided, and poorly organized. The exaggerated, even hysterical concern that the West should do nothing that could potentially be seen as offensive to even a small segment of the Muslim community has led Western governments to shrink from making the forceful statements of Western values that are critical to sharpening the ideological dividing lines and winning the debate. The interagency approach to public diplomacy that proved so effective under Reagan has been abandoned; as a result, America's public diplomacy efforts (particularly in the Muslim world) have been haphazard and ineffective in explaining American policy abroad and attacking the political repression fueling extremism. Moving government-wide control over public diplomacy efforts back to the National Security Council is a necessary first step to improving America's conduct of the political war against Islamic extremists. Just as it did in the Cold War, the United States needs to make clear that it supports prodemocracy movements in the Muslim world and to encourage private, nongovernmental support to these movements.

Finally, presidential leadership is absolutely critical in making clear the stakes of the current struggle; already public support for the GWOT is unclear, particularly within Europe. Just as Reagan made clear to America and the world the fundamental distinctions between the free West and the totalitarian East, so too must America's leaders remind the people of the West that the struggle with al

Qaeda is not over U.S. support for Israel, the Iraq War, or America's support for the Saudi regime, but rather is a battle for the survival of Western civilization that could last a generation or longer.

By necessity, much of the war on terrorism will continue to rely on the intelligence community. Even more so than during the Cold War, effectively targeting al Qaeda and preventing terrorist attacks requires robust, reliable, and timely intelligence, as well as the much more aggressive use of covert action. Yet, by their very nature, terrorist organizations are "hard targets" that are extraordinarily difficult for any intelligence agency to penetrate or disrupt. And while some progress has been made in the years since 9/11, the West's intelligence community still needs to place greater emphasis on human intelligence, particularly information obtained by individuals acting under unofficial cover, if it wants to have any hope of penetrating modern terrorist organizations. At the same time, American policymakers will need to come to terms with some uncomfortable facts—namely, that perfectly accurate information on the locations or plans of terrorist groups will be extremely rare, that policymakers will increasingly need to take action based on supposition or educated guesses, and that, in some cases, this information will be wrong. Preparing Western publics for the inevitable mistakes that will occur, while making clear the value these operations can have, is vital to maintaining national support for these operations. In addition to some of the more obvious forms of covert action that have been used in the GWOT, such as clandestine strikes against specific terrorist targets, consideration should be given to other efforts as well, such as the covert funding of moderate prodemocracy groups in the Muslim world and the covert distribution of pro-Western information.

Unlike in the Cold War, there is also an important domestic component to America's GWOT strategy worth noting. Largely subsumed today under the title of "homeland security," it includes a number of important tasks for the war on terrorism. Three, in particular, stand out. First, ensuring that federal, state, and local governments have the skills and equipment needed to respond effectively to a major terrorist attack is crucial to protecting the American people. Billions of dollars have already been allocated toward such efforts, yet there remain questions about how well prepared the United States as a whole is for such an attack. Regular, robust planning at every level of government is ultimately the key to such efforts.

Second, effective border and immigration controls are needed to prevent terrorists from entering the United States as easily as the nineteen hijackers did for the 9/11 attacks. While a great deal has been done to control the flow of legal immigrants and visitors to the United States, America's borders with Mexico and Canada remain largely unpatrolled and easily crossed, making it relatively easy for potential terrorists to enter.

Third, the United States and its allies need to improve their individual and collective ability to use domestic law enforcement tools to identify, track, arrest, and prosecute terrorists and their supporters. In the past several years, the threat of domestic terrorism has grown dramatically. Aggressive investigation and the free flow of information between the intelligence and law enforcement communities are critical to the successful use of the criminal justice system in fighting terrorism.

The strategy outlined represents a brief description of how the definition of grand strategy can be applied to the post-9/11 world. In doing so, it reinforces the notion that the development and implementation of grand strategy is an enduring and vitally important task of statecraft. Drawn as it is from this author's own personal views, it reinforces the argument that a state's grand strategy, and hence its behavior, reflects the basic beliefs, central goals, and preferred tools of its leader. Reagan's role in his administration's grand strategy provides strong evidence that key leaders matter. This study will, therefore, conclude with some general observations on the role of the individual in the development and implementation of grand strategy, as well as in international affairs as a whole.

ROLE OF THE INDIVIDUAL

In recent years, the role of the individual in political science—and particularly in the field of international affairs—has largely vanished as a topic considered worthy of consideration. For example, neither of the two dominant schools of thought in international relations, neorealism and neoliberalism, place any significant emphasis on the motivations, beliefs, or thought processes of national leaders.[18] Similarly, efforts to identify sources of state behavior typically focus on state-level factors, such as organizational processes or bureaucratic politics.

The reasons for this lack of interest in the individual are as understandable as they are unfortunate. Much of international relations theory focuses on developing, testing, refining, and debating various explanatory models. Yet, by definition, every model must simplify reality, identify variables that can be readily applied across cases, and assign a value and relative weight (numerical or otherwise) to each variable. Applying such an approach to individuals is extremely difficult, as factors that are extremely important to one world leader may be entirely irrelevant to another. Any effort to capture a sizable number of leaders in a single model would quickly degenerate into an extremely broad and unwieldy framework lacking either explanatory or predictive power. Even if one were to focus solely on psychological factors to the exclusion of other potentially important factors such as domestic politics, the complexity of the human psyche is far too great to be easily modeled.[19] In short, there is no suitable model capable of accurately capturing the nature of individual decision making.

However, the inability to model individual decision making poses a significant challenge to any effort to model strategic development, primarily because, as the Reagan strategy demonstrates, the individual statesman is the key source of grand strategy. As shown in chapter 6, Reagan himself was the ultimate source of his administration's grand strategy. It reflected his beliefs about the nature of the international system and the motivation of his adversary. Reagan, not his advisors or the bureaucracy or the international system itself, set forth the goals his administration would pursue. He either approved of or personally got involved in every major tool his administration used to achieve his goals.

Nor was Reagan's personal influence on his administration's grand strategy unusual; one can certainly see the guiding spirits of Nixon, Carter, and Clinton in their respective administrations' grand strategies. In fact, for the national leader, grand strategy represents the only viable way to guide and control a nation's foreign policy. Since bureaucracies are not capable of developing or implementing true grand strategies, absent such a strategy imposed from the top they will instead pursue their own agendas, often contrary to the wishes of the president. Thus, because strategic development is so tightly bound to the individual decision maker, conventional decision-making models are unsuitable for effectively understanding and explaining grand strategy. Rather than relying on these flawed models, those seeking to understand a specific nation's grand strategy would be better served by obtaining a thorough understanding of the beliefs, perceptions, and ambitions of the nation's leader.

This finding, that the key to understanding grand strategy lies in the study of the individual leader, offers some interesting logical consequences. To the extent that international affairs as a whole is a struggle among the competing grand strategies of various states, the finding tends to make individual leaders the crux of the international system and thus to move the analysis of these leaders toward the center of the study of international affairs. Other disciplines would certainly continue to play an important role but primarily as a means of better understanding the constraints, tendencies, and pressures with which leaders must content. System-level international relations theory, for example, could help students gauge whether a leader's perceptions regarding the nature of the international system were accurate, while regional studies could provide valuable insights into the influence of culture, history, and religion on international leaders. Moving the field in this direction would ultimately push the academic study of international affairs toward a much more history-centric, rather than theory-centric, approach. While such a radical change in the field is unlikely (at least in the near future) given the vested interests that would vehemently oppose it, at the very least greater attention should be paid to the role of the individual in international affairs. As Reagan demonstrated, individual statesmen have far greater influence over the international scene than most analysts—or even the leaders themselves—realize. Closer study of that influence can only benefit the field as a whole.

NOTES

CHAPTER 1: DEFINING GRAND STRATEGY

1 See, for example, John Karaagac, *Between Promise and Policy: Ronald Reagan and Conservative Reformism* (Lanham, MD: Lexington Books, 2000), 39, or Charles W. Kegley, Jr., and Eugene R. Wittkopf, "The Reagan Administration's World View," *Orbis* 26, no. 1 (Spring 1982): 223–44.

2 Alexander Dallin and Gail W. Lapidus, "Reagan and the Russians: United States Policy towards the Soviet Union and Eastern Europe," in *Eagle Defiant: United States Foreign Policy in the 1980s*, eds. Kenneth A. Oye, Robert J. Lieber, and Donald Rothchild (Boston: Little, Brown, 1983), 202.

3 Karaagac, *Between Promise and Policy*, 58.

4 Lou Cannon, *President Reagan: The Role of a Lifetime* (New York: Simon & Schuster, 1991), 362–63.

5 Godfrey Hodgson, *The World Turned Right Side Up: A History of the Conservative Ascendancy in America* (Boston: Houghton Mifflin, 1996), 246.

6 See Cannon, *President Reagan*, 306, for an example of this too-common (and deeply flawed) categorization of Reagan administration officials.

7 George Shultz, *Turmoil and Triumph: My Years as Secretary of State* (New York: Charles Scribner's Sons, 1993), 267.

8 In fact, Cannon's book (which is widely considered one of the most "accurate" biographies of Reagan) perpetuates both of these flawed views at various points throughout. See, for example, his denigration of Reagan's intellect (137–38), knowledge of foreign affairs (295), management style (182), and decision making (363).

9 Most notably, Kiron K. Skinner, Annelise Anderson, and Martin Anderson, eds., *Reagan, in His Own Hand: The Writings of Ronald Reagan That Reveal His*

Revolutionary Vision for America (New York: Free Press, 2001); Kiron K. Skinner, Annelise Anderson, and Martin Anderson, eds., *Reagan: A Life in Letters* (New York: Free Press, 2003); and Kiron K. Skinner, Annelise Anderson, and Martin Anderson, eds., *Reagan's Path to Victory: The Shaping of Ronald Reagan's Vision; Selected Writings* (New York: Free Press, 2004); as well as Ronald W. Reagan, *The Reagan Diaries*, ed. Douglas Brinkley (New York: HarperCollins, 2007).

10   Even Sir Basil H. Liddell Hart, one of the greatest strategic thinkers of the twentieth century, makes this fundamental mistake. See Basil H. Liddell Hart, *Strategy*, second revised ed. (London: Faber & Faber, 1967), 321–22.

11   Carnes Lord, *The Modern Prince: What Leaders Need to Know Now* (New Haven, CT: Yale University Press, 2003), 106.

12   Ibid., 24.

13   Even this delineation is, in one sense, incomplete, since the quality and capability of one's tools can serve as a limiting mechanism for the setting of goals.

14   Alexander L. George, "The 'Operational Code': A Neglected Approach to the Study of Political Leaders and Decision-Making," *International Studies Quarterly* 13, no. 222 (June 1969): 191.

15   Carl von Clausewitz, *On War*, ed. and trans. Michael Howard and Peter Paret (Princeton, NJ: Princeton University Press, 1984), 117.

16   George, "'Operational Code,'"191. While George deserves much credit for highlighting the influence that beliefs have on the actions and decisions of policymakers, his "operational code" suffers from some serious flaws. First, for no apparent reason, he wrongly excludes personal ethical beliefs from being part of a leader's operational code. Second, and more importantly, his set of core questions used to develop a picture of a given leader's operational code is inadequate. It both fails to capture key elements of a leader's belief structure and captures other information that is less important or relevant to some decision makers. As a result, this study will not explicitly use George's approach in subsequent chapters.

17   The approach this section takes is drawn heavily from the thinking of Dr. Carnes Lord.

18   Hans J. Morgenthau, *Politics among Nations: The Struggle for Power and Peace* (New York: Knopf, 1978), 146.

19   Joseph S. Nye, Jr., *Bound to Lead: The Changing Nature of American Power* (New York: Basic Books, 1990), 31.

CHAPTER 2: THE REAGAN ADMINISTRATION'S GRAND STRATEGY

1   While almost every senior administration official carefully avoids discussing these documents in their memoirs, Edwin Meese does make a statement about Reagan's

grand strategy that is largely consistent with the key NSC documents. See Edwin
Meese, III, *With Reagan: The Inside Story* (Washington, DC: Regnery, 1992), 167.

2   "X" (George F. Kennan), "The Sources of Soviet Conduct," *Foreign Affairs* 25,
    no. 4 (July 1947), 582.

3   See James Roosevelt, ed., *The Liberal Papers* (Chicago: Quadrangle Books, 1962),
    for an excellent example of liberal opposition to containment.

4   Press conference cited in Cannon, *President Reagan*, 281.

5   Ronald W. Reagan, *An American Life* (New York: Simon & Schuster, 1990), 265.

6   Anatoly Dobrynin, *In Confidence: Moscow's Ambassador to America's Six Cold War
    Presidents 1962–1986* (New York: Times Books, 1995), 475.

7   Allan A. Myer to William P. Clark, memorandum, October 5, 1982, "Basic
    Differences between Reagan Administration's National Security Strategy (NSDD-
    32) and Carter Administration's Strategy (PD-18 and PD-62)," obtained at the
    Ronald Reagan Presidential Library, NSC Executive Secretariat Collection, Box
    OA91311.

8   George Shultz, "U.S.-Soviet Relations in the Context of U.S. Foreign Policy,"
    testimony before the Senate Foreign Relations Committee, June 15, 1983.

9   For example, John Lewis Gaddis, "The Rise, Fall and Future of Détente," *Foreign
    Affairs* 62, no. 2 (Winter 1983–1984): 354–77.

10 Strobe Talbott, *The Russians and Reagan* (New York: Vintage Books, 1984), 7.

11 George F. Kennan, *At a Century's Ending: Reflections 1982–1995* (New York:
    Norton, 1996), 51.

12 George F. Kennan, *The Nuclear Delusion: Soviet-American Relations in the Atomic
    Age* (New York: Pantheon Books, 1983), 148.

13 Dimitri K. Simes, "The New Soviet Challenge," *Foreign Policy* 55 (Summer
    1984): 117–22.

14 Ibid., 115.

15 John M. Joyce, "The Old Russian Legacy," *Foreign Policy* 55 (Summer 1984):
    137, 150.

16 "Response to NSSD 11-82: U.S. Relations with the USSR," December 6, 1982,
    obtained at the Ronald Reagan Presidential Library, NSC Executive Secretariat
    Collection, Box 91287.

17 Ibid., 4.

18 Ibid., 9.

19 Ibid., 7–8.

20   See Dallin and Lapidus, "Reagan and the Russians," 207.

21   "Response to NSSD 11-82," 4.

22   "U.S. Relations with the USSR," National Security Decision Directive NSDD-75, dated January 17, 1983, 1. Hereinafter cited as NSDD-75.

23   Reagan, *An American Life,* 549.

24   Ibid., 267.

25   Talbott, *Russians and Reagan,* 7.

26   William G. Hyland, "Clash with the Soviet Union," *Foreign Policy* 49 (Winter 1982–1983): 4.

27   Kennan, *Nuclear Delusion,* 162.

28   Reagan, *An American Life,* 237.

29   Christopher Andrew, *For the President's Eyes Only: Secret Intelligence and the American Presidency from Washington to Bush* (New York: HarperCollins, 1995), 468.

30   "Response to NSSD 11-82," 5.

31   Ibid., 11.

32   Louis J. Walinsky, "Coherent Defense Strategy: The Case for Economic Denial," *Foreign Affairs* 61, no. 2 (Winter 1982–1983): 281–83.

33   "Response to NSSD 11-82," 10.

34   Ibid., 7.

35   Robert M. Gates, *From the Shadows: The Ultimate Insider's Story of Five Presidents and How They Won the Cold War* (New York: Simon & Schuster, 1996), 187.

36   "Response to NSSD 11-82," 8.

37   C. Robert Zelnick, "Pipe Dreams: The Foundering Soviets," *Foreign Policy* 57 (Winter 1984–1985): 93.

38   Ibid., 100.

39   Michael Binyon, *Life in Russia* (New York: Pantheon Books, 1983), 276.

40   Zelnick, "Pipe Dreams," 101.

41   Seweryn Bialer and Joan Afferica, "Reagan and Russia," *Foreign Affairs* 61, no. 2 (Winter 1982–1983): 263.

42   Binyon, *Life in Russia,* 3–4.

43   Cannon, *President Reagan,* 281.

44   Reagan, *An American Life,* 715.

45   Skinner et al., *Reagan, in His Own Hand*, 60.

46   NSDD-75, 3.

47   "U.S. National Security Strategy," National Security Decision Directive, NSDD-32, dated May 20, 1982, 1–2 (hereinafter cited as NSDD-32) and NSDD-75, 1.

48   NSDD-32, 1.

49   Caspar Weinberger, *Fighting for Peace: Seven Critical Years in the Pentagon* (New York: Warner Books, 1991), 293.

50   Martin Anderson, *Revolution: The Reagan Legacy* (Stanford, CA: Hoover Institution Press, 1990), 92.

51   NSDD-32, 1.

52   Christopher Layne, "The Real Conservative Agenda," *Foreign Policy* 61 (Winter 1985): 74.

53   Kenneth A. Oye, "International Systems Structure and American Foreign Policy," in Oye et al., eds., *Eagle Defiant*, 17.

54   Charles William Maynes, "Old Errors in the New Cold War," *Foreign Policy* 46 (Spring 1982): 101.

55   "Response to NSSD 11-82," 22.

56   Ibid., 33.

57   See Stephen S. Rosenfeld, "NATO: Read the Fine Print," *Washington Post*, May 8, 1981.

58   Cannon, *President Reagan*, 298.

59   "Response to NSSD 11-82," 38.

60   Talbott, *Russians and Reagan*, 67.

61   NSDD-75, 1.

62   "Response to NSSD 11-82," 39.

63   NSDD-75, 8.

64   Ibid., 1. See also NSDD-32, 1.

65   "Response to NSSD 11-82," 35.

66   NSDD-75, 4.

67   See ibid., 1, and NSDD-32, 2.

68   "Response to NSSD 11-82," 1.

69   Jeane Kirkpatrick, interview by author, January 10, 2002, American Enterprise Institute.

70   "Response to NSSD 11-82," 23.

71   The three risks outlined below are drawn from "Response to NSSD 11-82," 24.

72   Marshall D. Shulman, "Sensible Policy toward Moscow," *New York Times*, June 27, 1982.

73   Hyland, "Clash with the Soviet Union," 7.

74   Zelnick, "Pipe Dreams," 98.

75   Ronald Reagan, "Promoting Democracy and Peace," speech given to the British Parliament on June 8, 1982, in *Realism, Strength, Negotiation: Key Foreign Policy Statements of the Reagan Administration* (Washington, DC: Department of State, 1984), 80.

76   Reagan, *An American Life*, 267.

77   "Response to NSSD 11-82," 8.

78   For the former view, see Strobe Talbott, "Rethinking the Red Menace," *Time*, January 1, 1990, 66–73. For the latter view, see Richard Ned Lebow and Janice Gross Stein, "Reagan and the Russians," *Atlantic Monthly*, February 1994, 35–37.

79   Roger Robinson, interview by author, October 2, 2002, Center for Security Policy.

80   "East-West Economic Relations and Poland-Related Sanctions," National Security Decision Directive, NSDD-66, dated November 16, 1982, 1. Hereinafter cited as NSDD-66.

81   Ibid., 1. COCOM was created in 1949 to prevent the flow of controlled technology to the Soviet bloc. Under COCOM rules, the export of a controlled technology to the USSR was prohibited unless all members agreed to permit the transfer.

82   Ibid., 2.

83   Robinson interview, October 2, 2002.

84   NSDD-66, 2.

85   Peter Schweizer, *Victory: The Reagan Administration's Secret Strategy That Hastened the Collapse of the Soviet Union* (New York: Atlantic Monthly, 1994), 135.

86   John F. Burns, "Moscow: Arms Buildup Is Economic Warfare," *New York Times*, June 13, 1982.

87   NSDD-75, 6.

88   For a fuller discussion of the decline of public diplomacy prior to the Reagan administration, see Carnes Lord, "The Past and Future of Public Diplomacy," *Orbis* 42, no. 1 (Winter 1998): 49–73.

89   Ibid.

90   Ibid.

91   "United States International Broadcasting," National Security Decision Directive, NSDD-45, dated July 15, 1982, 1. Hereinafter cited as NSDD-45.

92   John Spicer Nichols, "Wasting the Propaganda Dollar," *Foreign Policy* 54 (Fall 1984): 129.

93   "Management of Public Diplomacy Relative to National Security," National Security Decision Directive, NSDD-77, January 14, 1983, 1. Hereinafter cited as NSDD-77.

94   "US International Information Policy," National Security Decision Directive, NSDD-130, March 6, 1984, 1. Hereinafter cited as NSDD-130.

95   Ibid., 1–3.

96   Lord, "Past and Future of Public Diplomacy."

97   "Transcript of President's First News Conference on Foreign and Domestic Topics," *New York Times*, January 30, 1981.

98   Lord, "Past and Future of Public Diplomacy."

99   Reagan, "Promoting Democracy and Peace," 80.

100 For a more detailed discussion of the creation and activities of the NED, see Peter Schweizer, *Reagan's War: The Epic Story of His Forty-Year Struggle and Final Triumph over Communism* (New York: Doubleday, 2002), 184–88.

101 Lord, "Past and Future of Public Diplomacy."

102 See NSDD-32, 1, and NSDD-75, 4.

103 Richard V. Allen, "The Man Who Changed the Game Plan," *The National Interest*, no. 44 (Summer 1996): 64–65.

104 Schweizer, *Victory*, 75.

105 Ibid., 173.

106 Vetrov's story can be found in Gus W. Weiss, "The Farewell Dossier," *Studies in Intelligence* 39, no. 5, 1996, available at http://www.odci.gov/csi/studies/96unclas/farewell.htm, as well as Schweizer, *Victory*, 187–89.

CHAPTER 3: BELIEFS

1   See Schweizer, *Reagan's War*, for an excellent overview of Reagan's lifelong interest in foreign policy.

2   "X" (Kennan), "Sources of Soviet Conduct," 566–82.

3 Ibid., 582.

4 George Nash, *The Conservative Intellectual Movement since 1945* (New York: Basic Books, 1976), 91, 149.

5 Zygmunt Nagorski, Jr., "NATO and the Captive Nations," *The Annals of the American Academy of Political and Social Science* 284 (July 1953): 79.

6 James Burnham, *The Coming Defeat of Communism* (New York: John Day, 1950), 24.

7 Ibid., 99.

8 Eugene Lyons, *Our Secret Allies: The Peoples of Russia* (New York: Duell, Sloan and Pearce, 1953), 297.

9 Charles J. Kersten, "The Liberation Policy and International Order," *The Annals of the American Academy of Political and Social Science* 284 (July 1953): 97.

10 Burnham, *Coming Defeat*, 25.

11 Ibid., 26.

12 Ibid., 134.

13 Lyons, *Our Secret Allies*, 302.

14 Kersten, "Liberation Policy," 101.

15 Robert R. Bowie and Richard H. Immerman, *Waging Peace: How Eisenhower Shaped an Enduring Cold War Strategy* (New York: Oxford University Press, 1998), 137. In this work, the terms "rollback" and "liberation" will be used interchangeably.

16 Robert Strausz-Hupé, William R. Kintner, James E. Dougherty, and Alvin J. Cottrell, *Protracted Conflict* (New York: Harper, 1959), 21. See also James Burnham, *The War We Are In* (New Rochelle, NY: Arlington House, 1967), 20.

17 Robert Strausz-Hupé, William R. Kintner, and Stefan T. Possony, *A Forward Strategy for America* (New York: Harper, 1961), 29.

18 David Sarnoff, "A Political Offensive against Communism," in *American Strategy for the Nuclear Age*, eds. Walter F. Hahn and John C. Neff (Garden City, NY: Doubleday, 1960), 425.

19 Barry M. Goldwater, "A Foreign Policy for America," *National Review* 10, no. 11 (March 25, 1961): 178–79.

20 Strausz-Hupé, *Forward Strategy*, 35, 45. See also Frank S. Meyer, "'New Ideas' or 'Old Truths,'" in *The Conservative Mainstream*, ed. Frank S. Meyer (New Rochelle, NY: Arlington House, 1969), 319.

21 James Burnham, "Some Proposals to a Goldwater Administration Regarding Foreign Policy," *National Review* 16, no. 28 (July 14, 1964): 590. For a fuller

discussion, see Jonathan Martin Kolkey, *The New Right, 1960–1968: With Epilogue, 1969–1980* (Washington, DC: University Press of America, 1983), 116–17.

22   Gerhart Niemeyer, "Détente and Ideological Struggle," in Gerhart Niemeyer, *Aftersight and Foresight: Selected Essays* (Lanham, MD: University Press of America, 1988), 134.

23   Frank J. Johnson, *No Substitute for Victory* (Chicago: Regnery, 1962), 33. See also, M. Stanton Evans, *The Politics of Surrender* (New York: Devin-Adair, 1966), 35–37.

24   Niemeyer, "Détente," 128, 132.

25   Barry M. Goldwater, *Why Not Victory?* (New York: McGraw-Hill, 1962), 25.

26   Gary Dorrien, *The Neoconservative Mind: Politics, Culture and the War of Ideology* (Philadelphia: Temple University Press, 1993), 19.

27   See Brian Crozier, *Strategy of Survival* (New Rochelle, NY: Arlington House Publishers, 1978), 151–56, for a good example of conservative criticisms of containment from this period.

28   For more information on the founding of the CPD, see Paul H. Nitze, *From Hiroshima to Glasnost: At the Center of Decision; A Memoir* (New York: Grove Weidenfeld, 1989), 353–54; Hodgson, *World Turned Right Side Up*, 236–37; and Jay Winik, *On the Brink: The Dramatic, Behind-the-Scenes Saga of the Reagan Era and the Men and Women Who Won the Cold War* (New York: Simon & Schuster, 1996), 110–12. For a more critical history of the CPD, see Jerry W. Sanders, *Peddlers of Crisis: The Committee on the Present Danger and the Politics of Containment* (Boston: South End, 1983).

29   Sanders, *Peddlers*, 282.

30   Marshall D. Shulman, "What Does Security Mean Today?" *Foreign Affairs* 49, no. 4 (July 1971): 613.

31   Theodore Draper, "Détente," *Commentary* 57, no. 6 (June 1974): 38. For the complete text of the agreement, see Richard Nixon, "Text of the 'Basic Principles of Relations Between the United States of America and the Union of Soviet Socialist Republics,'" May 29, 1972.

32   Leopold Labedz, "USA and the World Today: Kissinger and After," *Survey: A Journal of Soviet and East European Studies* 22, no. 1 (Winter 1976): 2.

33   Robert Conquest, *Present Danger: Toward a Foreign Policy* (Stanford, CA: Hoover Institution Press, 1979), 32.

34   Central Intelligence Agency, *Intelligence Community Experiment in Competitive Analysis, Soviet Strategic Objectives: An Alternative View, Report of Team "B,"* December 1976, 5. The "Team B Report" was conducted in response to complaints that the CIA's analysis of the Soviet military buildup was biased in favor of détente and overly optimistic about Soviet intentions. Team B was led by Richard Pipes and

included several other well-known conservatives, including William Van Cleave, Daniel Graham, and Paul Nitze.

35   Eugene V. Rostow, "The Safety of the Republic: Can the Tide Be Turned?" *Strategic Review* 4 (October 1976): 18.

36   Crozier, *Strategy of Survival*, 173. See also Patrick J. Buchanan, *Conservative Votes, Liberal Victories: Why the Right Has Failed* (New York: Quadrangle Books, 1975), 157.

37   Labedz, "USA and the World Today," 29. See also, Gerhart Niemeyer, *Deceitful Peace* (New Rochelle, NY: Arlington House, 1971), 162–72, and Norman Podhoretz, "The Future Danger," *Commentary* 71, no. 4 (April 1981): 47.

38   "X" (Kennan), "Sources of Soviet Conduct," 572.

39   Hannah Arendt, *The Origins of Totalitarianism* (New York: Harcourt, Brace, 1951), 316.

40   Ibid., 336–37.

41   Whittaker Chambers, *Witness* (New York: Random House, 1952), 9.

42   James Burnham, *The Struggle for the World* (New York: John Day, 1947), 60.

43   Ibid., 92. See also Lyons, *Secret Allies*, 299.

44   William Henry Chamberlin, *Appeasement: The Road to War* (New York: Rolton House, 1962), 36.

45   Lyons, *Our Secret Allies*, 312.

46   Ibid., 106.

47   Burnham, *Coming Defeat*, 83.

48   Nash, *Conservative Intellectual Movement*, 268.

49   McGeorge Bundy, "To Cap the Volcano," *Foreign Affairs* 48, no. 1 (October 1969): 12.

50   Strausz-Hupé et al., *Protracted Conflict*, 8. See also Johnson, *No Substitute for Victory*, 1, and William R. Kintner with Joseph Z. Kornfeder, *The New Frontier of War: Political Warfare, Present and Future* (Chicago: Regnery, 1962), xii.

51   Bertram D. Wolfe, "Communist Ideology and Soviet Foreign Policy," *Foreign Affairs* 41, no. 1 (October 1962): 167.

52   Strausz-Hupé et al., *Forward Strategy*, 22. See also, Frank S. Meyer, "Of Khrushchev, Stalin, and Sitting Ducks," in Meyer, *Conservative Mainstream*, 309.

53   Gerhart Niemeyer, "The Ideological Core of Communism," in Hahn and Neff, *American Strategy*, 56.

54   Gerhart Niemeyer, "The Communist Mind," in Niemeyer, *Aftersight and Foresight*, 73.

55   Goldwater, *Why Not Victory?*, 38–40.

56   George F. Kennan, *The Cloud of Danger: Current Realities of American Foreign Policy* (Boston: Little, Brown, 1977), 174. It is worth pointing out that Kennan's view of communism's influence on Soviet behavior changed over time. The view expressed in *The Cloud of Danger* does not, for example, correspond to the view he expressed in "The Sources of Soviet Conduct."

57   Shulman, "What Does Security Mean Today?," 614. In fairness, this view was also held by a few conservatives and neoconservatives. See, for example, Hans J. Morgenthau, "Changes and Chances in American-Soviet Relations," *Foreign Affairs* 39, no. 3 (April 1971): 432, and Irving Kristol, *Reflections of a Neoconservative: Looking Back, Looking Ahead* (New York: Basic Books, 1983), 23.

58   Richard Pipes, "Why the Soviet Union Thinks It Could Fight and Win a Nuclear War," *Commentary* 64, no. 1 (July 1977): 26.

59   Labedz, "USA and the World Today," 8. Similar arguments were made throughout the 1980s as well. See, for example, H. Joachim Maître, "Soviet Military Power," in *To Promote Peace: U.S. Foreign Policy in the Mid-1980s*, ed. Dennis L. Bark (Stanford, CA: Hoover Institution Press, 1984), 221.

60   Jeane Kirkpatrick, *Dictatorships and Double Standards* (New York: Simon & Schuster, 1982), 64.

61   Richard Pipes, "Soviet Global Strategy," *Commentary* 69, no. 4 (April 1980): 31–32. See also Barry M. Goldwater, "The Perilous Conjuncture: Soviet Ascendancy and American Isolationism," *Orbis* 15, no. 1 (Winter 1971): 53.

62   Jean-François Revel, *The Totalitarian Temptation* (New York: Doubleday, 1977), 30.

63   Richard Pipes, "Basic Soviet Institutions Have Not Changed," in *Decline of the West? George Kennan and His Critics*, ed. Martin F. Herz (Washington, DC: Ethics and Public Policy Center, Georgetown University, 1978), 62–63.

64   Conquest, *Present Danger*, 13. See also, Niemeyer, *Deceitful Peace*, 93.

65   Kirkpatrick, *Dictatorships*, 110. See also, Crozier, *Strategy of Survival*, 131.

66   Arthur M. Schlesinger, Jr., *The Vital Center: The Politics of Freedom* (Boston: Houghton Mifflin, 1949), 225.

67   Burnham, *Struggle for the World*, 95.

68   Arendt, *Origins*, 379.

69   Charles E. Osgood, "Reciprocal Initiative," in *Liberal Papers*, ed. Roosevelt, 168.

70   Bundy, "To Cap the Volcano," 17.

71   Bertram D. Wolfe, "Communist Vulnerabilities," in Hahn and Neff, *American Strategy*, 90. It is important to note that some anticommunist liberals agreed with this assessment. See, for example, Dean G. Acheson, "Premises of American Policy," in Hahn and Neff, *American Strategy*, 417.

72   Wolfe, "Communist Ideology," 161–62.

73   William R. Kintner, *Peace and the Strategy Conflict* (New York: Praeger, 1967), 3. See also, Burnham, *War We Are In*, 145.

74   Burnham, "Some Proposals," 590.

75   Shulman, "What Does Security Mean Today?," 607.

76   George F. Kennan, "After the Cold War: American Foreign Policy in the 1970s," *Foreign Affairs* 51, no. 1 (October 1972): 220.

77   Carl Gershman, "The Rise and Fall of the New Foreign Policy Establishment," *Commentary* 70, no. 1 (January 1980): 22. See also Crozier, *Strategy of Survival*, 40.

78   Committee on the Present Danger, "Peace with Freedom: A Discussion by the Committee on the Present Danger before the Foreign Policy Association, 14 March 1978," in *Alerting America: The Papers of the Committee on the Present Danger*, ed. Charles Tyroler II (Washington, DC: Pergamon-Brassey's, 1984), 28.

79   Fred Charles Iklé, "Arms Control and National Defense," in *The United States in the 1980s*, eds. Peter Duignan and Alvin Rabushka (Stanford, CA: Hoover Institution Press, 1980), 433.

80   Committee on the Present Danger, "Common Sense and the Common Danger," Policy Statement issued November 11, 1976, in Tyroler, *Alerting America*, 4.

81   Labedz, "USA and the World Today," 9. See also Conquest, *Present Danger*, 51.

82   Burnham, *Coming Defeat*, 111.

83   Burnham, *Struggle for the World*, 116.

84   Burnham, *Coming Defeat*, 113–22.

85   Arendt, *Origins*, 378.

86   Burnham, *Coming Defeat*, 124.

87   See, for example, Lyons, *Our Secret Allies*, 326.

88   It must be stressed, however, that the Soviets' shift from military intimidation to political subversion represented only a change in Soviet tactics, not goals.

89   Strausz-Hupé et al., *Protracted Conflict*, 142.

90   Stefan T. Possony, "The Challenge of Russian Totalitarianism," *Orbis* 8, no. 4 (1965): 765.

91   Strausz-Hupé et al., *Protracted Conflict*, 79. See also Johnson, *No Substitute*, 123, and Burnham, "Some Proposals," 590.

92   Kintner, *New Frontier of War*, 323. See also Evans, *Politics of Surrender*, 523.

93   Kintner, *New Frontier of War*, 324.

94   Ibid., 322. See also Sarnoff, "Political Offensive," 425–26.

95   Strausz-Hupé, *Forward Strategy*, 276–77. See also Wolfe, "Communist Vulnerabilities," 100.

96   Ralph James, "The Soviet Economy," in *Handbook on Communism*, eds. Joseph Bochenski and Gerhart Niemeyer (New York: Praeger, 1962), 444. See also, Kintner, *Peace and the Strategy Conflict*, 87–88.

97   G. Warren Nutter, "The Effects of Economic Growth on Sino-Soviet Strategy," in *National Security: Political, Military, and Economic Strategies in the Decade Ahead*, eds. David M. Abshire and Richard V. Allen (Stanford, CA: Hoover Institution Press, 1963), 162.

98   Brian Crozier, "Apocalyptic Thoughts," *National Review* 33, no. 10 (May 29, 1981): 604.

99   Richard Pipes, *Survival Is Not Enough* (New York: Simon & Schuster, 1984), 114. See also Niemeyer, *Deceitful Peace*, 96.

100   R. Sean Randolph, "Trading with the Enemy: A Happy Way to Die?," *National Review* 32, no. 19 (September 19, 1980): 1133. See also Robert Conquest, "A New Russia? A New World?," *Foreign Affairs* 53, no. 3 (April 1975): 485–95.

101   M. Stanton Evans, "Selling the West," *National Review* 31, no. 1 (January 5, 1979): 33.

102   Crozier, *Strategy of Survival*, 158. See also Buchanan, *Conservative Votes*, 152.

103   Conquest, *Present Danger*, 30.

104   Revel, *Totalitarian Temptation*, 267–68. See also Kristol, *Reflections*, 273, and Pipes, *Survival Is Not Enough*, 200.

105   Crozier, *Strategy of Survival*, 161–62 (emphasis in original). See also Walter Laqueur, "Containment for the 1980s," *Commentary* 70, no. 4 (October 1980): 41.

106   Edward N. Luttwak, "After Afghanistan, What?" *Commentary* 69, no. 4 (April 1980): 45.

107   Karaagac, *Between Promise*, 74.

108   Burnham, *Struggle for the World*, 187–89.

109   Burnham, *Coming Defeat*, 10. Similar concerns are expressed in Arendt, *Origins*, 379, and Niemeyer, *Deceitful Peace*, 176.

110   Frank S. Meyer, "The Relativist 'Re-evaluates' Evil," *National Review* 3, no. 18 (May 4, 1957): 429. See also Kersten, "Liberation Policy," 103, and Edmund A. Walsh, *Total Empire: The Roots and Progress of World Communism* (Milwaukee, WI: Bruce, 1951), 99–100.

111   William Henry Chamberlin, *Beyond Containment* (Chicago: Regnery, 1953), 348–49.

112   Schlesinger, *Vital Center*, 246.

113   J. David Hoeveler, *Watch on the Right: Conservative Intellectuals in the Reagan Era* (Madison: University of Wisconsin Press, 1991), 131. This belief in traditional American values was shared by much of the pro-Goldwater movement. See John A. Andrew, III, *The Other Side of the Sixties: Young Americans for Freedom and the Rise of Conservative Politics* (New Brunswick, NJ: Rutgers University Press, 1997), 19.

114   Strausz-Hupé et al., *Forward Strategy*, 11. His concern about Western materialism can be found in Strausz-Hupé et al., *Protracted Conflict*, 144.

115   Goldwater, *Why Not Victory?*, 34. See also Kintner, *New Frontier of War*, 341, and Labedz, "USA and the World Today," 36.

116   Osgood, "Reciprocal Initiative," 188.

117   James Warburg, "A Re-Examination of American Foreign Policy," in Roosevelt, *Liberal Papers*, 82.

118   Johnson, *No Subsitute*, 5.

119   George F. Kennan and George Urban, "From Containment to . . . Self-Containment" in Herz, *Decline of the West?*, 15. See also Kennan, *Nuclear Delusion*, 145.

120   Nathan Glazer, "American Values and American Foreign Policy," *Commentary* 62, no. 1 (July 1976): 37. See also Norman Podhoretz, "The Present Danger," *Commentary* 69, no. 3 (March 1980): 27–40.

121   Peter Steinfels, *The Neoconservatives: The Men Who Are Changing America's Politics* (New York: Simon & Schuster, 1979), 150.

122   Kirkpatrick, *Dictatorships*, 92. See also Michael Ledeen, *Grave New World* (New York: Oxford University Press, 1985), 25.

123   Revel, *Totalitarian Temptation*, 22, 33.

124   Conquest, *Present Danger*, 58–59. See also Committee on the Present Danger, "Common Sense and the Common Danger," 4, Buchanan, *Conservative Votes*, 159, and William R. Kintner, "A Program for America: Freedom and Foreign Policy," *Orbis* 21, no. 1 (Spring 1977): 148.

CHAPTER 4: GOALS

1   Bernard Brodie, "The Absolute Weapon," in *The Absolute Weapon: Atomic Power and World Order*, ed. Bernard Brodie (New York: Harcourt, Brace, 1946), 24, 76.

2   Ibid., 76.

3   Burnham, *Struggle for the World*, 36.

4   Burnham, *Coming Defeat*, 140.

5   This figure has been quoted widely and can be found in Lawrence Freedman, "The First Two Generations of Nuclear Strategists," in *Makers of Modern Strategy: From Machiavelli to the Nuclear Age*, ed. Peter Paret (Princeton, NJ: Princeton University Press, 1986), 758.

6   Strausz-Hupé et al., *Forward Strategy*, 95.

7   Ibid., 115 (emphasis in original).

8   Gerhart Niemeyer, "Political Requirements," in *National Security*, Abshire and Allen, 262.

9   Johnson, *No Substitute for Victory*, 7.

10 One must, as always, be very careful about such generalizations, as there were some "Cold War liberals" who were very uncomfortable with MAD and some conservatives who supported the concept.

11 Robert Jervis, "Why Nuclear Superiority Doesn't Matter," *Political Science Quarterly* 94, no. 4 (Winter 1979–1980): 618.

12 Paul H. Nitze, "The Relationship of Strategic and Theater Forces," *International Security* 2, no. 2 (Autumn 1977): 123.

13 Committee on the Present Danger, "What Is the Soviet Union Up To?," in Tyroler, *Alerting America*, 13. See also Robert Conquest, "The Limits of Détente," *Foreign Affairs* 46, no. 4 (July 1968): 736.

14 Colin S. Gray and Keith Payne, "Victory Is Possible," *Foreign Policy*, no. 39 (Summer 1980): 26–27.

15 Nitze, "Relationship of Strategic," 128. See also Iklé, "Arms Control," 438.

16 Richard Burt, "Reassessing the Strategic Balance," *International Security* 5, no. 1 (Summer 1980): 48. See also Charles Burton Marshall, "Strategy: The Emerging Dangers," in *National Security in the 1980s: From Weakness to Strength*, ed. W. Scott Thompson (San Francisco: Institute for Contemporary Studies, 1980), 439.

17 Gray and Payne, "Victory Is Possible," 16.

18 For a good example of liberal views on decolonization, see Chester Bowles, *The New Dimensions of Peace* (New York: Harper, 1955).

19   Burnham, *Coming Defeat*, 141.

20   Walsh, *Total Empire*, 219.

21   Burnham, *Coming Defeat*, 198.

22   Warburg, "A Re-Examination," 54.

23   Ibid., 85.

24   Goldwater, *Why Not Victory?*, 38. See also Johnson, *No Substitute*, 124.

25   Strausz-Hupé et al., *Forward Strategy*, 235.

26   Goldwater, "A Foreign Policy," 178.

27   Kennan and Urban, "From Containment," 13.

28   Ibid., 18.

29   Edward M. Kennedy, "Beyond Détente," *Foreign Policy* 16 (Fall 1974): 20.

30   See, for example, Layne, "Real Conservative Agenda," 74.

31   Richard J. Barnet, "U.S.-Soviet Relations: The Need for a Comprehensive Approach," *Foreign Affairs* 51, no. 4 (Spring 1979): 789.

32   Norman Podhoretz, "Future Danger," 41.

33   Niemeyer, *Deceitful Peace*, 201.

34   William F. Buckley, Jr., *Inveighing We Will Go* (New York: Putnam, 1972), 95.

35   Crozier, *Strategy of Survival*, 191.

36   Kirkpatrick, *Dictatorships and Double Standards*, 89.

37   Gershman, "Rise and Fall," 21. See also Pipes, "Soviet Global Strategy," 39.

38   Rostow, "Safety of the Republic," 25. See also Labedz, "USA and the World Today," 15.

39   Gary W. Reichard, "Divisions and Dissent: Democrats and Foreign Policy, 1952–1956," *Political Science Quarterly* 93, no. 1 (Spring 1978): 57.

40   The fundamental divide within the Democratic Party can be seen by comparing Dean G. Acheson, *A Democrat Looks at His Party* (New York: Harper, 1955), and Bowles, *New Dimensions*.

41   Edward Teller, "Alternatives for Security," *Foreign Affairs* 36, no. 2 (January 1958): 203.

42   Burnham, *Coming Defeat*, 37.

43   Ibid., 41. See Arendt, *Origins of Totalitarianism*, 379, for a fuller discussion of the differences between the West and totalitarian governments on this point.

44   Osgood, "Reciprocal Initiative," 175.

45   Strausz-Hupé et al., *Forward Strategy*, 222.

46   Goldwater, *Why Not Victory?*, 114.

47   Strausz-Hupé et al., *Forward Strategy*, 215.

48   Kintner, *Peace and the Strategy Conflict*, 137. See also Evans, *Politics of Surrender*, 30.

49   Kennedy, *Beyond Détente*, 8.

50   Barnet, *U.S.-Soviet Relations*, 780.

51   Niemeyer, *Deceitful Peace*, 172.

52   Committee on the Present Danger, "Where We Stand on SALT," in Tyroler, *Alerting America*, 16–17.

53   William R. Van Cleave, "SALT on the Eagle's Tail," *Strategic Review* 4, no. 2 (Spring 1976): 46. It is worth noting that the idea of equal limits would become a centerpiece of Reagan's arms control proposals.

54   Colin S. Gray, "SALT: Time to Quit," *Strategic Review* 4, no. 4 (Fall 1976): 15–16. See also Conquest, *Present Danger*, 51.

55   Schlesinger, *Vital Center*, 224.

56   Peter Grose, *Operation Rollback: America's Secret War behind the Iron Curtain* (Boston: Houghton Mifflin, 2000), 209.

57   Bowie and Immerman, *Waging Peace*, 137. Project Solarium (also known as the Solarium Exercise) was a strategic planning effort conducted early in the Eisenhower administration, in which three teams of analysts proposed three competing U.S. strategies for the president's consideration. While rollback was one of the proposed options, Eisenhower ultimately chose the containment approach.

58   Burnham, *Coming Defeat*, 27.

59   William Henry Chamberlin, *Beyond Containment* (Chicago:. Regnery, 1953), 294.

60   Burnham, *Struggle for the World*, 162.

61   Acheson, "Premises of American Policy," 410.

62   John Kenneth Galbraith, "An Agenda for American Liberals," *Commentary* 41, no. 6 (June 1966): 32.

63   Warburg, "A Re-Examination," 69.

64   Robert Strausz-Hupé, "The Protracted Conflict," in Hahn and Neff, *American Strategy*, 31.

65 Strausz-Hupé et al., *Forward Strategy*, 29–31.

66 See Goldwater, "A Foreign Policy," 181, and Johnson, *No Substitute for Victory*, 209.

67 It should be noted, however, that this opposition to rollback could also be found among a small number of conservatives. See Buchanan, *Conservative Votes*, 161.

68 Richard Rosecrance, "Détente or Entente?," *Foreign Affairs* 53, no. 3 (April 1975): 467.

69 Kennan, "After the Cold War," 217.

70 Kennan and Urban, "From Containment," 24.

71 Nash, *Conservative Intellectual Movement*, 322.

72 Crozier, *Strategy of Survival*, 124. See also Lev E. Dobriansky, *U.S.A. and the Soviet Myth* (Old Greenwich, CT: Devin-Adair, 1971), 60. Conservatives would make similar arguments in the 1980s. See, for example, Charles A. Moser, "Foreign Policy and the Conservative Blueprint," in Paul M. Weyrich and Connaught Coyne Marshner, eds. *Future 21: Directions for America in the 21st Century* (Greenwich, CT: Devin-Adair, 1984), 105.

73 James Burnham, "The Kissinger-Sonnenfeldt Doctrine I," *National Review* 28, no. 17 (May 14, 1976): 495.

74 Brian Crozier, "Rollback, New Style," *National Review* 34, no. 14 (July 23, 1982): 884.

75 Stefan Korbonski, "The Helsinki Agreement and Self-Determination," *Strategic Review* 4, no. 3 (Summer 1976): 54.

76 Podhoretz, "The Future Danger," 41.

77 Anthony R. Dolan, "Let's Take the Offensive," *National Review* 32, no. 11 (May 30, 1980): 662.

78 Barry M. Goldwater, *With No Apologies: The Personal and Political Memoirs of Senator Barry M. Goldwater* (New York: Morrow, 1979), 302.

79 Schlesinger, *Vital Center*, 235.

80 Ibid., 63, 68.

81 Lyons, *Our Secret Allies*, 303.

82 Burnham, *Coming Defeat*, 151.

83 See, for example, ibid., 109, and Lyons, *Our Secret Allies*, 319–20. See Sarnoff, "Political Offensive," 426, for a later example of conservatives' preference for political warfare over military conflict.

84 The most famous example, of course, was the "Daisy" ad, which implied that Goldwater was likely to start a nuclear war.

85 Warburg, "A Re-Examination," 56–58.

86 Bundy, "To Cap the Volcano," 12.

87 Theodore C. Sorensen, "Why We Should Trade with the Soviets," *Foreign Affairs* 46, no. 3 (April 1968): 579.

88 Strausz-Hupé, "The Protracted Conflict," 31.

89 Strausz-Hupé et al., *Forward Strategy*, 8.

90 Frank S. Meyer, "'New Ideas' or 'Old Truths,'" in *Conservative Mainstream*, Meyer, 322.

91 Gregory L. Schneider, *Cadres for Conservatism: Young Americans for Freedom and the Rise of the Contemporary Right* (New York: New York University Press, 1999), 20.

92 Frank S. Meyer, "Just War in the Nuclear Age," in *Conservative Mainstream*, Meyer, 375.

93 Goldwater, "A Foreign Policy," 177. See also Kintner, *New Frontier of War*, 339–41, for similar sentiments.

94 Shulman, "What Does Security Mean Today?," 613.

95 Rosecrance, "Détente or Entente?," 481. See also, Kennan, *Cloud of Danger*, 216.

96 Niemeyer, *Deceitful Peace*, 199.

97 Goldwater, *With No Apologies*, 302.

98 Crozier, *Strategy of Survival*, 185. See also Dobriansky, *U.S.A. and the Soviet Myth*, 60.

99 Brian Crozier, "Rollback, Mark II," *National Review* 31, no. 23 (May 8, 1979): 724.

100 William F. Buckley, Jr., "Marx Is Dead," *National Review* 32, no. 4 (February 22, 1980): 244.

101 Pipes, "Soviet Global Strategy," 39.

CHAPTER 5: TOOLS

1 Schlesinger, *Vital Center*, 239.

2 Burnham, *Struggle for the World*, 162. See also Chamberlin, *Appeasement*, 187.

3 Walsh, *Total Empire*, 209.

4 Burnham, *Coming Defeat*, 140.

5   Bundy, "To Cap the Volcano," 15.

6   Walter Millis, "A Liberal Military Defense Policy," in *Liberal Papers*, Roosevelt, 114.

7   Arthur Waskow, "The Theory and Practice of Deterrence," in *Liberal Papers*, Roosevelt, 138.

8   Goldwater, *Why Not Victory?*, 35.

9   Evans, *Politics of Surrender*, 527. See also Kintner, *New Frontier of War*, 343, and Frank S. Meyer, "The McNamara Policy: Road to Disaster," in *Conservative Mainstream*, ed. Meyer, 388. This point was also made by some anticommunist liberals. See Acheson, "Premises of American Policy," 417.

10 Robert Strausz-Hupé, "The Diminishing Freedom of Choice," in Hahn and Neff, *American Strategy*, 44.

11 Ibid., 48.

12 Johnson, *No Substitute for Victory*, 201.

13 Niemeyer, "Political Requirements," 263.

14 Hubert H. Humphrey, "The Course of Soviet Foreign Policy and Soviet-American Relations in the 1970s," *Orbis* 15, no. 1 (Winter 1971): 69. See also Kennedy, "Beyond Détente," 11, and Kennan, "After the Cold War," 220.

15 Kennedy, "Beyond Détente," 12.

16 Ibid., 13. See also Kennan, *Cloud of Danger*, 203, for similar calls for unilateral restraint in arms production.

17 For an example of this approach, see Paul C. Warnke, "Apes on a Treadmill," *Foreign Policy* 18 (Spring 1975): 12–29.

18 Iklé, "Arms Control," 438–39. See also Crozier, *Strategy of Survival*, 193, and Goldwater, *With No Apologies*, 302.

19 Pipes, "Soviet Global Strategy," 39. See also Daniel O. Graham, "Détente Adieu," *National Review* 28, no. 33 (September 3, 1976): 946–50.

20 Conquest, *Present Danger*, 49.

21 Bowie and Immerman, *Waging Peace*, 211.

22 Schlesinger, *Vital Center*, 221.

23 Bowie and Immerman, *Waging Peace*, 213.

24 Burnham, *Coming Defeat*, 258.

25 Chamberlin, *Appeasement*, 193.

26 Warburg, "A Re-Examination," 75.

27   Osgood, "Reciprocal Initiative," 166.

28   Bundy, "To Cap the Volcano," 14.

29   Strausz-Hupé et al., *Forward Strategy*, 174. While some conservatives, such as Burnham, clearly preferred an all-out boycott of all trade with the Soviet bloc, they reluctantly accepted a more selective boycott of strategic goods. See, for example, Burnham, "Some Proposals," 590, and Andrew, *Other Side*, 136.

30   Evans, *Politics of Surrender*, 527.

31   Strausz-Hupé et al., *Forward Strategy*, 205.

32   Schneider, *Cadres for Conservatism*, 101.

33   Burnham, *War We Are In*, 151. See also James, "Soviet Economy," 448.

34   Strausz-Hupé et al., *Forward Strategy*, 209.

35   Kennedy, *Beyond Détente*, 24. See also Adam B. Ulam, "Détente under Soviet Eyes," *Foreign Policy* 24 (Fall 1976): 517.

36   Humphrey, *Course of Soviet Foreign Policy*, 68. See also Kennan, *Cloud of Danger*, 219.

37   Sanders, *Peddlers of Crisis*, 177.

38   Hyland, "Clash with the Soviet Union," 17. It is important to note that a small number of conservatives agreed with this approach. See William R. Kintner and Wolfgang Klaiber, *Eastern Europe and European Security* (New York: Dunellen, 1971), 311–12.

39   Conquest, *Present Danger*, 42. For a detailed, comprehensive review of the impact of Western trade on the development of the Soviet military, see Antony Sutton, *Western Technology and Soviet Development, 1945–1965* (Stanford, CA: Hoover Institution Press, 1973).

40   Pipes, *Survival Is Not Enough*, 204.

41   See, for example, Goldwater, *With No Apologies*, 302, Richard Viguerie, *The New Right: We're Ready to Lead* (Falls Church, VA: Viguerie, 1981), 119, and Crozier, *Strategy of Survival*, 190.

42   Yuan-li Wu, "U.S. Foreign Economic Policy: Politico-Economic Linkages," in Duignan and Rabushka, *United States in the 1980s*, 615. See also, Pipes, *Survival Is Not Enough*, 133–34.

43   Richard F. Starr, "Soviet Union," in Duignan and Rabushka, *United States in the 1980s*, 741. See also Pipes, *Survival Is Not Enough*, 135.

44   Committee on the Present Danger, "Common Sense," 12.

45   Robert English, "Eastern Europe's Doves," *Foreign Policy* 56 (Fall 1984): 56.

46 Dobriansky, *U.S.A. and the Soviet Myth*, 231. See also Conquest, *Present Danger*, 63, and Moser, "Foreign Policy and the Conservative Blueprint," 112.

47 Strausz-Hupé et al., *Forward Strategy*, 222.

48 Schlesinger, *Vital Center*, 221.

49 Bowie and Immerman, *Waging Peace*, 129.

50 Ibid., 130.

51 Burnham, *Coming Defeat*, 176–79. See also Walsh, *Total Empire*, 218.

52 See Nagorski, "NATO and the Captive Nations," 77, and James Burnham, "The Third World War," *National Review* 1, no. 3 (December 7, 1955): 16.

53 Burnham, *Coming Defeat*, 143. See also Bowie and Immerman, *Waging Peace*, 135.

54 Burnham, *Coming Defeat*, 37.

55 Galbraith, "Agenda for American Liberals," 33.

56 Warburg, "A Re-Examination," 93.

57 Michael Nelson, *War of the Black Heavens: The Battles of Western Broadcasting in the Cold War* (New York: Syracuse University Press, 1997), 148. For the gradual decline of RFE's anticommunist tone during this period, see also Arch Puddington, *Broadcasting Freedom: The Cold War Triumph of Radio Free Europe and Radio Liberty* (Lexington: University Press of Kentucky, 2000), 142–43.

58 Bundy, "To Cap the Volcano," 9.

59 Schneider, *Cadres for Conservatism*, 66.

60 See, for example, Thomas W. Wolfe, "Soviet Strategy of Disarmament," in Hahn and Neff, *American Strategy*, 148, and William R. Kintner, *Peace and the Strategy Conflict*, 159.

61 Strausz-Hupé et al., *Forward Strategy*, 261–65.

62 See, for example, Chamberlin, *Appeasement*, 191, and Burnham, *War We Are In*, 62.

63 Goldwater, *Why Not Victory?*, 121–23.

64 Andrew, *Other Side*, 19.

65 Sarnoff, "Political Offensive," 426. See also Frank Rockwell Barnett, "What Is to Be Done?," in Hahn and Neff, *American Strategy*, 446.

66 Strausz-Hupé et al., *Protracted Conflict*, 133.

67 Nelson, *War of the Black Heavens*, 149.

68 Ibid., 148. See also George R. Urban, *Radio Free Europe and the Pursuit of Democracy: My War within the Cold War* (New Haven, CT: Yale University Press, 1997), 38.

69 Humphrey, "Course of Soviet Foreign Policy," 70. See also Dallin and Lapidus, "Reagan and the Russians," 220, and Shulman, "What Does Security Mean Today?," 616.

70 Kennedy, "Beyond Détente," 8. See also Kennan, "After the Cold War," 220.

71 See, for example, Committee on the Present Danger, "Common Sense," 4, and "Peace with Freedom: A Discussion by the Committee on the Present Danger before the Foreign Policy Association, 14 March 1978," in Tyroler, *Alerting America*, 30.

72 Jeane Kirkpatrick, *The Withering Away of the Totalitarian State . . . and Other Surprises* (Washington, DC: AEI Press, 1990), 17. See also Committee on the Present Danger, "Where We Stand on SALT," 17.

73 Dobriansky, *U.S.A. and the Soviet Myth*, 181.

74 Goldwater, "Perilous Conjuncture," 54.

75 Committee on the Present Danger, "Common Sense," 4.

76 Paul H. Nitze, "Living with the Soviets," *Foreign Affairs* 63, no. 2 (Winter 1984–1985): 363.

77 Crozier, *Strategy of Survival*, 190. See also Iklé, "Arms Control," 442, and Viguerie, *New Right*, 118.

78 Viguerie, *New Right*, 119.

79 Kirkpatrick, *Dictatorships and Double Standards*, 91. See also Niemeyer, *Deceitful Peace*, 201.

80 Conquest, *Present Danger*, 74. Moynihan was UN ambassador from 1975 to 1976.

81 Moser, "Foreign Policy and the Conservative Blueprint," 108. See also Starr, "Soviet Union," 754–55.

82 See Grose, *Operation Rollback*, for one such example.

83 Ibid., 139.

84 Ibid., 209.

85 Meyer, "Relativist 'Re-evaluates' Evil," 429.

86 Burnham, *Coming Defeat*, 143–44.

87 Chamberlin, *Beyond Containment*, 300. See also Lyons, *Our Secret Allies*, 319.

88 Burnham, *Coming Defeat*, 87.

89 Warburg, "A Re-Examination," 95.

90 Strausz-Hupé et al., *Forward Strategy*, 41.

91 Kintner, *New Frontier*, 321. See also Sarnoff, "Political Offensive," 426.

92 Barnett, "What Is to Be Done?," 448. See also Burnham, "Some Proposals," 593.

93 Johnson, *No Substitute*, 209.

94 Evans, *Politics of Surrender*, 527–29.

95 Gershman, "Rise and Fall," 16.

96 Shulman, "What Does Security Mean Today?," 614.

97 Iklé, "Arms Control," 441.

98 Crozier, *Strategy of Survival*, 189.

99 Viguerie, *New Right*, 121. See also Crozier, *Strategy of Survival*, 194.

CHAPTER 6: THE ROLE OF REAGAN AND HIS ADVISORS

1 This statement does not, of course, mean that all systems are equally effective, but rather that presidents dictate how they will make decisions.

2 In theory, this question should always be answered in the affirmative, as it is virtually unthinkable that a president would ever appoint or retain foreign policy advisors who disagree with him over something as fundamental as the nature of the adversary or the international system as a whole.

3 Interviews by author with Jeane Kirkpatrick, January 10, 2002, American Enterprise Institute; Caspar Weinberger, August 4, 2005, via telephone; Edwin Meese, August 17, 2005, Heritage Foundation; and Richard V. Allen, August 9, 2005, via e-mail.

4 "Remarks at the Presentation Ceremony for the Presidential Medal of Freedom," February 23, 1983, available at www.reagan.utexas.edu/archives/speeches/1983/22383c.htm.

5 Skinner et al., *Reagan: A Life in Letters*, 282, 399–400.

6 Reagan, *Reagan Diaries*, 331.

7 A far more detailed discussion of Reagan's struggle with communism can be found in Schweizer, *Reagan's War*.

8 Schweizer, *Reagan's War*, 25.

9 Weinberger, interview by author, August 4, 2005; Meese, interview by author, August 17, 2005; and Allen, interview by author, August 9, 2005.

10 For a broad array of similar analyses of Reagan's management style, see Anderson, *Revolution*, 284; Karaagac, *Between Promise and Policy*, 58–59; Cannon, *President*

Reagan, 182; and Carl M. Brauer, *Presidential Transitions: Eisenhower through Reagan* (New York: Oxford University Press, 1986), 222. This view was confirmed in interviews with Weinberger, August 4, 2005; Meese, August 17, 2005; and Allen, August 9, 2005.

11 Weinberger, interview by author, August 4, 2005; Meese, interview by author, August 17, 2005; and Allen, interview by author, August 9, 2005.

12 Richard V. Allen, interview by author, August 16, 2005, via e-mail.

13 Reagan, *An American Life*, 548. See also Shultz, *Turmoil and Triumph*, 246, and Caspar Weinberger, *Fighting for Peace: Seven Critical Years in the Pentagon* (New York: Warner Books, 1991), 309.

14 Kirkpatrick, interview by author, January 10, 2002.

15 Ronald Reagan, "Address at Commencement Exercises at the University of Notre Dame," May 17, 1981, in *Public Papers of the Presidents of the United States: Ronald Reagan, 1981* (Washington, DC: Government Printing Office, 1982), 434.

16 See Paul Kengor, *The Crusader: Ronald Reagan and the Fall of Communism* (New York: ReganBooks, 2006), 53–54, for a good discussion of this extraordinary conversation.

17 Reagan, *An American Life*, 266.

18 Skinner et al., *Reagan, in His Own Hand*, 118.

19 For more detail on these events, see Schweizer, *Reagan's War*, 5–16, and Peggy Noonan, *When Character Was King: A Story of Ronald Reagan* (New York: Viking, 2001), 54–65.

20 Skinner et al., *Reagan: A Life in Letters*, 703.

21 Skinner et al., *Reagan, in His Own Hand*, 60.

22 Reagan, *An American Life*, 265.

23 Skinner et al., *Reagan: A Life in Letters*, 546.

24 Ibid., 384.

25 Kirkpatrick, interview by author, January 10, 2002.

26 Reagan, *An American Life*, 294.

27 Skinner et al., *Reagan, in His Own Hand*, 113.

28 Ibid., 442.

29 Reagan, *An American Life*, 237.

30 Skinner et al., *Reagan, in His Own Hand*, 30.

31 Reagan, *An American Life*, 551.

32 Skinner et al., *Reagan, in His Own Hand*, 486.

33 Skinner et al., *Reagan: A Life in Letters*, 385.

34 Ibid., 375.

35 Skinner et al., *Reagan, in His Own Hand*, 61.

36 Skinner et al., *Reagan: A Life in Letters*, 261.

37 Skinner et al., *Reagan, in His Own Hand*, 472.

38 Ibid., 485.

39 Skinner et al., *Reagan: A Life in Letters*, 424.

40 Skinner et al., *Reagan, in His Own Hand*, 82.

41 See, for example, Skinner et al., *Reagan: A Life in Letters*, 424, 497.

42 Skinner et al., *Reagan, in His Own Hand*, 480.

43 Ibid., 481.

44 Ibid., 49.

45 Ibid., 112.

46 Reagan, *An American Life*, 271–73.

47 Skinner et al., *Reagan: A Life in Letters*, 410.

48 Skinner et al., *Reagan, in His Own Hand*, 473.

49 "Republican Party Platform of 1980" accessed July 22, 2005, available at http://www.presidency.ucsb.edu/showplatforms.php?platindex=R1980.

50 Skinner et al., *Reagan: A Life in Letters*, 378.

51 Kirkpatrick, interview by author, January 10, 2002.

52 Reagan, *An American Life*, 238.

53 Skinner et al., *Reagan: A Life in Letters*, 375.

54 Kirkpatrick, interview by author, January 10, 2002.

55 Skinner et al., *Reagan, in His Own Hand*, 31.

56 Quoted in Dinesh D'Souza, *Ronald Reagan: How an Ordinary Man Became an Extraordinary Leader* (New York: Free Press, 1997), 193.

57 Skinner et al., *Reagan's Path*, 353.

58 Ronald Reagan, "Time to Recapture Our Destiny," speech at the National Republican Convention on July 17, 1980, accessed June 13, 2005, www.reaganfoundation.org/reagan/speeches/speech.asp?spid=18.

59 Reagan, "Time to Recapture Our Destiny."

60 Skinner et al., *Reagan, in His Own Hand*, 86.

61 The best account of Reagan's decision to pursue SDI can be found in Paul Kengor and Patricia Clark Doerner, *The Judge: William P. Clark, Ronald Reagan's Top Hand* (San Francisco: Ignatius Press, 2007), 197–202. See also Weinberger, *Fighting for Peace*, 309, and Shultz, *Turmoil and Triumph*, 261.

62 See Frances FitzGerald, *Way Out There in the Blue: Reagan, Star Wars, and the End of the Cold War* (New York: Simon & Schuster, 2001), 22, for the erroneous claim. See Schweizer, *Reagan's War*, 84, for the story of Reagan's visit to Livermore. Schweizer's view is generally corroborated by Weinberger, *Fighting for Peace*, 296.

63 Schweizer, *Reagan's War*, 152.

64 Skinner et al., *Reagan, in His Own Hand*, 442.

65 Reagan, *An American Life*, 238.

66 Skinner et al., *Reagan: A Life in Letters*, 373.

67 Reagan, *An American Life*, 320.

68 Skinner et al., *Reagan, in His Own Hand*, 73.

69 Reagan, *An American Life*, 267.

70 Norman Podhoretz, "The Reagan Road to Détente," *Foreign Affairs* 63, no. 3 (America and the World 1984): 456.

71 Skinner et al., *Reagan: A Life in Letters*, 378. This explanation was corroborated by Roger Robinson, interview by author, October 2, 2002, Center for Security Policy.

72 Ronald Reagan, "Rendezvous with Destiny," speech of October 27, 1964, accessed June 17, 2005, available from www.reaganlibrary.com/reagan/speeches/rendezvous.asp.

73 Reagan, *An American Life*, 473.

74 Reagan, "Rendezvous with Destiny."

75 Skinner et al., *Reagan, in His Own Hand*, 472.

76 Lawrence W. Beilenson, *The Treaty Trap* (Washington, DC: Public Affairs, 1969). The role this book played in Reagan's thinking is discussed in Anderson, *Revolution*, 74–75, and Schweizer, *Reagan's War*, 86. See also Skinner et al.,

Reagan, in His Own Hand, 52, for direct evidence of Reagan's support for this argument.

77   Skinner et al., *Reagan, in His Own Hand*, 86.

78   Ibid., 484.

79   See Don Oberdorfer, "Kennan Urges Halving of Nuclear Arsenals," *Washington Post*, May 20, 1981, and Skinner et al., *Reagan: A Life In Letters*, 402.

80   A copy of the Rockefeller Commission Report can be obtained at http://www.aarclibrary.org/publib/church/rockcomm/contents.htm.

81   Andrew, *Other Side*, 459.

82   For a largely critical account of the Reagan administration's dealings with the CIA that nevertheless acknowledges Reagan's personal support for covert action, see Gates, *From the Shadows*, 197.

83   Meese, interview by author, August 17, 2005.

84   Weinberger, interview by author, August 4, 2005, and Meese, interview by author, August 17, 2005.

85   The same cannot, however, be said of Reagan's *political* advisors. Almost all accounts of the Reagan years note the opposition to every major "hard-line" element of the strategy by two key advisors: James Baker and Michael Deaver. See, for example, Kengor and Doerner, *The Judge*, 239 and 247–48.

86   Weinberger, *Fighting for Peace*, 30.

87   Weinberger, interview by author, August 4, 2005, and Meese, interview by author, August 17, 2005.

88   Cannon, *President Reagan*, 325 and 760. McFarlane was the Deputy National Security Advisor when SDI was announced in March 1983 but became National Security Advisor in October 1983.

89   Shultz, *Turmoil and Triumph*, 246.

90   Weinberger, *Fighting for Peace*, 31.

91   It was America's troubled experience in Lebanon that led Weinberger to issue his famous "rules" regarding the use of force.

92   Richard Perle, interview by author, October 8, 2004, American Enterprise Institute.

93   Perle, interview by author, October 8, 2004.

94   Fred Iklé, interview by author, July 5, 2005, Center for Strategic and International Studies.

95   Details of the structure of the SPG can be found in NSDD-77, 1–3, as well as Lord, "Past and Future of Public Diplomacy."

96   Meese, interview by author, August 17, 2005.

97   Shultz, *Turmoil and Triumph*, 266.

98   Iklé, interview by author, July 5, 2005. For more detail on the history of America's and DOD's efforts to develop these capabilities, see Lt. Col. Susan L. Gough, "The Evolution of Strategic Influence," a 2003 U.S. Army War College research project available at http://www.fas.org/irp/eprint/gough.pdf.

99   Weinberger made this point directly to Soviet ambassador Dobrynin in March 1981, as related in Weinberger, *Fighting for Peace*, 36. See also Caspar Weinberger, *In the Arena: A Memoir of the 20ᵗʰ Century* (Washington, DC: Regnery, 2001), 278–84, and Reagan, *Reagan Diaries*, 425, 433, for further discussion of Weinberger's views on arms control.

100 For information on Haig's opposition and Shultz's concerns, see Alexander M. Haig, *Caveat: Realism, Reagan, and Foreign Policy* (New York: Macmillan, 1984), 229, and Shultz, *Turmoil and Triumph*, 155–60.

101 Weinberger, *Fighting for Peace*, 320. See also Reagan, *An American Life*, 685.

102 Shultz, *Turmoil and Triumph*, 351.

103 Ibid., 377.

104 Perle, interview by author, October 8, 2004.

105 Gates, *From the Shadows*, 199.

106 Derek Leebaert, *The Fifty-Year Wound: The True Price of America's Cold War Victory* (New York: Little, Brown, 2002), 483.

107 Iklé, interview by author, July 5, 2005.

108 Leebaert, *Fifty-Year Wound*, 544–45.

109 Michael K. Deaver with Mickey Herskowitz, *Behind the Scenes* (New York: Morrow, 1987), 168. See also Shultz, *Turmoil and Triumph*, 278.

110 Schweizer, *Reagan's War*, 174–75, and Leebaert, *Fifty-Year Wound*, 541. For an opposing view, see Gates, *From the Shadows*, 237.

111 Leebaert, *Fifty-Year Wound*, 525–26. Casey's central role in this effort was reiterated in interviews with Perle (October 8, 2004) and Iklé (July 5, 2005).

112 Numerous examples can be found in Reagan, *Reagan Diaries*. See, for example, pages 277, 401, and 425.

CHAPTER 7: CONCLUSIONS

1   Woodrow Wilson, for example, was an extremely controversial figure in the years following his presidency, yet is now widely cited as one of America's most important figures. For a more recent example of how radically the popular view of a president can change, see Fred I. Greenstein, *The Hidden-Hand Presidency: Eisenhower as Leader* (Baltimore: Johns Hopkins University Press, 1982).

2   For examples of this view, see Beth A. Fischer, *The Reagan Reversal: Foreign Policy and the End of the Cold War* (Columbia: University of Missouri Press, 1997), and Don Oberdorfer, *From the Cold War to a New Era: The United States and the Soviet Union, 1983–1991* (Baltimore: Johns Hopkins University Press, 1998).

3   Cannon, *President Reagan*, 295. Ironically, Cannon himself makes the very same mistake repeatedly throughout his book. See, for example, the condescending way in which he portrays Reagan's decision-making process (362–63).

4   For the best example of such thinking, see Talbott, "Rethinking the Red Menace,"66–72, in which Talbott claims that American doves had been right all along about the Soviets.

5   Leebaert, *Fifty-Year Wound*, 516.

6   Ibid., 497–98.

7   For a good summary of this controversy, see Benjamin B. Fischer, *A Cold War Conundrum* (Washington, DC: Center for the Study of Intelligence, CIA, 1997) available at http://www.cia.gov/csi/monograph/coldwar/source.htm.

8   Leebaert, *Fifty-Year Wound*, 538.

9   Norman A. Bailey, *The Strategic Plan That Won the Cold War: National Security Decision Directive 75* (McLean, VA: Potomac Foundation, 1999), 5.

10 Ibid., 8.

11 This statement is based on the author's review of currently declassified NSC documents from the various administrations, as found at www.fas.org/irp/offdocs/direct.htm. It is, of course, possible that such documents exist for the Kennedy, Nixon, or Ford administrations but simply have not been released.

12 Carl von Clausewitz, *On War*, ed. and trans. Michael Howard and Peter Paret (Princeton, NJ: Princeton University Press, 1984), 136, 85.

13 Patrick E. Tyler, "U.S. Strategy Plan Calls for Insuring No Rivals Develop," *New York Times*, March 8, 1992.

14 See, for example, Michael McFaul, "To Fight a New 'Ism,'" *Washington Post*, September 22, 2001, and (far more extensively) David Frum and Richard Perle, *An End to Evil: How to Win the War on Terror* (New York: Random House, 2003).

15 For an example of this approach, see Robin Wright, "Don't Just Fund the War, Shell Out for Peace," *Washington Post*, March 10, 2002.

16 Reagan, "Promoting Democracy and Peace," 81.

17 National Commission on Terrorist Attacks upon the United States, *The 9/11 Commission Report* (Washington, DC: Government Printing Office, 2004), 169.

18 International relations theorists would rightly point out that both schools focus on levels of analysis above the individual (namely, at the international system level) and thus are specifically designed *not* to address the role of the individual. While that is certainly true, the fact that the greatest (and most persistent) debate in international relations completely ignores the individual simply proves the point that the field generally views other levels of analysis as more important than the individual.

19 For a good summary of the challenges in using psychological tools to model decision making, see James E. Dougherty and Robert L. Pfaltzgraff, Jr., *Contending Theories of International Relations: A Comprehensive Survey*, 4th ed. (New York: Addison-Wesley, 1997), 485–91.

BIBLIOGRAPHY

Abshire, David M., and Richard V. Allen, eds. *National Security: Political, Military, and Economic Strategies in the Decade Ahead*. Stanford, CA: Hoover Institution Press, 1963.

Acheson, Dean G. *A Democrat Looks at His Party*. New York: Harper, 1955.

Ackerman, Peter, and Christopher Kruegler. *Strategic Nonviolent Conflict: The Dynamics of People Power in the Twentieth Century*. Westport, CT: Praeger, 1994.

Adelman, Kenneth L. *Great Universal Embrace: Arms Summitry—A Skeptic's Account*. New York: Simon & Schuster, 1989.

Allen, Richard V. "The Man Who Changed the Game Plan." *The National Interest*, no. 44 (Summer 1996): 60–65.

———. *Peace or Peaceful Coexistence?* Chicago: American Bar Association, 1966.

Anderson, Martin. *Revolution: The Reagan Legacy*. Stanford, CA: Hoover Institution Press, 1990.

Andrew, Christopher M. *For the President's Eyes Only: Secret Intelligence and the American Presidency from Washington to Bush*. New York: HarperCollins, 1995.

Andrew, John A., III. *The Other Side of the Sixties: Young Americans for Freedom and the Rise of Conservative Politics*. New Brunswick, NJ: Rutgers University Press, 1997.

Arendt, Hannah. *The Origins of Totalitarianism*. New York: Harcourt, Brace, 1951.

Arquilla, John. *The Reagan Imprint: Ideas in American Foreign Policy from the Collapse of Communism to the War on Terror*. Chicago: Ivan R. Dees, 2006.

Art, Robert J. "To What End Military Power?" *International Security* 4, no. 4 (Spring 1980): 3–35.

Aspin, Les. "What Are the Russians Up To?" *International Security* 3, no. 1 (Summer 1978): 30–54.

Bailey, Norman A. *The Strategic Plan That Won the Cold War: National Security Decision Directive 75*. McLean, VA: The Potomac Foundation, 1999.

Bark, Dennis L., ed. *To Promote Peace: U.S. Foreign Policy in the Mid-1980s*. Stanford, CA: Hoover Institution Press, 1984.

Barnet, Richard J. "U.S.-Soviet Relations: The Need for a Comprehensive Approach." *Foreign Affairs* 57, no. 4 (Spring 1979): 779–95.

Beaufre, André. *An Introduction to Strategy*. New York: Praeger, 1965.

Beilenson, Laurence B. *Survival and Peace in a Nuclear Age*. Chicago: Regnery, 1980.

———. *The Treaty Trap: A History of the Performance of Political Treaties by the United States and European Nations*. Washington, DC: Public Affairs Press, 1969.

Bell, Coral. "From Carter to Reagan." *Foreign Affairs* 63, no. 3 (America and the World, 1984): 490–510.

———. *The Reagan Paradox: American Foreign Policy in the 1980s*. New Brunswick, NJ: Rutgers University Press, 1989.

Betts, Richard K. "A Nuclear Golden Age? The Balance before Parity." *International Security* 11, no. 3 (Winter 1986–1987): 3–32.

Bialer, Seweryn. "The Soviet Union and the West in the 1980s: Détente, Containment, or Confrontation?" *Orbis* 27, no. 1 (Spring 1983): 35–57.

———, and Joan Afferica. "Reagan and Russia." *Foreign Affairs* 61, no. 2 (Winter 1982–1983): 249–71.

Binyon, Michael. *Life in Russia*. New York: Pantheon Books, 1983.

Bloomfield, Lincoln P. "Foreign Policy for Disillusioned Liberals." *Foreign Policy* 9 (Winter 1972–1973): 55–68.

Blumenthal, Sidney. *The Rise of the Counter-Establishment*. New York: Times Books, 1986.

Bochenski, Joseph, and Gerhard Niemeyer, eds. *Handbook on Communism*. New York: Praeger, 1962.

Bowie, Robert R., and Richard H. Immerman. *Waging Peace: How Eisenhower Shaped an Enduring Cold War Strategy*. New York: Oxford University Press, 1998.

Bowles, Chester. *The New Dimensions of Peace*. New York: Harper, 1955.

Boyarsky, Bill. *Ronald Reagan: His Life and Rise to the Presidency*. New York: Random House, 1981.

Braley, Russ. *Bad News: The Foreign Policy of the* New York Times. Chicago: Regnery, 1984.

Brauer, Carl M. *Presidential Transitions: Eisenhower through Reagan*. New York: Oxford University Press, 1986.

Brennan, Donald G. "Commentary on 'Mutual Deterrence and Strategic Arms Limitation in Soviet Policy.'" *International Security* 3, no. 3 (Winter 1978–1979): 193–98.

Brewster, Kingman, Jr. "Reflections on Our National Purpose." *Foreign Affairs* 50, no. 3 (April 1972): 399–415.

Brodie, Bernard. "The Development of Nuclear Strategy." *International Security* 2, no. 4 (Spring 1978): 65–83.

———. "On the Objectives of Arms Control." *International Security* 1, no. 1 (Summer 1976): 17–36.

———, ed. *The Absolute Weapon: Atomic Power and World Order.* New York: Harcourt, Brace, 1946.

Brown, Archie, and Michael Kaser, eds. *Soviet Policy for the 1980s.* Bloomington: Indiana University Press, 1982.

Buchan, Alastair. "A World Restored?" *Foreign Affairs* 50, no. 4 (July 1972): 644–59.

Buchanan, Patrick J. *Conservative Votes, Liberal Victories: Why the Right Has Failed.* New York: Quadrangle Books, 1975.

Buckley, William F., Jr. "How to Read Ball." *National Review* 33, no. 16 (August 21, 1981): 978–79.

———. *Inveighing We Will Go.* New York: Putnam, 1972.

———. "Marx Is Dead." *National Review* 32, no. 4 (February 22, 1980): 244.

———. "Move to the Right." *National Review* 22, no. 43 (November 3, 1970): 1178–79.

———. "Neutralization: Liberal Assumptions." *National Review* 3, no. 8 (February 23, 1957): 177–78, 190.

———. "Opening Up Détente." *National Review* 28, no. 9 (March 19, 1976): 290.

———. "So Sonnenfeldt Is Jewish?" *National Review* 28, no. 17 (May 14, 1976): 522–23.

———. "Soviet Weakness?" *National Review* 34, no. 5 (March 19, 1982): 320.

———. "Understanding Solzhenitsyn." *National Review* 28, no. 17 (May 14, 1976): 522.

Bucy, J. Fred. "On Strategic Technology Transfer to the Soviet Union." *International Security* 1, no. 4 (Spring 1977): 25–43.

———. "Technology Transfer and East-West Trade: A Reappraisal." *International Security* 5, no. 3 (Winter 1980–1981): 132–51.

Bundy, McGeorge. "Maintaining Stable Deterrence." *International Security* 3, no. 3 (Winter 1978–1979): 5–16.

———. "To Cap the Volcano." *Foreign Affairs* 48, no.1 (October 1969): 1–20.

Bundy, William P. "Dictatorships and American Foreign Policy." *Foreign Affairs* 54, no. 1 (October 1975): 51–60.

———. "International Security Today." *Foreign Affairs* 53, no. 1 (October 1974): 24–44.

Burnham, James. "Angola: What Is Moscow Up To?" *National Review* 28, no. 9 (March 19, 1976): 260.

———. "The Atmosphere of Détente." *National Review* 27, no. 49 (December 19, 1975): 1465.

———. *The Coming Defeat of Communism.* New York: John Day, 1950.

———. "Communist or Russian?" *National Review* 3, no. 6 (February 9, 1957): 132.

———. "The Détente Party." *National Review* 29, no. 10 (March 18, 1977): 319.

———. "Does ADA Run the New Frontier?" *National Review* 14, no. 18 (May 7, 1963): 355–62.

———. "Estimates of the Situation." *National Review* 28, no. 25 (July 9, 1976): 731.

———. "The Gentle Khrushchev." *National Review* 13, no. 26 (December 31, 1962): 505.

———. "The Great Retreat." *National Review* 22, no. 49 (December 15, 1970): 1339.

———. "Jimmy Meets the World." *National Review* 30, no. 5 (February 3, 1978): 149–50.

———. "Joys and Sorrows of Empire." *National Review* 23, no. 27 (July 13, 1971): 749.

———. "Keep on the Premises." *National Review* 12, no. 18 (May 8, 1962): 324.

———. "The Kissinger-Sonnenfeldt Doctrine I." *National Review* 28, no. 17 (May 14, 1976): 495.

———. "The Kissinger-Sonnenfeldt Doctrine II." *National Review* 28, no. 19 (May 28, 1976): 560.

———. "The Kissinger-Sonnedfeldt Doctrine III." *National Review* 28, no. 21 (June 11, 1976): 611.

———. "Liberation: What Next?" *National Review* 3, no. 3 (January 19, 1957): 59–62, 71.

———. "On the Horns of Our Dilemma." *National Review* 11, no. 16 (October 21, 1961): 265.

———. "Questions Begging." *National Review* 15, no. 8 (August 27, 1963): 148.

———. "The Second Generation." *National Review* 22, no. 15 (April 21, 1970): 400.

———. "Sino-Soviet Sense and Nonsense." *National Review* 14, no. 2 (January 15, 1963): 16.

———. "Some Proposals to a Goldwater Administration Concerning Foreign Affairs." *National Review* 16, no. 28 (July 14, 1964): 589–93.

———. *The Struggle for the World*. New York: John Day, 1947.

———. "The Third World War." *National Review* 1, no. 3 (December 7, 1955): 16.

———. "The Third World War." *National Review* 2, no. 26 (November 17, 1956): 10.

———. "The Third World War." *National Review* 2, no. 32 (December 29, 1956): 12.

———. *The War We Are In*. New Rochelle, NY: Arlington House, 1967.

———. "Their World and Ours." *National Review* 2, no. 24 (November 3, 1956): 19–20.

———. "Waiting for Lefty." *National Review* 28, no. 5 (February 20, 1976): 140.

———. "Western, Yes, but Hard." *National Review* 12, no. 6 (February 13, 1962): 94.

———. "What the Gaffe Said." *National Review* 28, no. 45 (November 26, 1976): 1283.

———, Frank S. Meyer, and William S. Schlamm. "The Meaning of the Change." *National Review* 2, no. 21 (October 13, 1956): 9–13.

Burt, Richard. "Reassessing the Strategic Balance." *International Security* 5, no. 1 (Summer 1980): 37–52.

Byrnes, Robert F. "Russia in Eastern Europe: Hegemony without Security." *Foreign Affairs* 49, no. 4 (July 1971): 682–97.

Campbell, John C. "Negotiation with the Soviets: Some Lessons of the War Period." *Foreign Affairs* 34, no. 2 (January 1956): 305–19.

Cannon, Lou. *President Reagan: The Role of a Lifetime*. New York: Simon & Schuster, 1991.

———. *Reagan*. New York: G. P. Putnam's Sons, 1982.

Chamberlin, William Henry. *Appeasement: The Road to War*. New York: Rolton House, 1962.

———. *Beyond Containment*. Chicago: Regnery, 1953.

Chambers, Whittaker. *Witness*. New York: Random House, 1952.

Clausewitz, Carl von. *On War*. Michael Howard and Peter Paret, ed. and trans. Princeton, NJ: Princeton University Press, 1984.

Coffey, J. I. "Détente, Arms Control and European Security." *International Affairs* 52, no. 1 (January 1976): 39–52.

———. "Strategic Arms Limitation and European Security." *International Affairs* 47, no. 4 (October 1971): 692–707.

Cohen, S. T., and E. F. Black. "SALT and the Public Law." *National Review* 30, no. 3 (January 20, 1978): 82–89.

Conquest, Robert. "The Limits of Détente." *Foreign Affairs* 46, no. 4 (July 1968): 733–42.

————. "A New Russia? A New World?" *Foreign Affairs* 53, no. 3 (April 1975): 482–97.

————. *Present Danger: Toward a Foreign Policy*. Stanford, CA: Hoover Institution Press, 1979.

————. "Stalin's Successors." *Foreign Affairs* 48, no. 3 (April 1970): 509–24.

Coser, Lewis A., Oscar Gass, Hans J. Morgenthau, and Arthur Schlesinger, Jr. "America and the World Revolution." *Commentary* 36, no. 4 (October 1963): 278–96.

Crabb, Cecil V., Jr., and Kevin V. Mulcahy. *Presidents and Foreign Policy Making: From FDR to Reagan*. Baton Rouge: Louisiana State University Press, 1986.

Crozier, Brian. "Apocalyptic Thoughts." *National Review* 33, no. 10 (May 29, 1981): 604.

————. "Beyond Helsinki." *National Review* 34, no. 23 (November 26, 1982): 1468.

————. "Crash Course." *National Review* 32, no. 6 (March 21, 1980): 337.

————. "The Debate Goes On." *National Review* 31, no. 1 (January 5, 1979): 21.

————. "The Forgotten Ones." *National Review* 32, no. 17 (August 22, 1980): 1007.

————. "One-Way Traffic." *National Review* 32, no. 2 (January 25, 1980): 86.

————. "Pieties and Verities." *National Review* 33, no. 25 (December 25, 1981): 1533.

————. "The Polish Dilemma." *National Review* 32, no. 19 (September 19, 1980): 1129.

————. "Rollback, Mark II." *National Review* 31, no. 23 (May 8, 1979): 724.

————. "Rollback, New Style." *National Review* 34, no. 14 (July 23, 1982): 884.

————. *Strategy of Survival*. New Rochelle, NY: Arlington House Publishers, 1978.

————. "Thoughts on Sanctions." *National Review* 34, no. 18 (September 17, 1982): 1136.

————. "Weak Links." *National Review* 34, no. 4 (March 5, 1982): 216.

Crozier, Brian, Drew Middleton, and Jeremy Murray-Brown. *This War Called Peace*. New York: Universe Books, 1985.

Deaver, Michael K. *A Different Drummer: My Thirty Years with Ronald Reagan*. New York: HarperCollins, 2001.

————, with Mickey Herskowitz. *Behind the Scenes*. New York: William Morrow, 1987.

De Riencourt, Amaury. "Robert Strausz-Hupé's Thought in Retrospect." *Orbis* 17, no. 3 (1973): 1053–66.

Dobriansky, Lev E. *U.S.A. and the Soviet Myth*. Old Greenwich, CT: Devin-Adair Company, 1971.

Dobrynin, Anatoly. *In Confidence: Moscow's Ambassador to America's Six Cold War Presidents (1962–1986)*. New York: Times Books, 1995.

Dobson, Alan P. "The Reagan Administration, Economic Warfare, and Starting to Close Down the Cold War." *Diplomatic History* 29, no. 3 (June 2005): 531–56.

Dolan, Anthony R. "Let's Take the Offensive." *National Review* 32, no. 9 (May 30, 1980): 662.

Dorrien, Gary J. *The Neoconservative Mind: Politics, Culture, and the War of Ideology*. Philadelphia: Temple University Press, 1993.

Dougherty, James E., and Robert L. Pfaltzgraff, Jr. *Contending Theories of International Relations: A Comprehensive Survey*, 4th ed. New York: Addison-Wesley, 1997.

Draper, Theodore. "Appeasement and Détente." *Commentary* 61, no. 2 (February 1976): 27–38.

———. "Détente." *Commentary* 57, no. 6 (June 1974): 25–47.

D'Souza, Dinesh. *Ronald Reagan: How an Ordinary Man Became an Extraordinary Leader*. New York: Free Press, 1997.

Duignan, Peter, and Alvin Rabushka, eds. *The United States in the 1980s*. Stanford, CA: Hoover Institution Press, 1980.

Dulles, John Foster. "Challenge and Response in United States Policy." *Foreign Affairs* 36, no. 1 (October 1957): 25–43.

———. "Policy for Security and Peace." *Foreign Affairs* 32, no. 3 (April 1954): 353–64.

Dunn, Charles W., and J. David Woodard. *American Conservatism from Burke to Bush: An Introduction*. Lanham, MD: Madison Books, 1991.

"East-West Economic Relations and Poland-Related Sanctions." National Security Decision Directive, NSDD-66. November 16, 1982.

Edwards, Lee, ed. *The Collapse of Communism*. Stanford, CA: Hoover Institution Press, 2000.

———. *The Conservative Revolution: The Movement That Remade America*. New York: Free Press, 1999.

English, Robert. "Eastern Europe's Doves." *Foreign Policy* 56 (Fall 1984): 44–60.

Ermarth, Fritz W. "Contrasts in American and Soviet Strategic Thought." *International Security* 3, no. 2 (Autumn 1978): 138–55.

Evans, M. Stanton. *Clear and Present Dangers: A Conservative View of America's Government*. New York: Harcourt Brace Jovanovich, 1975.

———. "The Liberal against Himself." *National Review* 2, no. 31 (December 22, 1956): 11–13.

————. *The Politics of Surrender.* New York: Devin-Adair, 1966.

————. "Selling the West." *National Review* 31, no. 1 (January 5, 1979): 33.

Executive Office of the President. *A National Security Strategy of Engagement and Enlargement.* Washington, DC: Government Printing Office, 1995.

————. *National Security Strategy of the United States.* Washington, DC: Government Printing Office, 1991.

Fischer, Benjamin B. *A Cold War Conundrum.* Washington, DC: Center for the Study of Intelligence, CIA, 1997. Available at http://www.cia.gov/csi/monograph/coldwar/source.htm.

Fischer, Beth A. *The Reagan Reversal: Foreign Policy and the End of the Cold War.* Columbia: University of Missouri Press, 1997.

FitzGerald, Frances. *Way Out There in the Blue: Reagan, Star Wars, and the End of the Cold War.* New York: Simon & Schuster, 2001.

Francis, Samuel T. *Power and History: The Political Thought of James Burnham.* Lanham, MD: University Press of America, 1984.

Frum, David, and Richard Perle. *An End to Evil: How to Win the War on Terror.* New York: Random House, 2003.

Gaddis, John Lewis. "Containment: Its Past and Future." *International Security* 5, no. 4 (Spring 1981): 74–102.

————. "The Rise, Fall and Future of Détente." *Foreign Affairs* 62, no. 2 (Winter 1983–1984): 354–77.

Galbraith, John Kenneth. "An Agenda for American Liberals." *Commentary* 41, no. 6 (June 1966): 29–34.

Garthoff, Raymond L. "Mutual Deterrence and Strategic Arms Limitation in Soviet Policy." *International Security* 3, no. 1 (Spring 1977): 3–24.

————. "Negotiating with the Russians: Some Lessons from SALT." *International Security* 1, no. 4 (Summer 1978): 112–47.

————. "On Estimating and Imputing Intentions." *International Security* 2, no. 3 (Winter 1978): 22–32.

Gates, Robert M. *From the Shadows: The Ultimate Insider's Story of Five Presidents and How They Won the Cold War.* New York: Simon & Schuster, 1996.

Gati, Charles. "What Containment Meant." *Foreign Policy* 7 (Summer 1972): 22–40.

George, Alexander L. *Bridging the Gap: Theory and Practice in Foreign Policy.* Washington, DC: United States Institute for Peace Press, 1993.

————. "The 'Operational Code': A Neglected Approach to the Study of Political Leaders and Decision-Making." *International Studies Quarterly* 13, no. 222 (June 1969): 190–222.

Gershman, Carl. "The Rise and Fall of the New Foreign-Policy Establishment." *Commentary* 70, no. 1 (January 1980): 13–24.

Gerson, Mark. *The Neoconservative Vision: From the Cold War to the Cultural Wars.* Lanham, MD: Madison Books, 1996.

Glazer, Nathan. "American Values and American Foreign Policy." *Commentary* 62, no. 1 (July 1976): 32–37.

Godson, Roy. *Dirty Tricks or Trump Cards: U.S. Covert Action and Counterintelligence.* Washington, DC: Brassey's, 1995.

Goldwater, Barry M. "A Foreign Policy for America." *National Review* 10, no. 11 (March 25, 1961): 177–81.

————. "The Perilous Conjucture: Soviet Ascendancy and American Isolationism." *Orbis* 15, no. 1 (Winter 1971): 53–64.

————. *Why Not Victory?* New York: McGraw-Hill, 1962.

————. *With No Apologies: The Personal and Political Memoirs of United States Senator Barry M. Goldwater.* New York: Morrow, 1979.

————, and Jack Casserly. *Goldwater.* New York: Doubleday, 1988.

Gottfried, Paul. *The Conservative Movement.* Rev. ed. New York: Twyane, 1993.

Gough, Susan L. "The Evolution of Strategic Influence," U.S. Army War College research project, 2003. Available at http://www.fas.org/irp/eprint/gough.pdf.

Graebner, Norman A., Richard Dean Burns, and Joseph M. Siracusa. *Reagan, Bush, Gorbachev: Revisiting the End of the Cold War.* Westport, CT: Praeger Security International, 2008.

Graham, Daniel O. "Détente Adieu." *National Review* 28, no. 33 (September 3, 1976): 946–50.

Gray, Colin S. "The Arms Race Is About Politics." *Foreign Policy* 9 (Winter 1972–1973): 117–29.

————. *Modern Strategy.* New York: Oxford University Press, 1999.

————. "SALT: Time to Quit." *Strategic Review* 4, no. 4 (Winter 1976): 14–22.

————, and Michael E. Howard. "Perspectives on Fighting a Nuclear War." *International Security* 6, no. 1 (Summer 1981): 185–87.

————, and Keith Payne. "Victory Is Possible." *Foreign Policy* 39 (Summer 1980): 14–27.

Greenstein, Fred I. *The Hidden-Hand Presidency: Eisenhower as Leader*. Baltimore: Johns Hopkins University Press, 1982.

Grose, Peter. *Operation Rollback: America's Secret War behind the Iron Curtain*. Boston: Houghton Mifflin, 2000.

Grunwald, Henry. "Foreign Policy under Reagan II." *Foreign Affairs* 63, no. 2 (Winter 1984–1985): 219–39.

Guttmann, Allen. *The Conservative Tradition in America*. New York: Oxford University Press, 1967.

Hahn, Walter F. "Nuclear Balance in Europe." *Foreign Affairs* 50, no. 3 (April 1972): 501–16.

———, and John C. Neff, eds. *American Strategy for the Nuclear Age*. Garden City, NY: Doubleday, 1960.

Haig, Alexander Meigs. *Caveat: Realism, Reagan, and Foreign Policy*. New York: Macmillan, 1984.

Halloran, Richard. "Reagan Aide Tells of New Strategy on Soviet Threat." *New York Times*, May 22, 1982.

———. "U.S. Said to Revise Strategy to Oppose Threat by Soviet." *New York Times*, April 19, 1981.

Healey, Denis. "The Cominform and World Communism." *International Affairs* 24, no. 3 (July 1948): 339–49.

———. "When Shrimp Learn to Whistle: Thoughts after Geneva." *International Affairs* 32, no. 1 (January 1956): 1–10.

Herz, Martin F. *Decline of the West? George Kennan and His Critics*. Washington, DC: Ethics and Public Policy Center, Georgetown University, 1978.

Hodgson, Godfrey. *The World Turned Right Side Up: A History of the Conservative Ascendancy in America*. Boston: Houghton Mifflin, 1996.

Hoeveler, David. *Watch on the Right: Conservative Intellectuals in the Reagan Era*. Madison: University of Wisconsin Press, 1991.

Hoffman, Stanley. "The Uses of American Power." *Foreign Affairs* 56, no. 1 (October 1977): 27–48.

Howard, Michael E. "On Fighting a Nuclear War." *International Security* 5, no. 4 (Spring 1981): 3–17.

Humphrey, Hubert H. "The Course of Soviet Foreign Policy and Soviet-American Relations in the 1970s." *Orbis* 15, no. 1 (Winter 1971): 65–71.

Hyland, William G. "Clash with the Soviet Union." *Foreign Policy* 49 (Winter 1982–1983): 3–19.

————. "SALT and Soviet-American Relations." *International Security* 3, no. 2 (Autumn 1978): 156–62.

————. "U.S.-Soviet Relations: The Long Road Back." *Foreign Affairs* 60, no. 3 (America and the World 1981): 525–50.

Iklé, Fred Charles. "Can Nuclear Deterrence Last Out the Century?" *Foreign Affairs* 51, no. 2 (January 1973): 268–85.

————. "When the Fighting Has to Stop: The Arguments about Escalation." *World Politics* 19, no. 4 (July 1967): 692–707.

"Interview with George F. Kennan." *Foreign Policy* 7 (Summer 1972): 5–21.

Ionescu, Ghita. *Leadership in an Interdependent World: The Statesmanship of Adenauer, De Gaulle, Thatcher, Reagan, and Gorbachev.* Boulder, CO: Westview, 1991.

Jervis, Robert. "Why Nuclear Superiority Doesn't Matter." *Political Science Quarterly* 94, no. 4 (Winter 1979–1980): 617–33.

Johnson, Frank J. *No Substitute for Victory.* Chicago: Regnery, 1962.

Johnson, Robert H. *Improbable Dangers: U.S. Conceptions of Threat in the Cold War and After.* New York: St. Martin's, 1994.

Joyce, John M. "The Old Russian Legacy." *Foreign Policy* 55 (Summer 1984): 132–53.

Kaplan, Fred. *The Wizards of Armageddon.* New York: Simon & Schuster, 1983.

Karaagac, John. *Between Promise and Policy: Ronald Reagan and Conservative Reformism.* Lanham, MD: Lexington Books, 2000.

Kegley, Charles W., Jr., and Eugene R. Wittkopf. "The Reagan Administration's World View." *Orbis* 26, no. 1 (Spring 1982): 223–44.

Kelly, George Armstrong. "A Strange Death for Liberal America?" *Foreign Policy* 6 (Spring 1972): 3–24.

Kendall, Wilmoore. "The Liberal Line." *National Review* 1, no. 4 (December 14, 1955): 8.

Kengor, Paul. *The Crusader: Ronald Reagan and the Fall of Communism.* New York: ReganBooks, 2006.

————, and Patricia Clark Doerner. *The Judge: William P. Clark, Ronald Reagan's Top Hand.* San Francisco: Ignatius Press, 2007.

Kennan, George F. "After the Cold War: American Foreign Policy in the 1970s." *Foreign Affairs* 51, no. 1 (October 1972): 210–27.

————. *At a Century's Ending: Reflections 1982–1995.* New York: Norton, 1996.

————. *The Cloud of Danger: Current Realities of American Foreign Policy.* Boston: Little, Brown, 1977.

————. *The Nuclear Delusion: Soviet-American Relations in the Atomic Age.* New York: Pantheon Books, 1983.

————. "The United States and the Soviet Union, 1917–1976," *Foreign Affairs* 54, no. 4 (July 1976): 670–90.

Kennedy, Edward M. "Beyond Détente." *Foreign Policy* 16 (Fall 1974): 3–29.

Kennedy, John F. "A Democrat Looks at Foreign Policy." *Foreign Affairs* 36, no. 1 (October 1957): 44–59.

Kersten, Charles J. "The Liberation Policy and International Order." *The Annals of the American Academy of Political and Social Science* 284 (July 1953): 93–104.

Kesler, Charles R. "Jeane Kirkpatrick: Not Quite Right." *National Review* 34, no. 21 (October 29, 1982): 1341–43.

Kincade, William H. "Arms Control or Arms Coercion?" *Foreign Policy* 62 (Spring 1986): 24–45.

Kintner, William R. *Peace and the Strategy Conflict.* New York: Praeger, 1967.

————. "A Program for America: Freedom and Foreign Policy." *Orbis* 21, no. 1 (Spring 1977): 139–56.

————. "Soviet Morality and U.S. Nuclear Strategy." *National Review* 30, no. 35 (September 1, 1978): 1071–75.

————, and Robert L. Pfaltgraff, Jr. *Strategy and Values: Selected Writings of Robert Strausz-Hupe.* Lexington, MA: Lexington Books, 1974.

Kintner, William R., and Stefan T. Possony. "Strategic Asymmetries." *Orbis* 9, no. 1 (Spring 1965): 23–48.

Kintner, William R., and Wolfgang Klaiber. *Eastern Europe and European Security.* New York: Dunellen, 1971.

Kintner, William R., with Joseph Z. Kornfeder. *The New Frontier of War: Political Warfare, Present and Future.* Chicago: Regnery, 1962.

Kirkpatrick, Jeane J. *Dictatorships and Double Standards.* New York: Simon & Schuster, 1982.

————. *The Strategy of Deception: A Study in World-Wide Communist Tactics.* New York: Farrar, Straus, 1963.

————. "U.S. Security and Latin America." *Commentary* 71, no. 1 (January 1981): 29–40.

————. "Why Not Abolish Ignorance?" *National Review* 34, no. 13 (July 9, 1982): 829–31.

————. *The Withering Away of the Totalitarian State . . . and Other Surprises.* Washington, DC: AEI Press, 1990.

Kissinger, Henry A. "Force and Diplomacy in the Nuclear Age." *Foreign Affairs* 34, no. 3 (April 1956): 351–66.

———. "Reflections on American Diplomacy." *Foreign Affairs* 35, no. 1 (October 1956): 37–56.

———. "The Search for Stability." *Foreign Affairs* 37, no. 4 (July 1959): 537–60.

Kolkey, Jonathan Martin. *The New Right, 1960–1968: With Epilogue, 1969–1980.* Washington, DC: University Press of America, 1983.

Korbonski, Stefan. "The Helsinki Agreement and Self-Determination." *Strategic Review* 4, no. 3 (Summer 1976): 48–58.

Kramer, Hilton. *The Twilight of the Intellectuals: Culture and Politics in the Era of the Cold War.* Chicago: Ivan R. Dee, 1999.

Kristol, Irving. "American Intellectuals and Foreign Policy." *Foreign Affairs* 45, no. 4 (July 1967): 594–609.

———. *Neoconservatism: The Autobiography of an Idea.* New York: Free Press, 1995.

———. *Reflections of a Neoconservative: Looking Back, Looking Ahead.* New York: Basic Books, 1983.

Kunz, Diane B. *Butter and Guns: America's Cold War Economic Diplomacy.* New York: Free Press, 1997.

Labedz, Leopold. "USA and the World Today: Kissinger and After." *Survey: A Journal of Soviet and East European Studies* 22, no. 1 (Winter 1976): 1–37.

Lagon, Mark P. *The Reagan Doctrine: Sources of American Conduct in the Cold War's Last Chapter.* Westport, CT: Praeger, 1994.

Laqueur, Walter. "Containment for the 1980s." *Commentary* 70, no. 4 (October 1980): 33–42.

Layne, Christopher. "The Real Conservative Agenda." *Foreign Policy* 61 (Winter 1985): 73–93.

Lebow, Richard Ned, and Janice Gross Stein. "Reagan and the Russians." *Atlantic Monthly* 273, no. 2 (February 1994): 35–37.

Ledeen, Michael Arthur. *Grave New World.* New York: Oxford University Press, 1985.

Leebaert, Derek. *The Fifty-Year Wound: The True Price of America's Cold War Victory.* New York: Little, Brown, 2002.

Lichtheim, George. "The Cold War in Perspective." *Commentary* 37, no. 6 (June 1964): 21–26.

Liddell Hart, Basil H. *Strategy*, 2nd rev. ed. London: Faber & Faber, 1967.

Lord, Carnes. *The Modern Prince: What Leaders Need to Know Now*. New Haven, CT: Yale University Press, 2003.

———. "The Past and Future of Public Diplomacy." *Orbis* 42, no. 1 (Winter 1998): 49–72.

Lucas, Scott. *Freedom's War: The American Crusade against the Soviet Union*. New York: New York University Press, 1999.

Luttwak, Edward N. "After Afghanistan, What?" *Commentary* 69, no. 4 (April 1980): 40–49.

———. *Strategy: The Logic of War and Peace*. Cambridge, MA: Belknap Press, 1987.

Lyons, Eugene. *Our Secret Allies: The Peoples of Russia*. New York: Duell, Sloan and Pearce, 1953.

"Management of Public Diplomacy Relative to National Security." National Security Decision Directive, NSDD-77. January 14, 1983.

Mandelbaum, Michael. "The Luck of the President." *Foreign Affairs* 64, no. 3 (America and the World 1985): 393–412.

Manning, Bayless. "Goals, Ideology and Foreign Policy." *Foreign Affairs* 54, no. 2 (January 1976): 271–84.

Matlock, Jack F., Jr. *Reagan and Gorbachev: How the Cold War Ended*. New York: Random House, 2004.

Mayers, David. *George Kennan and the Dilemmas of U.S. Foreign Policy*. New York: Oxford University Press, 1988.

Maynes, Charles William. "Lost Opportunities." *Foreign Affairs* 64, no. 3 (America and the World 1985): 413–34.

———. "Old Errors in the New Cold War." *Foreign Policy* 46 (Spring 1982): 86–104.

McEvoy, James. *Radicals or Conservatives? The Contemporary American Right*. Chicago: Rand McNally, 1971.

McFaul, Michael. "To Fight a New 'Ism.'" *Washington Post*, September 22, 2001.

McLaughlin, John. "The Accession of Shultz." *National Review* 34, no. 14 (July 23, 1982): 882.

Meese, Edwin, III. *With Reagan: The Inside Story*. Washington, DC: Regnery, 1992.

Meissner, Boris. "Soviet Russia's Foreign Policy: Ideology and Power Politics." *Modern Age* 8, no. 1 (Winter 1963–1964): 7–24.

Menges, Constantine Christopher. *Inside the National Security Council: The True Story of the Making and Unmaking of Reagan's Foreign Policy*. New York: Simon & Schuster, 1988.

————. *The Twilight Struggle*. Washington, DC: AEI Press, 1990.

Meyer, Frank S. "An American Tragedy." *National Review* 2, no. 29 (December 8, 1956): 12.

————. "Nature of the Enemy." *National Review* 3, no. 12 (March 23, 1957): 283.

————. "The Relativist 'Re-evaluates' Evil." *National Review* 3, no. 14 (May 4, 1957): 429.

————. "World Government: Last Refuge of Liberalism." *National Review* 14, no. 10 (March 12, 1963): 197.

Meyer, Frank S., ed. *The Conservative Mainstream*. New Rochelle, NY: Arlington House, 1969.

Mikheyev, Dmitry F. "The Soviet Union: Might It Collapse?" *National Review* 33, no. 8 (May 1, 1981): 478–89.

Miles, Michael. *The Odyssey of the American Right*. New York: Oxford University Press, 1980.

Molnar, Thomas. *The Two Faces of American Foreign Policy*. New York: Bobbs-Merrill, 1962.

Morgenthau, Hans J. "Changes and Chances in American-Soviet Relations." *Foreign Affairs* 49, no. 3 (April 1971): 429–41.

————. *Politics among Nations: The Struggle for Power and Peace*. New York: Knopf, 1978.

————. "Senator Fulbright's New Foreign Policy." *Commentary* 37, no. 5 (May 1964): 68–71.

Mosely, Philip E. "Soviet Foreign Policy: New Goals or New Manners?" *Foreign Affairs* 34, no. 4 (July 1956): 541–53.

Moser, Charles A., ed. *Combat on Communist Territory*. Washington, DC: Free Congress Research and Education Foundation, 1985.

Myer, Allan A. "Basic Differences between Reagan Administration's National Security Strategy (NSDD-32) and Carter Administration's Strategy (PD-18 and PD-62)." Memorandum to William P. Clark, October 5, 1982. Ronald Reagan Presidential Library, National Security Council Executive Secretariat Collection, Box 91311.

Nagorski, Zygmunt, Jr. "NATO and the Captive Countries." *The Annals of the American Academy of Political and Social Science* 288 (July 1953): 74–81.

Nash, George H. *The Conservative Intellectual Movement in America since 1945*. New York: Basic Books, 1976.

National Commission on Terrorist Attacks upon the United States. *The 9/11 Commission Report: Final Report of the National Commission on Terrorist Attacks upon the United States.* Washington, DC: Government Printing Office, 2004.

Nelson, Michael. *War of the Black Heavens: The Battles of Western Broadcasting in the Cold War.* Syracuse, NY: Syracuse University Press, 1997.

Nichols, John Spicer. "Wasting the Propaganda Dollar." *Foreign Policy* 56 (Fall 1984): 129–40.

Niemeyer, Gerhart. *Aftersight and Foresight: Selected Essays.* Lanham, MD: University Press of America, 1988.

———. *Deceitful Peace.* New Rochelle, NY: Arlington House, 1971.

———. "The Evil Society." *National Review* 28, no. 47 (December 10, 1976): 1354.

———. "The Probability of War in Our Time." *Orbis* 1, no. 2 (July 1957): 161–83.

Nitze, Paul H. "Assuring Strategic Stability in an Era of Détente." *Foreign Affairs* 54, no. 2 (January 1976): 207–32.

———. "Atoms, Strategy and Policy." *Foreign Affairs* 32, no. 2 (January 1956): 187–98.

———. *From Hiroshima to Glasnost: At the Center of Decision; A Memoir.* New York: Grove Weidenfeld, 1989.

———. "Living with the Soviets." *Foreign Affairs* 63, no. 2 (Winter 1984–1985): 360–74.

———. "The Relationship of Strategic and Theater Forces." *International Security* 2, no. 2 (Autumn 1977): 122–32.

Nixon, Richard. "Text of the 'Basic Principles of Relations Between the United States of America and the Union of Soviet Socialist Republics.'" May 29, 1972. American Presidency Project, http://www.presidency.ucsb.edu/ws/index.php?pid=3438#axzz1kIf1qiDn.

Noonan, Peggy. *When Character Was King: A Story of Ronald Reagan.* New York: Viking, 2001.

Nutter, G. Warren. *Kissinger's Grand Design.* Washington, DC: American Enterprise Institute, 1975.

Nye, Joseph S., Jr. *Bound to Lead: The Changing Nature of American Power.* New York: Basic Books, 1990.

———. "Can America Manage Its Soviet Policy?" *Foreign Affairs* 62, no. 4 (Spring 1984): 857–78.

Oberdorfer, Don. *From the Cold War to a New Era: The United States and the Soviet Union, 1983–1991.* Baltimore: Johns Hopkins University Press, 1998.

———. "Kennan Urges Halving of Nuclear Arsenals." *Washington Post,* May 20, 1981.

Oye, Kenneth A., Robert J. Lieber, and Donald Rothchild, eds. *Eagle Defiant: United States Foreign Policy in the 1980s.* Boston: Little, Brown, 1983.

Paolucci, Henry. "Carter's Kissinger." *National Review* 28, no. 37 (October 1, 1976): 1054–60.

Paret, Peter, ed. *Makers of Modern Strategy: From Machiavelli to the Nuclear Age.* Princeton, NJ: Princeton University Press, 1986.

Pemberton, William E. *Exit with Honor: The Life and Presidency of Ronald Reagan.* Armonk, NY: M. E. Sharpe, 1998.

Percy, Charles H. "The Partisan Gap." *Foreign Policy* 45 (Winter 1981–1982): 3–15.

Pipes, Richard. "Soviet Global Strategy," *Commentary* 69, no. 4 (April 1980): 31–39.

———. *Survival Is Not Enough.* New York: Simon & Schuster, 1984.

———. *Vixi: Memoirs of a Non-Belonger.* New Haven, CT: Yale University Press, 2003.

———. "Why the Soviet Union Thinks It Could Fight and Win a Nuclear War." *Commentary* 64, no. 1 (July 1977): 21–34.

Podhoretz, Norman. "The Future Danger." *Commentary* 71, no. 4 (April 1981): 29–47.

———. "Making the World Safe for Communism." *Commentary* 61, no. 4 April 1976): 31–41.

———. *My Love Affair with America : The Cautionary Tale of a Cheerful Conservative.* New York: Free Press, 2000.

———. "The Present Danger." *Commentary* 69, no. 3 (March 1980): 27–40.

———. "The Reagan Road to Détente." *Foreign Affairs* 63, no. 3 (America and the World 1984): 447–64.

Possony, Stefan T. *A Century of Conflict: Communist Techniques of World Revolution.* Chicago: Regnery, 1953.

———. "The Challenge of Russian Totalitarianism." *Orbis* 8, no. 4 (Winter 1965): 761–89.

Possony, Stefan T., and J. E. Pournelle. *The Strategy of Technology: Winning the Decisive War.* Cambridge, MA: Dunellen, 1970.

Powell, Colin L., and Joseph E. Persico. *My American Journey.* New York: Random House, 1995.

Powers, Richard Gid. *Not Without Honor: The History of American Anticommunism.* New Haven, CT: Yale University Press, 1998.

Prados, John. *Keepers of the Keys: A History of the National Security Council from Truman to Bush.* New York: Morrow, 1991.

President's Commission on CIA Activities within the United States (Rockefeller Commission). *Report to the President by the Commission on CIA Activities within the United* States. Washington, DC: Government Printing Office, 1975.

Public Papers of the Presidents of the United States: Ronald Reagan, 1981. Washington, DC: Government Printing Office, 1982.

Puddington, Arch. *Broadcasting Freedom: The Cold War Triumph of Radio Free Europe and Radio Liberty.* Lexington, KY: University Press of Kentucky, 2000.

Randolph, R. Sean. "Trading with the Enemy: A Happy Way to Die?" *National Review* 32, no. 19 (September 19, 1980): 1132–37.

Ravenal, Earl C. "The Case for Strategic Disengagement." *Foreign Affairs* 51, no. 3 (April 1973): 505–21.

Reagan, Ronald W. *An American Life.* New York: Simon & Schuster, 1990.

———. "Time to Recapture Our Destiny." National Republican Convention, July 17, 1980 speech. Available from www.reaganfoundation.org/reagan/speeches/speech.asp?spid=18.

———. *The Reagan Diaries.* Edited by Douglas Brinkley. New York: HarperCollins, 2007.

———. "Rendezvous with Destiny." Televised speech, October 27, 1964. Available from www.reaganlibrary.com/reagan/speeches/rendezvous.asp.

Reeves, Richard. *President Reagan: The Triumph of Imagination.* New York: Simon & Schuster, 2005.

———. *The Reagan Detour.* New York: Simon & Schuster, 1985.

Regan, Donald T. *For the Record: From Wall Street to Washington.* New York: Harcourt Brace Jovanovich, 1988.

Rehyansky, Joseph A. "Fire One on SALT." *National Review* 31, no. 19 (May 11, 1979): 612, 641.

Reichard, Gary W. "Divisions and Dissent: Democrats and Foreign Policy, 1952–1956." *Political Science Quarterly* 93, no. 1 (Spring 1978): 51–72.

Republican Party Platform of 1980. Available at http://www.presidency.ucsb.edu/showplatforms.php?platindex=R1980.

Revel, Jean-François. "The Myths of Eurocommunism." *Foreign Affairs* 56, no. 2 (January 1978): 295–305.

———. *The Totalitarian Temptation.* New York: Doubleday, 1977.

Roberts, Henry L. "The Crisis in the Soviet Empire." *Foreign Affairs* 35, no. 2 (January 1957): 191–200.

Roche, John P. "Bucks vs. Barbarism." *National Review* 34, no. 6 (April 2, 1982): 378.

Roosevelt, James, ed. *The Liberal Papers*. Chicago: Quadrangle Books, 1962.

Root, William A. "Trade Controls That Work." *Foreign Policy* 56 (Fall 1984): 61–80.

Rosecrance, Richard. "Détente or Entente?" *Foreign Affairs* 53, no. 3 (April 1975): 464–81.

Rosenfeld, Stephen S. "The Guns of July." *Foreign Affairs* 64, no. 4 (Spring 1986): 698–714.

———. "NATO: Read the Fine Print." *Washington Post*, May 8, 1981.

———. "Testing the Hard Line." *Foreign Affairs* 61, no. 3 (America and the World 1982): 489–510.

Rostow, Eugene V. "The Safety of the Republic: Can the Tide Be Turned?" *Strategic Review* 4, no. 2 (Spring 1976): 12–25.

Sanders, Jerry W. *Peddlers of Crisis: The Committee on the Present Danger and the Politics of Containment*. Boston: South End, 1983.

Schieffer, Bob, and Gary Paul Gates. *The Acting President*. New York: Dutton, 1989.

Schlesinger, Arthur M., Jr. *The Vital Center: The Politics of Freedom*. Boston: Houghton Mifflin, 1949.

Schlesinger, James R. "The Evolution of American Policy towards the Soviet Union." *International Security* 1, no. 1 (Summer 1976): 37–48.

Schneider, Gregory L. *Cadres for Conservatism: Young Americans for Freedom and the Rise of the Contemporary Right*. New York: New York University Press, 1999.

Schulz, William. "Trading with the Enemy." *National Review* 11, no. 8 (August 26, 1961): 116.

Schweizer, Peter. *Reagan's War: The Epic Story of His Forty-Year Struggle and Final Triumph over Communism*. New York: Doubleday, 2002.

———. *Victory: The Reagan Administration's Secret Strategy That Hastened the Collapse of the Soviet Union*. New York: Atlantic Monthly, 1994.

Seton-Watson, Hugh. "Soviet Foreign Policy on the Eve of the Summit." *International Affairs* 36, no. 3 (July 1960): 287–98.

Shub, Anatole. "Lessons of Czechoslovakia." *Foreign Affairs* 47, no. 2 (January 1969): 266–80.

Shulman, Marshall D. "Sensible Policy toward Moscow." *New York Times*, June 27, 1982.

———. "Toward a Western Philosophy of Coexistence." *Foreign Affairs* 52, no. 1 (October 1973): 35–58.

———. "What Does Security Mean Today?" *Foreign Affairs* 49, no. 4 (July 1971): 607–18.

Shultz, George P., *Turmoil and Triumph: My Years as Secretary of State*. New York: Scribner's, 1993.

Sienkiewicz, Stanley. "SALT and Soviet Nuclear Doctrine." *International Security* 2, no. 4 (Spring 1978): 84–100.

Simes, Dimitri K. "America's New Edge." *Foreign Policy* 56 (Fall 1984): 24–43.

———. "The New Soviet Challenge." Foreign Policy 55 (Summer 1984): 113–31.

Skinner, Kiron K., Annelise Anderson, and Martin Anderson, eds. *Reagan: A Life in Letters*. New York: Free Press, 2003.

———. *Reagan, in His Own Hand*. New York: Free Press, 2001.

———. *Reagan's Path to Victory: The Shaping of Ronald Reagan's Vision; Selected Writings*. New York: Free Press, 2004.

Slessor, Sir John. "A New Look at Strategy for the West." *Orbis* 2, no. 3 (October 1958): 230–36.

Slocombe, Walter. "The Countervailing Strategy." *International Security* 5, no. 4 (Spring 1981): 18–27.

Sonnenfeldt, Helmut. "Russia, America and Détente." *Foreign Affairs* 56, no. 2 (January 1978): 275–94.

Sorensen, Theodore C. "Why We Should Trade with the Soviets." *Foreign Affairs* 46, no. 3 (April 1968): 575–83.

Spielman, Richard. "Crisis in Poland." *Foreign Policy* 49 (Winter 1982–1983): 20–36.

Steel, Ronald. "A Sphere of Influences Policy." *Foreign Policy* 5 (Winter 1971–1972): 107–118.

Steinfels, Peter. *The Neoconservatives: The Men Who Are Changing America's Politics*. New York: Simon & Schuster, 1979.

Stivers, William. "Doves, Hawks, and Détente." *Foreign Policy* 45 (Winter 1981–1982): 126–44.

Strauss, Lewis L. "Thoughts on Helsinki." *National Review* 22, no. 51 (December 29, 1970): 1398.

Strausz-Hupé, Robert. *Democracy and American Foreign Policy: Reflections on the Legacy of Alexis de Tocqueville*. New Brunswick, NJ: Transaction, 1995.

———. "The Crisis of International Communism." *Confluence* 6, no. 3 (October 1957): 228–44.

———. "The Kremlin's Undiminished Appetite." *National Review* 20, no. 8 (February 27, 1968): 180–82, 205.

———. "The Real Communist Threat." *International Affairs* 41, no. 4 (October 1965): 611–23.

———. "The Sino-Soviet Tangle and U.S. Policy." *Orbis* 6, no. 1 (Spring 1962): 25–37.

———, William R. Kintner, James E. Dougherty, and Alvin J. Cottrell. *Protracted Conflict*. New York: Harper, 1959.

Strausz-Hupé, Robert, William R. Kintner, and Stefan T. Possony. *A Forward Strategy for America*. New York: Harper, 1961.

Sun Tzu. *Sun Tzu: The Art of Warfare*, trans. Roger T. Ames. New York: Ballantine Books, 1993.

Sutton, Antony. *Western Technology and Soviet Development, 1945–1965*. Stanford, CA: Hoover Institution Press, 1973.

Talbott, Strobe. "Rethinking the Red Menace." *Time*, January 1, 1990.

———. *The Russians and Reagan*. New York: Vintage Books, 1984.

Tatu, Michel. "U.S.-Soviet Relations: A Turning Point?" *Foreign Affairs* 61, no. 3 (America and the World 1982): 591–610.

Teller, Edward. "Alternatives for Security." *Foreign Affairs* 36, no. 2 (January 1958): 201–208.

Thompson, W. Scott, ed. *National Security in the 1980s: From Weakness to Strength*. San Francisco: Institute for Contemporary Studies, 1980.

Tonelson, Alan. "Nitze's World." *Foreign Policy* 35 (Summer 1979): 74–90.

Trofimenko, Henry A. "Counterforce: Illusion of a Panacea." *International Security* 5, no. 4 (Spring 1981): 28–48.

Tyler, Patrick E. "U.S. Strategy Plan Calls for Insuring No Rivals Develop." *New York Times,* March 8, 1992.

Tyroler, Charles, II, ed. *Alerting America: The Papers of the Committee on the Present Danger*. Washington, DC: Pergamon-Brassey's, 1984.

"U.S. International Information Policy." National Security Decision Directive, NSDD-130. March 6, 1984.

"U.S. National Security Strategy." National Security Decision Directive, NSDD-32. May 20, 1982.

"U.S. Relations with the USSR." National Security Decision Directive, NSDD-75. January 17, 1983.

Ulam, Adam B. "The Cold War according to Kennan." *Commentary* 55, no. 1 (January 1975): 66–69.

————. *Dangerous Relations: The Soviet Union in World Politics, 1970–1982*. New York: Oxford University Press, 1983.

————. "Détente under Soviet Eyes." *Foreign Policy* 24 (Fall 1976): 145–59.

————. "Forty Years of Troubled Coexistence." *Foreign Affairs* 64, no. 1 (Fall 1985): 12–32.

————. "Soviet Ideology and Soviet Foreign Policy." *World Politics* 11, no. 2 (January 1959): 153–72.

United States Central Intelligence Agency. *Intelligence Community Experiment in Competitive Analysis, Soviet Strategic Objectives: An Alternative View, Report of Team "B,"* December 1976.

United States Congress. Senate Foreign Relations Committee. "U.S.-Soviet Relations in the Context of U.S. Foreign Policy." Testimony of Secretary of State George P. Shultz. June 15, 1983.

United States Department of State. *Realism, Strength, Negotiation: Key Foreign Policy Statements of the Reagan Administration*. Washington, DC: Department of State, 1984.

"United States International Broadcasting." National Security Decision Directive, NSDD-45. July 15, 1982.

United States National Security Council. "Response to NSSD 11-82: U.S. Relations with the USSR," December 6, 1982.

United States President. "Remarks at the Presentation Ceremony for the Presidential Medal of Freedom," February 23, 1983.

Urban, G. R. *Radio Free Europe and the Pursuit of Democracy: My War within the Cold War*. New Haven, CT: Yale University Press, 1997.

Van Cleave, William. "SALT on the Eagle's Tail." *Strategic Review* 4, no. 2 (Spring 1976): 44–55.

————, and W. Scott Thompson, eds. *Strategic Options for the Early Eighties: What Can Be Done?* White Plains, MD: Automated Graphic Systems, 1979.

Van Hassel, Kai-Uwe. "Détente through Firmness." *Foreign Affairs* 42, no. 2 (January 1964): 184–94.

Viguerie, Richard. *The New Right: We're Ready to Lead*. Falls Church, VA: Viguerie, 1981.

Walinsky, Louis J. "Coherent Defense Strategy: The Case for Economic Denial." *Foreign Affairs* 61, no. 2 (Winter 1982–1983): 272–91.

Walker, Martin. *The Cold War: A History*. New York: Holt, 1995.

Walsh, Edmund A. *Total Empire: The Roots and Progress of World Communism*. Milwaukee, WI: Bruce, 1951.

Warnke, Paul C. "Apes on a Treadmill." *Foreign Policy* 18 (Spring 1975): 12–29.

Warren, James A. *Cold War: The American Crusade against World Communism, 1945–1991*. New York: Lothrop, Lee & Shepard Books, 1996.

Weinberger, Caspar. *Fighting for Peace: Seven Critical Years in the Pentagon*. New York: Warner Books, 1991.

———, with Gretchen Roberts. *In The Arena: A Memoir of the 20th Century*. Washington, DC: Regnery, 2001.

Weiss, Gus W. "The Farewell Dossier." *Studies in Intelligence* 39, no. 5 (1996): 121–26.

Weyrich, Paul M., and Connaught Coyne Marshner. *Future 21: Directions for America in the 21st Century*. Greenwich, CT: Devin-Adair, 1984.

Wilentz, Sean. *The Age of Reagan: A History, 1974–2008*. New York: Harper, 2008.

Winik, Jay. *On the Brink: The Dramatic, Behind-the-Scenes Saga of the Reagan Era and the Men and Women Who Won the Cold War*. New York: Simon & Schuster, 1996.

Windsor, Philip. "America's Moral Confusion: Separating the Should from the Good." *Foreign Policy* 13 (Winter 1973–1974): 139–53.

Wright, Robin. "Don't Just Fund the War, Shell Out for Peace." *Washington Post*, March 10, 2002.

Wolfe, Bertram D. "Communist Ideology and Soviet Foreign Policy." *Foreign Affairs* 41, no. 1 (October 1962): 152–70.

———. "The New Gospel according to Khrushchev." *Foreign Affairs* 38, no. 4 (July 1960): 576–87.

Woodward, Bob, *Veil: The Secret Wars of the CIA: 1981–1987*. New York: Simon and Schuster, 1987.

"X" (George F. Kennan), "The Sources of Soviet Conduct." *Foreign Affairs* 25, no. 4 (July 1947): 566–82.

Zelnick, C. Robert. "Pipe Dreams: The Foundering Soviets." *Foreign Policy* 57 (Winter 1984–1985): 92–107.

Zyzniewski, Stanley J. "Soviet Foreign Economic Policy." *Political Science Quarterly* 73, no. 2 (June 1958): 206–33.

Able Archer exercise (1983), 164–65
Acheson, Dean, 83, 89
Afghanistan: in post-9/11 environment, 173, 175; rollback of Soviet control, 25, 34, 88, 157; Soviet invasion of, 17, 34, 63, 145
al Qaeda, 170–77
Allen, Richard V., 22, 133, 149, 152, 157
American Federal of Labor and Congress of Industrial Organization (AFL-CIO), 125, 158
Anderson, Martin, 22
Angola: U.S. aid to anti-Soviet rebels, 34, 157; Soviet support to, 17, 52
Anti-Ballistic Missile (ABM) Treaty: Reagan administration interpretation of, 155, 156; Soviet violations of, 28, 121, 156. See also Strategic Defense Initiative
Arendt, Hannah, 48, 54, 55
arms control: conservative view of, 47, 57, 84–86, 115–17, 119–21; liberal and mainstream view of, 13, 84–86, 96, 100, 103, 105, 111, 116, 118, 119, 146; Reagan administration view of, 23–24, 149, 150, 151, 155–57, 159; Ronald Reagan view of, 140, 146, 147. See also diplomacy

Bailey, Norman, 153
Baker, James, 2, 154, 165, 166, 168
Barnett, Frank Rockwell, 148
Brezhnev Doctrine, 25, 92, 140, 141
Brezhnev, Leonid, 20, 23, 53, 140
Brodie, Bernard, 72, 73, 102
Bryen, Stephen, 152, 153
Buckley, James, 153
Buckley, William F., 66
Burnham, James, 39, 40, 43, 45, 65, 73, 78, 85, 102, 104, 123; on communism, 48–49, 52; on economic warfare, 108, 145; on liberation, 94, 95, 148; Reagan familiarity with, 130; on Soviet vulnerabilities, 58-59
Bush, George H.W., 165-66, 168–69, 170

Carter, Jimmy, 13, 16, 26, 31, 52, 145, 157, 167, 168, 179
Casey, William, 2, 18, 19, 148, 149, 151, 152, 154, 157, 158
Central Intelligence Agency (CIA), Reagan administration, 18, 19, 34, 122, 123, 125, 131, 136, 144, 148, 152, 154, 157
Chambers, Whittaker, 48–49, 134
China, People's Republic of, 18, 19, 139, 167; in post–Cold War strategy, 170
Clark, William P., 13, 149, 152, 154, 157

Clausewitz, Carl von, 3, 6, 9, 168

Clifford, Clark, 1

Clinton, Bill, 169–170

Committee on the Present Danger (CPD), 45, 120

communism, role of: conservative view of, 40, 42, 43, 44, 47-53, 54, 55, 56-57, 59–62, 62–64, 65, 66-67, 68, 78, 79, 81, 83, 85, 88, 90–91, 93, 96-97, 99, 104, 117, 118, 120, 121, 123; liberal and mainstream view of, 14–15, 44–45, 48, 51–52, 53, 67, 78, 89, 94–95, 96, 119, 124; Reagan administration view of, 15–17, 18–20, 21, 25, 31, 32, 154; Ronald Reagan view of, 18, 27, 32, 131, 134–35, 136, 140–41, 146

Congress for Cultural Freedom, 122

containment, 12–13, 72, 87, 88, 91, 92, 94, 98, 102, 166; criticism of, 13, 26, 39–43, 45, 73, 95; Reagan administration and, 12, 14, 35, 149; Ronald Reagan opposition to, 132–33

Coordinating Committee for Multilateral Export Controls (COCOM), 29–30, 153

covert action, 8–9; conservative view of, 68, 122–26; liberal and mainstream view of, 122–23, 124, 125; in post-9/11 strategy, 177; Reagan administration use of, 33–35, 68, 123, 125, 127, 157–58; Ronald Reagan view of, 141, 147–48

Crozier, Brian, 81, 99, 131

Crusade for Freedom, 131

Cuba, 13, 31, 52, 55, 90, 92, 104, 125, 141, 143, 152

Deaver, Michael, 2, 154

Defense, Department of, Reagan administration, 131, 143, 152, 153, 155

democracy, superiority of: conservative view of, 47, 64–69, 78, 79, 81, 91, 92–93, 95, 97, 99, 115, 121, 124; liberal and mainstream view of, 65, 67, 80, 114, 116, 124; neoconservatives and,

64, 67–68, 81; in post-9/11 strategy, 172, 174, 176, 177; Reagan administration view of, 12, 20–21, 32–33, 154; Ronald Reagan view of, 21, 64, 136–37, 139, 140–41, 141–42, 146

détente, 13, 17, 26, 43–46, 51, 55–56, 62, 80, 85, 89, 91–92, 96, 98, 105, 110–13, 116, 118–19, 125, 170; conservative opposition to, 37, 41, 43–47, 85, 98, 110, 112–13; Reagan administration and, 12–14, 16, 38, 149; Ronald Reagan opposition to, 13–14, 133, 145, 146, 147; Soviet view of, 13, 16, 43–44, 46

deterrence, 8, 87; conservative view of, 54–57, 71–76, 90, 100, 101–4, 106; liberal and mainstream view of, 22, 54, 55, 56, 72, 73–74, 75, 100, 012, 103, 105, 143; Reagan administration approach to, 16–17, 21–22, 24, 28, 30, 151; Ronald Reagan view of, 22, 138, 143. *See also* Strategic Defense Initiative

diplomacy, 8; conservative view of, 84, 87, 114, 115–16, 117, 119–20; liberal and mainstream view of, 56, 114, 116; in post–Cold War strategy, 169–70; in post-9/11 strategy, 174, 175; Reagan administration view of, 22–24, 152, 156; Ronald Reagan view, 139–40, 146; Strausz-Hupé tasks of, 84, 114, 140. *See also* arms control *and* public diplomacy

Dobrynin, Anatoly, 13

economic warfare, 9; conservative support for, 107–13; liberal and mainstream opposition to, 108, 109, 111–12; in post-9/11 strategy, 175–76; Reagan administration use of, 12, 23, 26, 27, 28, 29–30, 34–35, 131, 136, 151, 152–53; Ronald Reagan view of, 136, 144–45

Eisenhower, Dwight, 26, 41, 88, 97, 108–109, 122, 167

Evans, M. Stanton, 52

Farewell. *See* Vladimir Vetrov

Ford, Gerald, 13, 31, 131, 133, 148, 167

Fulbright, William, 84, 119

Graham, Daniel, Lt. Gen., 22

grand strategy: beliefs as component of, 5–6; definition of, 3–4; goals, as component of, 6; individual's role in, 178–80; necessity of, 166–168; post-9/11, 170–78; post-Cold War, 168–70; relationship to statecraft, 4–5; tools, as component of, 7–9.

Gray, Colin, 45

Grenada, 28–29, 92, 104, 152

George, Alexander, 6

Goldwater, Barry, 38, 41–43, 52, 66, 79, 90–91, 104, 133, 159; on economic warfare, 144, 145; on liberation, 90, 97, 99; 1964 presidential campaign of, 41, 91, 96, 131

Gorbachev, Mikhail, 27, 132, 134–35, 139, 142, 165, 168; and end of the Cold War, 163–64

Hook, Sidney, 68

Hungary, 1956 uprising in, 41, 60, 97, 124

Iklé, Fred, 153

influence, expansion of U.S., 21, 24, 76, 82, 87; conservative view of, 42–43, 57, 67, 76–82, 103, 104, 117, 121, 126; liberal and mainstream view of, 46, 67, 77, 78–79, 80, 102, 114–15, 116, 124, 125; in post-9/11 strategy, 175; Reagan administration view of, 22–23, 28–29, 154–55; Ronald Reagan view of, 139, 143

intermediate-range nuclear forces (INF), 23, 152, 155; INF Treaty, 134, 155–157

John Paul II, Pope, 137, 158. *See also* Solidarity, Polish

Kennan, George, 14–15, 39, 41, 48, 51, 53, 80, 84, 88, 94, 114, 123

Kennedy, Edward, 105

Kennedy, John F., 43, 116, 167

Keyworth, George, 22

Khrushchev, Nikita, 48, 50, 53

Kirkpatrick, Jeane, 2, 45, 52, 81, 149, 154, 157–158

Korean War, 37, 77, 82, 88, 107

Lake, Anthony, 125

Lebanon, 28, 152

Lenin, Vladimir, 14, 32, 49, 94, 134. *See also* communism

Leninism. *See* communism

liberation: conservative view of, 38, 41, 87–99, 102, 103, 104, 107–26; of Eastern Europe, 3, 10, 21, 24–26, 38, 41, 42, 87–93, 103, 107–26; liberal and mainstream view of, 41, 72, 87–88, 89, 91–92, 94, 96, 98; Reagan administration pursuit of, 24–27, 29–35, 149, 152–55, 157–58; Ronald Reagan support for, 131, 140–42, 144, 145

Libya, 28, 104, 152

Lord, Carnes, 33

Lyons, Eugene, 40

Marxism. *See* communism

McFarlane, Robert, 151

McNamara, Robert, 73

Meese, Edwin, III, 2, 22, 149, 151, 157

Meyer, Frank, 65

military buildup: conservative support for, 101–6, 107, 110–11; liberal opposition to, 102, 103, 105, 109; of Reagan administration, 12, 28–29, 30, 151–52; Ronald Reagan view on, 142–44

Mondale, Walter, 6

Moynihan, Daniel Patrick, 121

Mutual Assured Destruction (MAD). *See* deterrence

National Endowment for Democracy (NED), 33

National Review, 39, 130

National Security Council (NSC), Reagan
    administration, 11, 15, 32, 131, 152–
    153, 154, 160
National Security Decision Directive 32
    (NSDD-32), 21, 22, 34
National Security Decision Directive 45
    (NSDD-45), 31
National Security Decision Directive 66
    (NSDD-66), 29
National Security Decision Directive 75
    (NSDD-75), 15, 16, 21, 25, 29, 34,
    163, 166, 167
National Security Decision Directive 77
    (NSDD-77), 32, 154
National Security Decision Directive 130
    (NSDD-130), 32
National Union for the Total
    Independence of Angola (UNITA). See
    Angola
neoconservatives, 38, 44–45, 52, 64, 67–68,
    81, 91, 92, 97, 99, 117, 121, 137, 139
Nicaragua, 17, 34, 157–58
Niemeyer, Gerhart, 81, 159
Nitze, Paul, 45, 138
Nixon, Richard, 13, 31, 81, 133, 134,
    145, 164, 167, 179
North Atlantic Treaty Organization
    (NATO), 23, 28, 29, 32, 39, 57, 81,
    115, 126, 156

Peaceful coexistence. See détente
Perle, Richard, 45, 152, 153
Pershing II See Intermediate-Range
    Nuclear Forces
Pipes, Richard, 52, 99
Project Democracy, 32, 33, 154
Project Solarium, 88, 108
Project Truth, 32, 154, 155
Podhoretz, Norman, 68, 81
political warfare, 44; conservative view of,
    90, 104, 113–21; liberal and mainstream
    view of, 114, 116, 118–19; in post-9/11
    strategy, 176; Reagan administration use
    of, 31–33, 35, 149, 153–57; Ronald
    Reagan view of, 132, 146–47

power, importance of: conservative view
    of, 46, 54–58, 60, 69, 71, 73, 74–76,
    79, 102–7; liberal and mainstream view
    of, 17, 53–55, 56, 72, 75, 80, 89, 102,
    103, 105–6; in post-9/11 strategy, 171;
    Reagan administration view of, 16–17,
    28; Ronald Reagan view of, 135, 138,
    143
Prague Spring movement, 91, 116
public diplomacy, 8; conservative view of,
    114, 115, 117–18, 120–21; liberal and
    mainstream view of, 114, 116, 118–19;
    in post-9/11 strategy, 176; Reagan
    administration use of, 31–33, 34, 68,
    152, 154–55; Ronald Reagan view of,
    146–47

Radio Free Europe/ Radio Liberty
    (RFE/RL), 31, 116, 117, 119
Reagan administration: arms control, view
    of, 23–24, 149, 150, 151, 155–57,
    159; communism, view of, 15–17, 18–
    20, 21, 25, 31, 32, 154; containment,
    opposition to, 12, 14, 35, 149; covert
    action, use of, 33–35, 68, 123, 125,
    127, 157–58; Defense Department,
    131, 143, 152, 153, 155; democracy,
    view of, 12, 20–21, 32–33, 154;
    détente, opposition to, 12–14, 16, 38,
    149; deterrence, approach to, 16–17,
    21–22, 24, 28, 30, 151; diplomacy,
    view of, 22–24, 152, 156; economic
    warfare, use of, 12, 23, 26, 27, 28, 29–
    30, 34–35, 131, 136, 151, 152–53;
    expansion of U.S. influence, view of,
    22–23, 28–29, 154–55; grand strategy,
    risks of, 164–66; liberation, pursuit of,
    24–27, 29–35, 149, 152–55, 157–58;
    military buildup, 12, 28–29, 30, 151–
    52; National Security Council, 11, 15,
    32, 131, 152, 153, 154, 160; political
    warfare, use of, 31–33, 34, 35, 149,
    154–57; public diplomacy, use of, 31–
    33, 34, 68, 152, 154–55; State
    Department, 131, 132, 143, 152, 153,

154; Third World, involvement in, 23, 25, 29, 33–34, 91, 123, 157–58; Soviet vulnerabilities, view of, 12, 17–19, 26, 31–33, 131

Reagan Doctrine, 25, 33, 91, 123, 157–58

Reagan, Ronald: arms control, view of, 140, 146, 147; communism, view of, 18, 27, 32, 131, 134–35, 136, 140–41, 146; containment, opposition to, 132–33; conventional view of, 1–2, 11, 159, 161–63; covert action, support for, 141, 147–48; democracy, view of, 21, 64, 136–37, 139, 140–41, 141–42, 146; détente, opposition to, 13–14, 133, 145, 146, 147; deterrence, view of, 22, 138, 143; diplomacy, view of, 139–40, 146; economic warfare, support for, 136, 144–45; foreign policy knowledge of, 2–3, 130–31, 159; expansion of U.S. influence, view of, 139, 143; liberation, support for, 131, 140–42, 144, 145; management style of, 129–32; military buildup, support for, 142–44; 1976 primary campaign, 13, 131; political warfare, view of, 132, 146–47; power, view of, 135, 138, 143; public diplomacy, support for, 146–47; Strategic Defense Initiative, creation of, 22, 132, 143–44, 151; Third World, view of, 137, 139, 141, 146, 148; Soviet vulnerabilities, view of, 133, 136–37, 163

Revel, Jean-François, 68

Robinson, Roger, 29, 153

rollback. See liberation.

Rostow, Eugene, 45

Schlesinger, Arthur, 65, 66, 94

Shulman, Marshall, 125

Shultz, George, 2, 14, 149, 151, 154–56, 157–59

Solidarity, Polish, 18; US support to, 33, 34, 124–25, 158; Vatican support to, 34, 158

Soviet Union. See Union of Soviet Socialist Republics

Stalin, Joseph, 48, 49, 50, 53, 82

State, Department of, Reagan administration, 131, 132, 143, 152–53, 154

Strategic Arms Limitation Talks (SALT), 85, 86, 143

Strategic Defense Initiative (SDI), 138, 143, 155; arms control and, 132, 151, 156; creation of, 22, 143–44, 151; as economic warfare, 30, 144; military buildup and, 28; Reagan role in, 22, 132, 143–44, 151, 156; Soviet fears of, 30, 144, 165. See also deterrence

Strausz-Hupé, Robert, 41–43, 45, 66, 79, 104, 106, 146, 148, 159; on deterrence, 74, 76, 138; on economic warfare, 144, 145; on liberation, 90, 99; Reagan familiarity with, 103–31; on Soviet vulnerabilities, 60, 61, 63; three pillars of diplomacy of, 84, 114, 140

Sun Tzu, 3, 9

Talbott, Strobe, 17

Teller, Edward, 22

third world: conservative view of, 76–82, 90, 92, 93, 104, 106, 115, 117, 121, 124, 125, 126; liberal and mainstream view of, 77, 78, 80, 91–92, 95, 116, 124, 125; Reagan administration involvement in, 23, 25, 29, 33–34; Reagan view of, 137, 139, 141, 146, 148; Soviet involvement in, 13, 17, 18, 22, 24, 28, 30, 31, 40, 41, 42, 43, 44, 52, 60, 74, 89, 90, 92, 104, 113, 133, 165; U.S. involvement in, 13, 44, 57, 78, 122. See also Reagan Doctrine

Union of Soviet Socialist Republics (USSR): Afghanistan invasion, 17, 34, 63, 145; Angola, support to, 17, 52; détente, view of, 13, 16, 43–44, 46; Strategic Defense Initiative, fear of,

30, 144, 165; Third World,
involvement in, 13, 17, 18, 22, 24,
28, 30, 31, 40, 41, 42, 43, 44, 52, 60,
74, 89, 90, 92, 104, 113, 133, 165;
treaty violations of, 28, 46, 82, 83,
114, 116, 120, 121, 147, 156, 163
United States Information Agency (USIA),
32, 117, 154, 155

Van Cleave, William, 22
Vetrov, Vladimir, 34–35, 158
Vietnam War, 1, 13, 21, 22, 29, 37, 44,
56, 67, 78, 80, 93, 103, 106, 110, 111,
113, 119, 124, 125, 126, 164; Reagan
views of, 138–39, 143
Voice of America (VOA), 31, 116, 117, 119

vulnerability, Soviet: conservative view of,
58–64, 92, 95, 96 103, 108–11, 121;
economic, 17–18, 26, 29–30, 58–59,
61–64, 108–9, 136; political, 18–19,
26, 59–61, 63–64, 121, 136–37, 165;
Reagan administration view of, 12, 17–
19, 26, 31–33, 131; Ronald Reagan
view of, 133, 136–37, 163

Walker, Charls, 45
Warburg, James, 109
Weinberger, Caspar, 2, 149, 151–52, 155–
56, 157, 159
Wick, Charles, 32

Young Americans for Freedom, 97, 110

ABOUT THE AUTHOR

Francis H. Marlo is assistant professor of strategic studies at the Command and Staff College, Marine Corps University (MCU), in Quantico, Virginia. Prior to joining MCU in 2008, he taught at the National Defense University. From 2002 to 2005, he served as assistant for counterproliferation policy in the Office of the Assistant Secretary of Defense for International Security Policy. This is his first book. He lives in Vienna, Virginia.